Buy, Own and Sell a Flat

About the author

Michael Haley is a solicitor and professor of law at Keele University, specialising in the law of landlord and tenant, on which he has written extensively.

Other contributors

Derek O'Carroll, author of the chapter on Scotland, is an advocate at the Scottish bar. He speaks and writes frequently on housing issues.

Jeremy Hinds, author of the chapter on Northern Ireland, works for a firm of solicitors in Belfast. He specialises in property law, including landlord and tenant law.

Buy, Own and Sell a Flat

Michael Haley

CONSUMERS' ASSOCIATION

Which? Books are commissioned and researched by
Consumers' Association and published by
Which? Ltd, 2 Marylebone Road, London NW1 4DF
Email: books@which.net

Distributed by The Penguin Group:
Penguin Books Ltd, 80 Strand, London WC2R 0RL

First edition March 1996
This edition April 2004

Copyright © 1996, 2000, 2002, 2004 Which? Ltd

British Library Cataloguing in Publication Data
A catalogue record for *Buy, Own and Sell a Flat* is available from the British Library

ISBN 0 85202 976 4

For a full list of Which? books, please call 0800 252100, access our website at
www.which.net, or write to Which? Books, Freepost, P.O. Box 44, Hertford SG14 1SH

Original cover concept by Sarah Harmer
Cover photograph: D-Bernd Ducke/A1PIX
Index: Marie Lorimer
Editorial and production: Joanna Bregosz, Nithya Rae

Typeset by Saxon Graphics Ltd, Derby
Printed and bound in Wales by Creative Print and Design

Contents

★An asterisk next to the name of an organisation in the text indicates that the address can be found in this section

Introduction

Prospective buyers of flats are nowadays spoilt for choice as they have a wide range of properties to pick from. In addition to new, purpose-built flats, many large buildings (such as former churches, warehouses and office blocks), especially in major cities, are being converted to meet the ever-increasing demand for flats.

Purchasers of flats, as well as of houses, are also faced with a confusing array of mortgage packages. The pros and cons of different kinds of mortgages, the growing public awareness of over-charging by lenders and the justifiable lack of faith in the traditional endowment mortgage are discussed in Chapter 4.

Leasehold reform

In England, Wales and Northern Ireland a person buying a flat will usually have to do so by taking a lease of the property. Under a lease, the tenant acquires only a limited type of ownership, for a fixed period of time. Simply put, a lease is the legal right to occupy property, often for a specified number of years, which is granted to the tenant in return for payment of a premium and/or rent. The law regulating leases in Northern Ireland (see Chapter 22) is somewhat different to that operating in England and Wales; moreover, the concept of leasehold does not apply in Scotland (see Chapter 21).

A variety of steps have been taken during the last decade to address the inadequacies of the leasehold system, especially to calm the often troubled landlord–tenant relationship. This has been achieved by giving tenants – both individually and collectively – extra rights, and by imposing on the landlord additional obligations. In particular, flat-owners are allowed either to appoint a manager of the building, in circumstances where the landlord does not carry out management obligations effectively (see Chapter 15), or, provided that certain requirements are met, to buy out the landlord's freehold in the property collectively. The latter situation is known as collective enfranchisement and is discussed in Chapter 18. Although an individual tenant cannot compulsorily purchase the landlord's interest, an individual tenant does enjoy the right to buy an extension to the lease.

Also important for buyers of leases granted after 1995 is the abolition of original tenant liability under a leasehold covenant. Previously, the original tenant could always be sued for a subsequent tenant's breach of covenant even though the lease had been sold on years before (see Chapter 10). Flat-owners have also been given extra protection against unscrupulous landlords who attempt to milk their tenants by charging exorbitantly high service charges and management fees: they are now able to challenge the amount of the service charge levied, as well as the quality and suitability of the maintenance work undertaken (see Chapters 13 and 15).

This extension of tenants' rights is continuing and further reforms are introduced by the Commonhold and Leasehold Reform Act 2002. Part II of the Act offers tenants new rights and enhances other existing ones. The changes are intended to assist those leaseholders who are unable, or might not want, to convert to the new system of commonhold as mentioned below. For example, a new right has been established to enable leaseholders to take over the management of their building without having to show default on the part of the landlord and without having to pay compensation. The legislation makes it easier for tenants to buy the landlord's freehold collectively and to extend their leases individually. Greater safeguards are put in place to shield tenants against unreasonable service charges and other payments. The legislation also extends the jurisdiction of the Leasehold Valuation Tribunal (LVT) and strengthens the current requirements for landlords to consult tenants about proposed major works. It restricts the charging of penalties for late payment of ground rent, prevents the initiation of forfeiture proceedings until the facts have been established, and makes it easier to vary the terms of a defective lease.

Most of these provisions are now in force, but some will be on stream only in spring 2004. Although this guide assumes that all of them are now operational, the following will commence only in 2004:

- the landlord's obligation to demand ground rents before taking action or imposing penalties for late payment
- the landlord's need to show that the lease has been breached before taking forfeiture action
- the prevention of forfeiture for trivial debts
- the introduction of new accounting requirements and the right to withhold service charges where certain information is not provided.

Nevertheless, the leasehold system will never be perfect and there will always be tenants who have legitimate complaints against their landlords. This is because both landlord and tenant simultaneously have a stake in the flat and their different interests do not necessarily coexist well. The new scheme, known as commonhold (see Chapter 2), appears to be the solution because the buyer will purchase the freehold title to an individual flat and own the common parts with other flat-owners: commonhold does not involve leases or landlords. The new laws introducing commonhold will not directly affect existing leases and new leases will still be created if that is the preference of the freeholder. Although these provisions are contained in the 2002 Act, commonhold is likely to be introduced in spring 2004.

Making buying and selling flats easier

In 1999, the government put forward proposals aimed at making the conveyancing process in England and Wales faster, more transparent and consumer-friendly (see Chapter 6). The suggestions were intended to shorten the period of uncertainty between acceptance of offer and exchange of contracts, thereby minimising the prospects of gazumping, and to reduce the need for negotiations, cutting the overall timescale of the transaction from an average of three months to three weeks. The package of reforms sounds promising and proved to work well in trials. When implemented, they should take much of the hassle out of buying and selling property, particularly if the professionals and lenders involved pull together and attempt to make it work successfully.

Fortunately, the government appears to have rekindled its interest in this and proposals are in the process of being put before Parliament.

The Starter Home Initiative (SHI)

This recent development takes the form of a government-funded scheme which is designed to help key public-sector workers (including, among others, teachers, health workers, social workers, fire fighters and police officers) to purchase a home in areas where high house prices are undermining recruitment. At present this covers London, the south-east and so-called housing 'hot spots' in eastern and south-western England. The scheme is operated by local scheme providers, usually housing associations: a list of providers will be available from your employer. The type of assistance available, and its extent, depends upon the local provider. Most commonly, it takes the form of a subsidised loan or shared ownership (i.e. a part-own part-rent basis). Most schemes allow the purchase on the open market. Some schemes cater for all key workers whereas others might be limited to, say, occupational therapists. In order to qualify, you must show that you cannot afford a home without SHI assistance, that you do not own another home and that you are entitled to reside permanently in the UK. This assistance is currently available until March 2004, but it is possible that it will be renewed beyond this time.

Which? campaign on estate agents

Which? is campaigning for the government to call time on the voluntary regulation of estate agents: agents should be licensed, and training and membership of an Ombudsman scheme should be made compulsory. Robust monitoring and sanctions regimes should be introduced to ensure that the industry is adequately policed.

Signing up with an estate agent can leave you out of pocket if you've signed up to an unfair contract. To help protect you from rogue estate agent contracts Which? lawyers have put together a standard contract. For a free copy visit *www.which.co.uk*

Chapter 1

An introduction to leaseholds

Buying a flat is for many the first step in home ownership. This chapter explains the concept of leasehold, terms associated with it and the peculiarities of leasehold conveyancing and ownership.

Demographics of flat ownership

Of the over 1 million long leaseholders in England and Wales:

- one-quarter are under the age of 35; half are aged between 35 and 64; and the rest are over 65
- 57 per cent are in full-time employment, and one-quarter are retired
- the majority live in purpose-built flats; only 16 per cent live in converted properties
- 40 per cent have fewer than 75 years remaining on their leases; 11 per cent have fewer than 50 years.

Over half of the leasehold *flats* are in London and the south-east of England; interestingly, over half of the leasehold *houses* are in the north-west of England and Merseyside.

What is a leasehold?

Conveyancing is the legal and administrative process involved in transferring the ownership of land and/or any buildings on it from one owner to another. Buying and selling a flat is similar to buying and selling a house, apart from one crucial difference – the nature of what is bought and sold.

Unlike a freehold, which gives the buyer what is, to all intents and purposes, complete ownership of the land and the buildings on it, a leasehold gives only a limited type of ownership for a fixed period of time. It is essentially permission to occupy property, given by the land-owner (known as the freeholder, reversioner or landlord) to the buyer (known as the leaseholder, lessee or tenant) in return for payment. In a loose sense, leasing can be compared with hiring land for a definite period and subject to a variety of rights and obligations. Nevertheless, a properly executed lease (the document setting out the terms and conditions of the leasehold)

What you should know about a leasehold

- Mortgage money is not automatically available for the purchase of every type of flat. Banks and building societies are generally unwilling to lend money on freehold flats. Even in the case of leaseholds, they will look at the nature and state of repair of the property before making a loan and will usually be reluctant to advance funds on a lease which has less than 60 years to run or on a property which has substantial defects (see Chapter 4).
- All flat-owners have to pay a ground rent (usually nominal) to their landlord. In addition, if the landlord retains control and management of the premises (as occurs with a block of flats), the tenant will be obliged to pay an annual service charge to cover a share of the costs of repair, maintenance and insurance of the entire building, usually to a management company (see Chapters 12, 13 and 14).
- The lease normally imposes obligations (in the form of covenants) on the tenant: for example, to repair and maintain the interior; to take out buildings insurance if the landlord does not do so; to pay service charges; and to use the flat only for the purposes of a dwelling (see Chapter 9).
- The flat-owner has the right to occupy the flat and can be dispossessed only on certain grounds. These include defaults on the mortgage agreement (for example, non-payment of the interest and capital; see Chapter 4) and breaches of the leasehold covenants (for example, alterations carried out without the landlord's consent; see Chapter 10). All these possibilities are regulated by Parliament which offers the tenant some protection against unjust action (see Chapters 10 and 17).

---

gives the tenant a legal estate in land. For reasons that will become clear in the rest of this chapter, people who own flats generally own the leasehold, not the freehold.

A leasehold is carved out of a landlord's freehold estate and can adopt various forms. At one end of the spectrum there is the tenancy of a furnished bedsit, providing short-term accommodation at a weekly market rent. (For all types of short tenancies at market rents see *Renting and Letting* published by Which? Books.) At the other end is the long-term lease for a fixed number of years – for example, 99, 199 or 999 years. Once a long lease is taken and the capital premium (the purchase price of the property) is paid, the tenant's financial responsibility to the landlord is limited to a small ground rent (payable annually or quarterly) and any service or management charge levied by the lease in respect of the premises. It is with the long, fixed-term lease that this book is concerned.

Basic vocabulary

Lawyers have devised a language of technical terms and expressions that is often baffling to the general public. This is certainly true in relation to leasehold conveyancing and, in particular, the wording of leases and the covenants they contain. Coming to grips with some of the terminology is, however, a necessary chore. Some of these basic terms are explained below and a more detailed glossary is provided at the back of the book.

A **freehold** is property held absolutely (until the end of time, as it were). Normally, in the case of a flat, the freehold will be the title owned by the landlord and will relate to the whole building and the land on which the building stands. A **freeholder** is, simply, the person who owns the freehold. When this person creates or grants a lease (that is, sells a flat) he or she is known as the **lessor**, **landlord** or **reversioner**.

A **leasehold** is ownership of property for a specified time, the terms and conditions of ownership being set out in a contract known as a **lease.** A lease may also be called a **tenancy, term of years** or **demise. A leaseholder** (or **lessee** or **tenant**) is the person to whom a lease is granted (that is, the person who buys the flat).

A landlord can **assign** (sell) the freehold and a tenant can usually assign the unexpired period of a lease. This **assignment** can be of the whole or just part of the premises. Although this is unlikely, and is subject to the lease prohibiting this, the tenant can structurally convert the flat and sell off parts of it. The effect of an assignment is that the property has a new landlord or a new tenant (the **assignee**). Assignments can occur any number of times during the course of a lease. At any given time there must be two owners of the property: the landlord, who owns the freehold, and the tenant, who owns the leasehold.

When a lease is granted, the landlord retains the freehold of the property. This is described as the landlord's **reversion** because at the end of the lease the property traditionally reverts back to the landlord.

A tenant can also carve out from the lease a shorter tenancy in favour of someone else, known as a **sub-lease**, **sub-demise** or **underlease.** The tenant's own lease will then be known as the **head-lease.** This can be of the whole or just part of the premises, so the tenant could sub-let one room in the flat, for example. Unlike assignment, this transaction does not dispose of the entire interest under the lease. The parties to the transaction creating an underlease are often known as the **sub-lessor** and the **sub-lessee** or **sub-tenant.**

A sub-tenant can either assign the existing sub-lease or create a further **sub-letting** (sometimes called a **sub-underlease**) of the flat for a shorter term than the first.

It should be noted that the terms **landlord** and **tenant** can be used to describe various levels of relationship. A sub-tenant will regard the person from whom he or she is sub-leasing as the landlord

---

EXAMPLES

In 1977 Janet leases a flat for 99 years to Sammy. In 2004, Sammy sells the entire lease to Sadek. Janet remains the landlord, Sammy ceases to be the tenant, and Sadek takes the assignment of the rest of that 99-year lease, which then has 72 years to run.

In 1990 Janet leases a flat for 99 years to Sammy, who immediately creates a sub-lease of 25 years for Sadek. Janet remains the head landlord, Sammy is the tenant of Janet and the sub-lessor of Sadek, and Sadek is the sub-tenant. At the end of 25 years, the remaining 74 years revert back to Sammy and, when that period expires, the premises revert back to Janet.

(technically called a mesne landlord), in which case that landlord's lessor (in other words, the freeholder) might become known as the **head landlord.** Furthermore, the words landlord/tenant apply equally to both short-term leases, in which a tenant pays a market rent to the landlord, and long-term leases, for which the tenant pays only ground rent. To confuse matters even further, a sub-tenant might in everyday language be referred to simply as a 'tenant'.

The diagram below illustrates the transactions possible for a single flat.

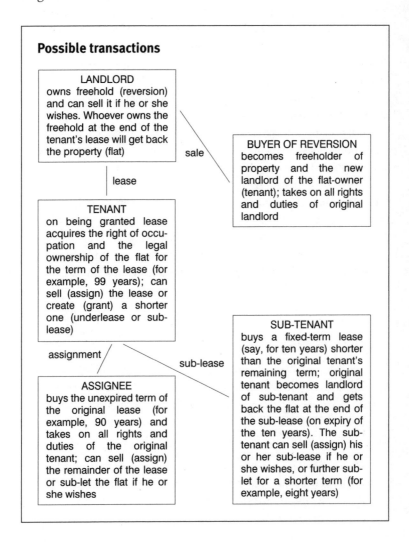

Possible transactions

LANDLORD
owns freehold (reversion) and can sell it if he or she wishes. Whoever owns the freehold at the end of the tenant's lease will get back the property (flat)

sale

BUYER OF REVERSION
becomes freeholder of property and the new landlord of the flat-owner (tenant); takes on all rights and duties of original landlord

lease

TENANT
on being granted lease acquires the right of occupation and the legal ownership of the flat for the term of the lease (for example, 99 years); can sell (assign) the lease or create (grant) a shorter one (underlease or sublease)

assignment

sub-lease

SUB-TENANT
buys a fixed-term lease (say, for ten years) shorter than the original tenant's remaining term; original tenant becomes landlord of sub-tenant and gets back the flat at the end of the sub-lease (on expiry of the ten years). The sub-tenant can sell (assign) his or her sub-lease if he or she wishes, or further sub-let for a shorter term (for example, eight years)

ASSIGNEE
buys the unexpired term of the original lease (for example, 90 years) and takes on all rights and duties of the original tenant; can sell (assign) the remainder of the lease or sub-let the flat if he or she wishes

What you should know about a lease

Leases tend to follow a certain format, although the precise terms will vary according to the nature of the property and the wishes of the parties involved. Whatever form a lease takes, it must satisfy certain conditions.

- The parties to a lease must enter a legally binding relationship. A lease cannot, for example, be a purely domestic arrangement.
- The lease must be for a certain duration which can be calculated precisely. This is why leases are often granted for, say, 99 or 999 years. Such arrangements as 'until the landlord seeks possession of the property for road-widening purposes', 'until the landlord pays off a debt to the occupier', or 'for the duration of the present government' would fall foul of this rule.
- The date when the lease is to commence must be stated.
- The lease will contain covenants (that is, contractual obligations) between the parties, either spelled out or implied into the lease (for example, to pay ground rent).
- The landlord must retain the reversion.
- The transaction must convey to the tenant what is called 'exclusive possession', which is the legal right to exclude all others, including the landlord, from the property.
- If it is for a fixed period of more than three years, the lease must be created by deed. A deed is a formal document which is signed by the parties in the presence of a witness.

Problem leases

The fact that a lease details the obligations of the landlord and tenant, and that these obligations can be enforced between the parties, does not offer any guarantee that the flat is saleable or mortgageable. Many long leases of flats are problematic. The main points to watch out for are the following:

- **Insurance** It is imperative that the lease makes adequate insurance arrangements (see Chapter 12 for details). There must be an obligation to insure comprehensively. A block policy covering the entire building, usually arranged by the landlord or a management company with the premium shared among the flat-owners by means of a service charge, is preferable to individual flat-owners taking out separate cover, with different insurers and for differing amounts. In the event of a claim it is easier if a single insurer and policy deals with it. Most mortgage lenders will not lend on flats if the insurance clauses are inadequate.

- **Repairs** Like insurance, it is preferable for one person or company (usually the landlord or a management company) to take on the legal responsibility for the main fabric of the building. The roof, foundations, main timbers and so on must be legally covered. The covenant to repair must be enforceable and workable. The cost of repair is normally shared by means of the service charge. Again, if the lease does not deal properly with such matters, the flat will be difficult to sell or to secure a mortgage on. See Chapter 15 for more details.

- **Management structures** For larger buildings, the lease must provide a proper management structure. It is normal for a management company to be formed by the landlord, but it is possible for the tenants to set up a company themselves and manage the property (see Chapter 14). If the tenants do take over management of the building, each flat-owner becomes a shareholder or member of the management company, which will own the common parts of the building and assume the major responsibilities. This way the tenants run the property collectively, and there is one vote per flat. There is legislation to force bad landlords to comply with the lease (see Chapter 15), but having to resort to litigation is hardly the best way to manage a block of flats. Obviously in small conversions of flats, management structures will not usually be needed, as the lease will impose liability on the tenants individually and/or collectively. For example, if you have the top-floor flat in a Victorian house, you will usually be personally liable for repairs to the roof.

- **Mutual enforceability** It is essential that each tenant can enforce the obligations which the other flat-owners have entered into. The simplest way to do this is to ensure that the landlord or management company is legally obliged to enforce the obligations at the request of each flat-owner. If those obligations cannot be enforced by the other flat-owners, the lease is defective. A clause in the lease obliging such enforceability is the best answer.

Why leasehold flats?

From the freeholder's point of view, selling long leases for the flats in a building will raise capital (from the first tenants of the leases and re-sales at the end of those leases) and income from ground rent. As ground rent for individual flats is very low (never comparable to the market rent for a flat), such income is probably worthwhile only if the freeholder has numerous properties or some other interest in the property: for example, if he or she lives in one of the flats.

Some landlords may view the long-term prospect of a property reverting back at the end of the lease as an inheritance to leave for future generations. However, this notion is now threatened by the recent rights given to groups of tenants to buy the landlord's freehold jointly – collective enfranchisement – and to individual tenants to obtain an extension of their respective leases (see Chapter 18).

From the tenant's point of view, owning a leasehold flat may not seem very different from owning a freehold property. For many purposes this is very near to the truth. The leaseholder can sell the unexpired period of the tenancy for such price as the market will pay. The lease, although declining in value with the passing of time, will for many years be a saleable asset. Indeed, for the greater part of the lease, the tenant has a more valuable interest than that held by the landlord.

Apart from the financial advantages to both landlord and tenant, the main practical reason why flats are traditionally leased out rather than sold freehold is maintenance. Landlords usually wish to retain a high degree of control over the premises. The simplest way to do this is to set up a management scheme covering all the flats in the building, whereby the upkeep of the whole property is ensured. As has been mentioned before, leases generally impose a variety of conditions (covenants) on a tenant. In a block of flats, for example, it is essential that the covenants regulating maintenance, repair and insurance are enforceable against each flat-owner, so that ceilings, walls, floors and other important parts are kept in good repair.

While positive covenants (that is, obligations to do something, like repair or pay money) are enforceable between landlords and tenants of a leasehold flat, they are not enforceable between the parties in a freehold flat. Although it has always been possible, in theory, to buy a freehold flat (sometimes called a 'flying freehold'), such purchases are unusual because banks and building societies are very reluctant to lend on them. This reluctance is due to the fact that, as positive covenants cannot be enforced against freeholders, the security for the loan is not as well protected as with a leasehold flat. Even though most flat-owners would prefer to own a freehold estate rather than a leasehold estate, the general unavailability of mortgage finance for freehold flats is the major reason why leasehold flats are the norm. In contrast, freehold titles of flats are to be found throughout the rest of the world, for example, in the USA in the form of condominiums and in Australia and New Zealand in the form of 'strata' titles. As long ago as 1990, the government proposed a new 'commonhold' scheme of freehold ownership of flats and communal management of common parts, and this legislation was finally introduced in 2002 (see Chapter 2). Importantly, this new type of flat ownership allows all covenants to be enforced against future owners of the flat. The introduction of commonhold title during 2004 should mean that the number of leasehold flats will diminish over future years.

A wasting asset

A lease becomes less marketable below a certain number of years (usually estimated at 60 years), or marketable only to a cash buyer because of the difficulty of obtaining mortgage finance for a comparatively short lease. New statutory rights allowing tenants to buy the freehold collectively or to obtain a new lease go some way towards overcoming the problems associated with the wasting nature of a lease (see Chapter 18).

The value of the property may also be depressed by lack of maintenance and unchecked deterioration of adjacent flats. This can be a major cause of concern for flat-owners and gives rise to many legal difficulties.

What happens when a lease is assigned?

When the unexpired term of the lease is sold on (assigned), the original tenant, and any intervening assignees, drop out of the picture for most purposes. The first tenant, however, is in an unusual position. As regards leases that were granted before 1 January 1996, he or she will always remain liable on the contractual covenants contained in the original lease.

Sadly, since the recession of the 1990s, there has been an increasing number of legal cases in which action has been brought against an original tenant when a landlord has been unable to sue a current, insolvent tenant for breach of covenant. This has happened even when the first tenant sold the flat at a market price a long time ago and had nothing to do with the current tenant's breach of covenant.

As a step in the right direction, however, the Landlord and Tenant (Covenants) Act 1995 has altered the law relating to leasehold covenants. With new leases granted since 1 January 1996, the first tenant is automatically released from liability on tenants' covenants when the lease is assigned. When a freehold is sold, the former landlord can apply to the court to be released from landlord's covenants.

The Act does not affect the rules that apply to sub-leases. With a sub-lease, the original tenant should ensure that the covenants in the head-lease, which still bind him or her, will be honoured ('performed') by the sub-tenant.

Chapter 2

Commonhold

In England and Wales there are currently only two ways to own land: freehold and leasehold. Freehold is the closest to absolute ownership, whereas leasehold offers ownership for a temporary period. The Commonhold and Leasehold Reform Act 2002 introduces a new way of land-owning known as 'commonhold' which offers a new alternative to leasehold. This development is designed primarily – but not exclusively – to cover blocks of flats. Unlike leasehold, it allows the occupier (the 'unit-holder') to own the freehold of an individual flat while collectively – with other flat-owners – owning and managing the common parts through a 'commonhold association'. Great things are expected from commonhold: the 1997 Labour Party manifesto declared that it 'will provide a complete answer to many of the problems which have plagued flat-owners over the decades'. It is probably the best method of empowering flat-owners. Commonhold title will be available some time during 2004 although many fine details still have to be worked out.

Why the change?

Commonhold was proposed fundamentally because of the rules which govern the enforceability of covenants (promises in a deed). There are two types of covenant: first, the positive covenant, which is a promise to do something (for example, to keep the property in repair and to pay rent and service charges); second, the negative (or restrictive) covenant which is a promise *not* to do something (for example, not to make alterations or use the property for business purposes). It has always been the case that both positive and negative covenants can bind future tenants of leasehold property.

In contrast, positive covenants (unlike negative covenants) cannot bind a subsequent purchaser of freehold property. The potential difficulties are well illustrated in the case of a block of flats where each flat-owner depends upon the other flat-owners to help keep the block in proper maintenance and repair. This simply could not be guaranteed if the flats were held on a freehold basis. Accordingly, the overwhelming majority of flats are held under a leasehold title.

Leasehold ownership, however, is traditionally beset with a number of problems, such as the following.

- In many parts of the country, a leasehold flat is not as readily marketable as a freehold house.
- Towards the end of the lease, the tenant can feel saddled with an asset which is wasting away and losing value with each passing year.
- The tenant may face high service charges levied by the landlord.
- In order for tenants to safeguard their financial interests, they may feel compelled to buy out the landlord's freehold and to form a company to manage the block for themselves.
- If the tenant fails to carry out all the leasehold covenants, the lease can be terminated prematurely (that is, forfeited) by the landlord.
- Throughout the lease, the tenant is required to pay an annual ground rent to the landlord.

The introduction of commonhold is designed to offer the security of freehold ownership while ensuring that positive covenants bind each and every current and future flat-owner. The scheme lays down a local set of dos and don'ts for a block of flats, which would be enforceable by and against each owner and the commonhold association. Despite these obvious attractions to the flat-owner, the scheme will only be voluntary. This means that whether or not a commonhold system applies to a new development will be solely at the discretion of the freeholder. It remains to be seen whether commonhold will be favoured by property developers or, as it is a novel scheme, viewed with suspicion.

The key features of commonhold

A new vocabulary

Commonhold introduces a range of new terms and expressions into the flat-owner's vocabulary.

- Each flat within a commonhold development will be called a **unit**.
- A flat-owner will be known as a **unit-holder**.
- The common parts will be owned and managed by a body called a **commonhold association**. Members of the association are the unit-holders themselves; there is no separate landlord.
- The rights and obligations of the owners and association will be governed by a formal document called a **commonhold community statement**.
- The payments made by the occupiers towards the running costs of the block (in leasehold known as service charges) are retitled as the **commonhold assessment**.

The units

For a commonhold scheme to operate there will have to be a minimum of two units. It does not matter whether the units are detached, separated vertically (as with terraced houses) or horizontally (as with flats and maisonettes). If horizontally, however, no part of the scheme can be over any part of a building which is not part of the commonhold scheme. The units will be identified in the commonhold community statement that sets out the details of an individual scheme; this statement will also include a written description of the units comprised in the scheme, and a plan depicting them. It will be possible for a unit to comprise two or more separate areas of land (for example a flat and a detached garage). Obviously, the community statement will have to be certain and comprehensive because any future changes to the size of a unit can only be made with the consent of all the occupiers and, where relevant, any lender with a mortgage interest in a unit affected by the change.

The commonhold association

Under the provisions of the new legislation, a commonhold association must be formed before registration of the commonhold can take place. The association must be a private company limited by guarantee (that is, its members' liability is limited to a fixed guarantee, in this case £1) and its members will comprise the unit-holders within the development. The purpose of the company is to manage the block, including its maintenance and insurance. The company will be registered at Companies House in the usual fashion and will have a standard set of documents of incorporation (memorandum and articles of association). These documents will deal with such matters as the voting rights of members, the minimum requirements for the keeping of accounts and the method for calculating and collecting the commonhold assessment. Copies of these documents will have to be deposited at the Land Registry before registration of the commonhold can take place.

As with any company, the association must have directors and provision for their appointment and removal. As the flats are sold, the purchasers will automatically become members of the company, but the rule is that there can be only one member per unit. When all the flats are sold, the developer's interest in the association will, understandably, cease.

The members will elect the directors of the commonhold association. This means that individual unit-holders, being members of the association, will then have direct control over the common parts and the commonhold assessment levied to look after them. Disputes between members will be determined by internal procedures as set out in the association's documents of incorporation. If this does not work, the matter will go to arbitration under an approved ombudsman scheme to be set up by the government.

The commonhold community statement

This lays down the scheme for governing the collective management of the development; it must be drafted before the commonhold can be registered at the Land Registry, and will be of particular interest to prospective purchasers of the units. The scheme will come into full operation when the first flat is sold and the purchaser is registered as proprietor with commonhold title.

The community statement will set out the reciprocal rights and duties of the association and the unit-holders and will require mutual cooperation by the parties for specified purposes (for example, access to inspect and to carry out repair works). Other rights will be reserved to allow car parking, the use of communal drains, cables and the like, waste disposal etc. The statement will also impose restrictions upon individual occupiers, for example, not to cause a nuisance, not to make alterations to the unit without the consent of the association and not to carry on a business from the premises. General restrictions on use might be imposed such as prohibiting ball games on the communal lawn or controlling the placing of goods in a common hallway.

The statement will normally impose duties on the unit-holder to pay the commonhold assessment, to undertake prescribed works (for example, relating to the internal decoration and repair of the flat), to give notice of dealings with the unit (any sale, lease or sub-lease of the flat), and to indemnify the association against costs arising from a breach of his or her obligations. The commonhold association will have to ensure that occupiers comply with their obligations; equally, it must indemnify the unit-holders against a breach of its own obligations.

Registration

The commonhold title to the site will need to be registered by the developer at the Land Registry. The developer will need to produce to the Land Registry the commonhold association's documents of incorporation and the commonhold community statement. Any person with an interest in the land (for example, the developer's mortgage lender) must, however, consent before the title to the site can be registered as commonhold. Once the appropriate documents and consents have been obtained, the commonhold will be registered in the name of the developer. From then on, a register will be maintained at the Land Registry, including details of the scheme and copies of the documents supplied. This initial registration will occur before any of the units in the development are sold. As soon as the first unit is sold, the common parts (for example, communal landings, lifts, entrance halls and gardens) will be registered in the name of the commonhold association. The developer will retain title to the units until after the sale of each unit, when the purchaser will be registered with commonhold title of the property bought.

Conversion to commonhold

It is planned that existing leasehold schemes may be converted to commonhold, although the change can only happen with the consent of all leaseholders and the freeholder. This consensus is likely to be difficult to achieve. The government is, however, likely to relax this rule. It will not be possible to have commonhold of only part of a building – simply put, it is an all-or-nothing affair. Conversion will be more suited to blocks where the freehold is already vested in the tenants' management company, and in this instance no purchase costs will be involved other than Land Registry fees and legal costs. The management company will apply for the registration as commonhold and, if conversion goes ahead, the company will be adapted to become a commonhold association. From the moment of registration as commonhold, the leasehold interests will end, the commonhold association will take control and the commonhold community statement will regulate the management of the block.

In other cases, conversion is likely to prove more problematic and expensive. If, for example, the freeholder is not the tenants' management company then that landlord will be in receipt of rents and service charges. The freehold then has a value that exists outside the interests of the tenants. The landlord's consent, needed for conversion to commonhold, may not be forthcoming. In that situation, the tenants will be able to buy the freehold collectively (under 'collective enfranchisement') and subsequently take the decision to switch to the commonhold system. Indeed, collective enfranchisement has been made more straightforward under the Commonhold and Leasehold Reform Act 2002 – the new rules simplify the eligibility criteria and reduce the scope for costly dispute over the price to be paid (see Chapter 18).

Future dealings

Under the commonhold rules, the individual units/flats can be dealt with freely by their owners and they could, for example, be mortgaged, sold or bequeathed by will. But subdivisions of the unit will be prohibited and the unit-holder's ability to lease the unit is restricted. Dealings with the unit will, of course, have ramifications for the membership of the commonhold association, and the new purchaser should be registered with the association as the replacement member as soon as possible after completion of the sale.

Financial matters

The scourge of leaseholders is the service charge levied by the free-holder for the management of their block. When the tenants' management company is the freeholder, the threat of excessive charges is, of course, reduced, and so it would be with commonhold. The service charge, to be called the commonhold assessment, would be detailed in the commonhold community statement and the directors of the commonhold association would be required annually to make an assessment of the income necessary to meet the running expenses of the block. The services to be charged for would usually cover insurance premiums for the entire block, maintenance of common parts, and security. A sinking fund might be built up in order to pay for any major repairs that might be needed at a future date.

The total amount of the assessment would be allocated between the individual units according to a formula set out in the commonhold community statement. This allocation might be geared to the relative sizes of the units or according to council-tax bands. The commonhold association would notify the individual unit-holders of the amount required each year. If arrears build up, interest could be charged. Unlike the situation with leasehold flats, the association would not be able to forfeit the lease for non-payment. Commonholders will not be able to refer disputes about the reasonableness of the commonhold assessment to the Leasehold Valuation Tribunal*. Instead, the new scheme will contain an internal dispute resolution procedure. The details are still to be finalised.

Chapter 3

Buyers, sellers and estate agents

There are various types of flats and, while the law applies equally to all, there are different considerations to take into account depending on the nature of the flat bought. The main descriptions that are applied to flats are the following:

- **Conversions** This is where the freeholder of a building converts it into a number of dwellings. In most cases of small conversions, each flat will have a separate entrance and there will be no common parts retained by the landlord and shared between the tenants. The tenants will be responsible for main-taining and repairing the interior and exterior of their flats. Maintenance of the roof, for example, will normally rest with the owner of the upper-storey flat. As regards larger conver-sions (e.g. of a warehouse), they will operate as a block of flats (see below). During conveyancing a surveyor's report (see Chapter 6) will indicate how well the conversion work has been carried out and alert the buyer to potential problems. Conversions of older properties can lead to higher risks of expensive repair work and structural problems. Often there will be no service charges payable under leases taken in small conversions.

- **Mansion flats** This term, often used by estate agents, does not have any legal significance, but it does, however, carry a certain prestige. It simply refers to the character of the building in which the flats are contained – normally a large, imposing, resi-dential building. In such large-scale conversions, the landlord will retain common parts and, as with purpose-built blocks of flats, enter into a series of mutual covenants with each tenant. A service charge will be payable to reimburse the landlord's costs of managing the premises.

- **Purpose-built blocks of flats** In purpose-built blocks, the legal relationship between the landlord and the tenants (and between the tenants themselves) is close and there is a greater degree of interdependency between them all. The individual tenant has little direct control over the external structure of the building, and the quality of life and the value of the flat are influenced by the actions of the landlord as well as those of the other tenants. The tenants will pay the landlord an annual service charge (which can be substantial) to finance the costs of managing the premises. The problem with purpose-built blocks is that they may not be well constructed. To detect any structural problems the whole building may have to be surveyed, thus adding substantially to the surveyor's fees. If the block falls into serious disrepair, the tenants may be faced with hefty service charges and flats that cannot be sold except at a knock-down price. Moreover, banks and building societies will not lend money to buy a flat in a block that is rundown.

- **Studio flats** These are essentially one-room flats (the living room normally doubles as a bedroom) with a separate kitchen and bathroom. Some studios, however, may have a raised gallery to accommodate a bed. Obviously, studios are cheaper than one-bedroom flats, but tend to be more difficult to sell. It is often worth spending a little extra to acquire a separate bedroom.

- **Basement flats** These are, as the name suggests, flats that are below ground level. Such flats may have problems with damp and lighting. Generally speaking, they are not as easy to sell (and do not retain their value as much) as flats on the ground (or higher) floors.

- **Lofts** These are flats situated within converted warehouses or other commercial buildings. The term 'loft' has nothing to do with which floor the flat is situated on. Such conversions are normally characterised by exposed brickwork, iron beams and industrial-style staircases, but blended with state-of-the-art kitchens, bathrooms and security systems. Loft living is marketed at the younger, unmarried and affluent professional class of buyer. There are, however, some potential drawbacks with buying a loft conversion. Due to the nature of the planning permission often granted for such developments, the lease might permit 'live–work' occupation of the loft. Consequently, landlords might argue that, because some business use is permitted, the loft-owner is deprived of important legal rights afforded to residential tenants of more conventional properties. In particular, this potential for mixed use might take the tenant outside the laws which govern collective enfranchisement (buying the landlord's freehold estate) or the right to buy an extension to the lease. This different type of flat appears to give rise to some novel problems.

- **Maisonettes** Generally speaking, maisonettes are similar to flats, but they have their own entrance and are on two floors, with their own internal staircases. They may have a common garden or a shared water tank in the roof space. Maisonettes could be in purpose-built blocks or in houses which have been divided up. The law applies similarly to leases of property whether horizontally or vertically divided.

- **Pieds à terre** This expression sometimes finds its way into estate agents' particulars. It applies to flats in cities and large towns, and means that the flat would make a small and convenient second property (a stop-over) for those who live outside the city/town.

- **Newly constructed flats** Whether such flats are in a large block or a small development, the buyer has some protection offered by the National House Building Council (NHBC).★ This is a non-profit-making body with a register of some 25,000 builders and developers who undertake to build flats and houses to a set of standards drawn up by the Council. NHBC inspectors will have examined the property and, if the builder is registered with the Council, issue a ten-year Buildmark warranty. This offers the buyer some protection if faults emerge (see Chapter 8 for details). It is also generally easier to raise mortgage finance on a newly constructed flat than on an old property. Clearly, the newer the building, the less likely it is that it will require repair or maintenance in the short term.

- **Local authority flats** Tenants who have lived in council property for a certain number of years have the right to buy at a substantial discount (see Chapter 20). Ownership of such flats is the same as that of any other flat, except that there is a clawback of the discount if the flat is sold on within a set period (currently three years but soon to rise to five years). Problems may arise, however, on buying a flat in a council block. Often, such blocks fall into severe disrepair. If that happens, the tenants could face service charges beyond their means, and more importantly, the property will become 'red-lined', which means that no prospective purchaser (if one can be found) will be able to obtain mortgage finance. Consequently, the tenant will have to sell at auction at a considerable loss or hope that the council will buy it back.

- **Housing association flats** Housing associations and other social landlords exist to give people the opportunity to buy their own home. The development projects are financed by government grants and the properties are normally situated in poorer housing areas. These properties are subject to similar 'right-to-buy' rules as council properties (see Chapter 20).
- **Repossessed flats** Flats which have been repossessed by the mortgage lender can be bought in the same way as any other property. The lender will not, however, be able to supply comprehensive details about the property and will not know whether the previous tenants had any disputes with the neighbours. Sales of repossessed homes often take place at a public auction or by tender, and there is no doubt that the lucky buyer can snap up a bargain.

Buying a flat

Flat-hunting

Once you have decided to buy a flat the process of looking for one can begin. You may even have chosen the area in which you would like to live. This choice can be influenced by a combination of factors such as: closeness to work, public transport or family and friends; price; safety; or general attractiveness in terms of amenities and natural beauty. If you have not yet selected an area, it might be helpful to compile a list of features that you are looking for and check out different locations.

Estate agents

By far the most common way of finding a flat is through the use of an estate agent. Contact estate agents in the area you have chosen, give them your specifications (the number of rooms you want, whether you want a garage or garden, how much you are prepared to pay, etc.) and ask to be put on their mailing lists. This will ensure that details of suitable properties ('particulars') are sent to you at regular intervals. A growing number of agents now have their own web pages on the Internet.

Although estate agents are prevented by law from actually misdescribing property that they are trying to sell, you should remember that they tend to use the most flattering terms possible in their particulars. Do not get carried away by their use of adjectives. 'Desirable residence', 'deceptively spacious', 'conveniently situated', 'luxury kitchen', 'exceptionally well presented' and similar expressions adorn many agents' descriptions. They have, however, no legal significance and are merely designed to get the prospective buyer into the flat. Photographs of properties will also tend to flatter.

When you want to view the properties that seem attractive, the estate agents, who act as negotiators between the seller and you, will arrange appointments for you to do so, and very often will accompany you there. Estate agents can also offer advice about mortgages, surveys and solicitors. As a buyer, you do not have to pay the agents: they get their commission from the seller.

Some estate agents (roughly a third of all agents) are members of the Ombudsman for Estate Agents (OEA)★ Scheme. Members will display an OEA logo on their premises. This is a voluntary scheme which obliges its members to comply with the OEA Code of Practice. The code offers tight regulation of the estate-agency business and provides for dispute resolution between members and their clients. The estate agent is required to operate an internal complaints procedure, which must be set out in writing and available for inspection. All complaints are to be recorded and all written complaints acknowledged within three working days. The complaint, however, has to be made within 12 months of the alleged wrongdoing. At the same time, the estate agent must give a commitment to send a formal written outcome within 21 days. An in-house appeals procedure must also exist for those clients dissatisfied with the initial outcome. A final written statement should then be sent to the client; this letter should include information about the possible referral of the dispute to the Ombudsman. The client must, however, apply to the Ombudsman within six months of the closure of the agent's internal complaints procedure.

If the complaint is upheld and concerns unfairness, inefficiency or delay, the Ombudsman has the power to award you compensation up to a maximum of £25,000 although most awards are under £500. A common grievance is the refusal of the estate agent to pass on offers made by prospective buyers unless they agree to obtain financial services through the agent.

If you have genuinely been misled by the estate agents' particulars, or have another grievance against the agents, complain first to

---

The new Code of Practice

The Ombudsman for Estate Agents has issued a new Code of Practice for estate agents which came into operation in 2003. The key features of this code are:

- never deliberately to misrepresent the price of a property or recklessly make misleading statements
- at the outset, to give clients a written copy of the contract with the client as well as details of fees, expenses and business terms. Information as to how the agreement can be cancelled must also be given
- as appropriate, to provide an explanation of the phrases 'sole selling rights', 'sole agency' or 'ready, willing and able purchaser'
- to inform the client of the Ombudsman for Estate Agents Scheme and to make available the Code of Practice free of charge
- not to harass or cause offence in order to gain instructions
- not to erect a 'For Sale' sign, allow unsupervised viewing or give out keys without the client's permission
- to record all offers made and to pass them on to the client as soon as is reasonably practicable. There is to be no discrimination against a prospective purchaser on the ground that the purchaser will not take financial services offered by the estate agent
- to tell the seller if the purchaser does take advantage of its services and thereby disclose any potential conflict of interest.

---

the firm and then, if necessary, contact the association of which the estate agent is a member, or the Ombudsman (if relevant). General and legal advice may be sought from your local Citizens Advice Bureau or a solicitor. Recourse to the courts should be viewed as a measure of last resort.

Other sources

There are other ways in which a buyer can find out what is on the market. Flats for sale are advertised in specialised property magazines and local and national newspapers. The Internet is a useful and popular source of information. It is also helpful to drive or walk round the area chosen, looking for 'For Sale' signs and to ask friends and acquaintances about any properties they might know of.

First impressions

Apart from the dimensions and the internal layout – which are arguably the most important considerations when choosing a flat – there are a variety of other factors that a prospective purchaser should bear in mind. It is worth writing down a list of the features that are important for you in a flat, so you know what to look out for when viewing. Compromising on some of them will almost certainly be called for – no single flat will provide all you want – so it would help to decide before you start viewing which factors are absolutely essential and which you can forgo. Some of the more important things to look out for are listed below. Many of them are specific to flats, so even an experienced house-buyer will find the tips useful.

The exterior

- Notice the state of decoration and repair of the outside of the building: as far as possible, look at the condition of the roof, pointing, chimney stacks, down pipes and gutters. Look at the common parts of the building – the stairways, gardens, parking areas – to see whether they are clean, reasonably decorated and well lit. Look for puddles which might indicate poor drainage.
- In a block of flats, check whether there is a lift and examine the width and incline of the stairways. If possible, ask other residents about the reliability of any lift fitted. If there is no lift and you are considering buying a flat above ground-floor level,

imagine facing the daily climb up to the flat carrying shopping, children, etc. It is also advisable to find out about rubbish disposal and window-cleaning facilities.

- Check on the rights to use (and the obligation to maintain) access areas and gardens, and verify what the price does and does not include.
- Note how close the building is to the road, schools, pubs, railway lines, etc. These factors are potential irritants. Conversely, check on how conveniently located the flat is for public transport and amenities which are important to you – parks, banks, shops, medical facilities.
- Check whether there is a garage (large enough for your car) or a parking space which comes with the flat. A garage, in particular, can add to the selling price and make the property more marketable. You should also check on where visitors can park.

The interior

- Inside the flat, look for any tell-tale signs of damp: for example, a musty smell, crumbling plaster, stained ceilings and mould around the windows. With ground-floor or basement flats, ask if a damp-proof course has been fitted. If so, ask whether it is still under guarantee. If you visit the flat in winter and the seller has the windows wide open, this might be an attempt to disguise the odour of damp. Look also for cracks in the ceiling, sloping floors, and ill-fitting doors and bulges and cracks in the walls, which may indicate settlement problems.
- Check whether there is central heating and double or secondary glazing. It is always wise to ask the seller to turn on the central heating to see if it is in working order. Listen for unusual noises and check that all the radiators come on. Turn on the taps.
- A number of factors which may seem trivial at this stage could prove to be problematic later on. Check, therefore, on things like how well the doors and windows fit and whether they open and close easily; how many electric sockets there are in each room and whether they are fitted firmly; how many telephone and television points there are; how old the central heating boiler is; what state the bath and other sanitary facilities are in;

and whether the storage space and loft space available are adequate.

- If in a block, see if the windows open inwards. If they do they will be easier to clean and might be outside the service charge clause. It is cheaper to clean them yourself than to employ a window cleaner or pay the landlord for doing so.

One of the most important tips is that if you are interested in a flat you should visit it more than once and at different times of the day. By doing so you could discover, for example, loud neighbours, barking dogs, noisy lifts or increased traffic. If you can, talk to the neighbours to settle any queries you may have about the area. It is also likely that one visit might leave a more favourable impression about the flat than is deserved. For example, you may not realise on your first visit that the carpets are stained or that few rooms benefit from natural light. A second or even third visit may be necessary for you to put your doubts at rest.

Running costs

You should also ask about the following:

- the band of council tax the flat falls under
- the heating bills and water rates (including whether the water used is measured by a meter) – ask the seller if you can see recent fuel bills
- the annual ground rent payable on the flat
- the level of service charges: what they cover and when they are payable. It may be that every three years or so an extra charge is made for painting the exterior, so ask to see bills over a few years
- whether the landlord is intending to carry out any major repairs or maintenance work on the building or block (if so, there may be extra charges to pay in future).

Selling a flat

Although there are alternative means of finding a buyer (for example, placing an advert in a local newspaper), employing an estate agent is the most effective and efficient means of doing so. An estate agent (or a valuer working with one) will help you fix a price for the flat, based on the local market. The agency will conduct negotiations with prospective buyers, advertise and market the flat, and arrange (conducted or unconducted) viewings of your property.

Estate agents work for the seller of the property. They have a duty to obtain the best price reasonably available and an obligation to disclose offers made in respect of the property. Choosing an estate agent to sell your property can, however, be perplexing: there are likely to be numerous firms in your area. It is possible that one may be personally recommended to you or that you have used a particular agent before and were satisfied with the service provided. It could be that, when looking for a property to buy, you have come across an agency which impresses you by its professionalism. A local agent might have a special expertise in selling flats in your area – you can tell if you see many more 'For Sale' signs from one particular firm than any other outside flats being marketed. Decisive factors may be what an agent is prepared to do to advertise and sell the property (and at what price), and whether it can help arrange a favourable mortgage or put you in touch with other professionals (for example, a solicitor).

An agent's right to payment will depend on the contract entered into with the seller. Agents are obliged to explain their charges before the contract is signed. Some require a fee to be paid at the outset and most require the seller to pay a percentage of the purchase price (usually 1½–2 per cent for sole agency – see below – and 2–3½ per cent for multiple agency) or, alternatively, a fixed fee, when a buyer is introduced. The contract may provide that if a willing buyer is introduced, but the seller decides not to proceed, the fee still remains payable. It is also possible that the agent will operate on a 'no-sale, no-fee' basis, but beware of this ploy as some agents require the payment of expenses even if a buyer is not found.

Two types of arrangement with estate agents are commonly found: 'sole selling rights' and 'sole agency'. The sole selling rights agreement means that, even if the flat is sold privately without the agent's involvement, the fee becomes payable. Generally, this type of agreement should be avoided. The sole agency agreement, however, allows a private sale without fee. It also allows other estate agents to be employed in addition to the original agent. However, if one of the other agents finds a buyer, the seller must pay double commission (that is, to the original agent as well as to the selling agent).

Other arrangements that might be encountered are the 'joint agency' (whereby two agents are instructed and they agree between them as to how the commission is to be split) and the more expensive 'multiple agency' (whereby the seller chooses how many agents to employ, with the commission being paid to the one who finds the buyer). The latter is usually best if a quick sale is required. The Ombudsman for Estate Agents Scheme requires the agent to explain such arrangements in clear language.

Chapter 4

Mortgages

The majority of residential purchases are financed by a mortgage, which is a major form of credit. Strictly speaking, the word does not mean a loan; it refers to the security provided by the borrower to the lender. A loan helps you (the mortgagor) buy a flat, which you pledge as security for the loan – that is, you cannot sell the flat without repaying the loan, and if you do not keep up your repayments, the lender (the mortgagee) has the right to go to court to repossess the flat.

The major characteristics of a mortgage are:

- A person borrows a sum of money for a fixed period of time – often between 20 and 25 years – from a lender to buy a property.
- The borrower gives the lender a legal right over the flat, but retains legal ownership of it.
- The borrower has a right to redeem the mortgage – that is, he or she can repay the capital and interest (and any redemption fee or penalty) and so terminate the mortgage at any time.
- If the borrower defaults, the lender has certain rights and remedies through which the security for the loan may be safeguarded and enforced.
- If the borrower becomes insolvent, the lender has priority over other creditors and is entitled to be repaid in full.

Home-ownership: dream or nightmare?

A mortgage is the largest financial commitment in the lives of millions of people. By offering a flat as security for the loan, the buyer can borrow a substantial sum which is normally repayable over 20 or 25 years. The attraction is that the borrower has the opportunity to become an owner-occupier, which would otherwise not generally be possible. The borrower not only acquires a place to live but also makes a speculative capital investment: even though the buyer owes the lender the amount borrowed, if the flat rises in value then the increase belongs to the buyer and does not affect the amount owed.

In the 1990s, however, there was a disturbing number of mortgage defaults. In 1991, for example, there were 75,500 repossessions in England and Wales (see 'Lender's remedies', on pages 55–6). Although in 1995 the number had fallen to 49,410, by 1999 it had risen to 71,000. It has been estimated that during the 1990s over 500,000 households were affected by repossession. The recession in the 1990s was characterised by high rates of inflation, high interest rates and rising levels of unemployment. Withdrawal of tax relief on mortgage interest payments and increasing numbers of divorces and separations also contributed to the mortgage arrears problem. Although the lender has wide powers for enforcing the debt (particularly taking repossession), if there is a substantial decline in property values, selling the property may not recoup the value of the mortgage. The borrower then remains liable to the lender for any excess outstanding, plus interest and the lender's legal and administration charges. This concept of 'negative equity', that is, where the value of the property is less than the outstanding mortgage debt, became a major problem in some parts of the UK in the early and mid 1990s. Particularly affected were first-time buyers who purchased during the property boom of the late 1980s.

Therefore, the best advice to a potential borrower is not to over-extend yourself financially. If you are seeking a mortgage, it is imperative that you should find out exactly how much it is going to cost you each month and be sure that you can meet those payments, and cope with higher payments if interest rates rise. Taking out insurance (home loan protection or a mortgage payment protection policy) against being unable to make mortgage repayments is generally advisable (see Chapter 12 for details). If you do face problems about repayments, it is advisable to contact either a solicitor or the Citizens Advice Bureau and let them undertake debt negotiations. Professional debt counsellors now advertise widely, but may promise more than they can deliver. First, they will usually require a fee (which, of course, puts you further into debt) and, second, your mortgage lender might refuse to do business with them. If you take this route, proceed with some scepticism and caution.

Kinds of mortgages

When you have a mortgage you have to pay back the money you borrowed (the capital) and the cost of borrowing the money (the interest). This is done by making regular monthly payments over the life of the mortgage. Although there are now thousands of different products on the market, there are two main types of mortgage: repayment mortgages and interest-only mortgages, the majority of which used to be endowment mortgages.

With a **repayment** mortgage, interest and capital are repaid over a set number of years (for example, 25) by monthly payments. In the first few years of the mortgage the repayments go mainly towards paying off the interest. The proportion of the monthly repayment being used to pay off capital gradually increases over the years. In later years, therefore, the balance outstanding will be greatly reduced. The borrower might be obliged (or at least advised) to take out separate life insurance cover (term insurance), so that if he or she dies during the life of the mortgage the balance owed will be repaid.

With most repayment mortgages, the amount of the loan discharged used to be adjusted only once a year and so, for 11 months per year, the borrower was paying interest on a sum greater than that actually owed. This practice was described as the £350 million scam. Not surprisingly, there was a growing demand for fairer mortgage deals. Lenders have developed a new range of flexible repayment mortgages under which interest is calculated on a daily basis rather than annually. This means that when the borrower makes a payment, the outstanding debt is reduced immediately and interest is then calculated on that reduced sum.

With an **interest-only** mortgage, two separate payments are made each month. First (this is the bulk of the repayment) is the money which goes to the lender towards repaying the interest, that is, for servicing the loan. In the most common type of interest-only mortgages, until now endowment mortgages, the second amount went into an investment administered by a life insurance company, and also acted as the premium for a life insurance policy (tax relief for these premiums was abolished some years ago). There were many kinds of policies available; many lenders were 'tied' to an insurer and so would encourage borrowers to take a policy with that insurer. The idea was that the money paid into such a company – which would invest it for you – would build up over the years to enable you to repay the capital outstanding in one lump sum when the policy matured. A **'with profits' endowment** policy was designed not only to pay enough to cover the capital borrowed but in addition, if the company invested your premiums well and profited from it, to give you a share of the profits when the policy matured. The other main kind of endowment policy was the **unit-linked endowment** (see page 46), which was more risky than the 'with profits' variety. The possibility of getting a surplus amount on maturity, and the benefit of built-in life insurance (so that the mortgage was paid off by the insurer should you die during the period) were the usual reasons for choosing an endowment mortgage.

Pension mortgages, another type of interest-only mortgage, are normally relevant only for self-employed people (or those with a personal pension) above the age of 35 years. With a pension mortgage, the borrower arranges for a mortgage loan alongside a suitable pension policy (and sometimes a life insurance policy as well). During the term of the mortgage, the borrower pays the interest due each month and regular premiums to a pension plan. There is no capital repayment. The premiums under the pension scheme generate a (tax-free) cash sum that is ultimately used to pay off the mortgage debt and also provide a pension for life (an annuity) which is then taxed as earned income.

Although somewhat similar to an endowment mortgage, a pension mortgage is more tax-efficient because of the relief on the premiums paid into the pension scheme. The borrower should, however, be aware that the lump sum used for repayment of the mortgage loan reduces the capital upon which the pension is based, so that the pension will be a reduced one. So, unless you really want to use part of your retirement fund to pay off your mortgage, do not go in for a pension mortgage.

Individual savings account (ISA) mortgages are a common type of interest-only mortgage. An ISA mortgage is similar to endowment and pension mortgages. The borrower sets up the finance for the purchase of a flat through a mortgage lender, but repays only the interest (and not the capital) on the debt each month. He or she also takes out an ISA and makes monthly deposits. The expectation is that the money in this savings scheme will grow over the mortgage term and cover the loan. The borrower gets to keep any excess there may be. However, like other interest-only mortgages, ISA mortgages involve an element of risk. The rule of thumb is that one should save £15 per month for every £10,000 borrowed. This type of mortgage is more flexible than an endowment mortgage, is cheaper to set up, has tax advantages and can be cashed in early. Normally the lender will insist on a life insurance policy being taken out. The government has guaranteed the continued existence of ISAs until 2009.

The amount paid monthly on both interest-only and repayment mortgages usually changes when interest rates go up or down (see page 47).

Repayment versus interest-only mortgages

The question of which type of mortgage to choose vexes most first-time buyers. Endowment mortgages have come in for severe criticism recently because there is no guarantee that the maturity value will be sufficient to discharge the whole mortgage. *Which?* magazine has suggested that most people are better off avoiding them because they are old-fashioned, risky and inflexible. However, there is no simple answer: thinking about your circumstances now and in the future is the best way to come to a decision.

A **repayment** mortgage is probably better for you if:

- you are unwilling to take a risk – all interest-only mortgages have an element of risk built into them
- you expect to come into a lump sum of money that can be used to pay off all or part of the debt outstanding: it is relatively easy to arrange this on a repayment mortgage
- you want to make modest regular payments
- you think you may experience difficulties in paying the monthly amounts: under the repayment scheme, the overall mortgage term can be increased more easily so that those payments are reduced
- you are not likely to stay in the UK housing market for the whole 25 years – with an endowment mortgage the benefit arises only when the policy matures
- you want a mortgage term of less than 20 years.

On the other hand, an **interest-only** mortgage may be better for you if:

- you are willing to take a small risk; if the investment you make performs well you could end up paying off the capital and have a tax-free lump sum left over. On the downside, and as indicated above, there is no guarantee that the policy will provide a surplus lump sum on maturity, or even that it will be enough to cover the capital.

Disadvantages of endowment mortgages

Low-cost endowments were, until recently, the most common policy used as the means of repaying an interest-only mortgage. The policy contained both life cover and savings and the policy was supposed to grow enough during this term to build up sufficient capital to pay off the mortgage. Often these policies were sold on the basis that there would even be extra capital available after the mortgage was paid off as a 'nest egg'. While people who took out endowments in the 1970s saw their policies mature with more than enough money to pay off their policies, endowments are now struggling. Today many thousands of these policies are falling behind and will not produce enough to pay off the capital owed. A large number of people with endowment mortgages have had to make decisions about whether to increase their premiums, or put in place alternative arrangements to cover the shortfalls. If you have been affected by the mis-selling of an endowment mortgage, you should first make a formal complaint to the individual or company that was the source of advice. If this does not resolve matters you should contact the Financial Ombudsman Service.*

The problem with endowment policies sold in the past was that they had very high charges, which often meant that little or no investment would take place in the early years of the policy. This made them very poor value if you were forced to stop paying cash in during the early years. They were also very inflexible. You could not decrease the premiums or extend the term, and if you increased the premium you incurred yet more charges. This meant that often, if you increased or extended your mortgage, you would have to take out yet another endowment to cover the new mortgage, rather than being able simply to restructure your original plan. Despite this, endowments were sold as the 'flexible' option, with many advisers criticising repayment mortgages for their rigidity.

Mortgages for the self-employed

Traditionally, the self-employed have not been treated well by the mortgage market, apart from the availability of pension mortgages. Until recently, it was the case that, in order to obtain a mortgage, the borrower would always have to produce audited accounts for the previous three years as proof of income. Audited accounts are not, however, a true reflection of disposable income – they are merely the individual's tax returns, usually massaged by an accountant to keep tax liability down. Recently, new self-certification mortgages have been introduced which operate on the basis of self-certified accounts – these are designed for people who cannot produce audited accounts that will satisfy mortgage lenders' traditional requirements (for example, people with less than three years of accounts, or low net earnings, and contract workers and company directors). The lender will assess the borrower's credit-worthiness by looking at bank statements, carrying out a credit reference check and obtaining an accountant's letter.

As a further safeguard, lenders do not usually allow the self-employed to borrow 100 per cent of the value of the property, in the absence of audited accounts; on average, the advance will be some-where between 70 and 80 per cent of the value of the property to be bought. You can get advice on the availability of such mortgage deals from one of the more than 3,000 mortgage brokers now registered in England and Wales: the FSA has a register of members, which can be consulted.

If you have a bad credit history

If, in the past, you have been declared bankrupt, gone into arrears with a mortgage and/or have county court judgments outstanding against you, then obtaining a mortgage is likely to prove difficult. Certainly, the major lenders will not contemplate making an advance in those circumstances. Specialist mortgage lenders (sometimes called 'sub-prime lending sources') now exist and they deal with such higher-risk cases, but they will not advance 100 per cent of the property's value and will charge a higher interest rate than with standard mortgages. Albeit an expensive form of credit, this is much better than borrowing money from disreputable loan sharks.

Council housing: right-to-buy mortgages

Various statutory provisions give local authorities the power to sell freehold or leasehold council housing stock to tenants. Since 1993 tenants no longer have the right to a mortgage from public funds in order to finance the transaction. The traditional local authority mortgage is repayable over a period of up to 25 years. Each prospective buyer has an individual income limit, although a local authority may, if appropriate, advance a sum greater than this income would normally warrant. The detailed calculations of the income limits are given in regulations laid down by the government.

Drip mortgages

This is a method of home-buying more properly known as a rental purchase. It is technically not a mortgage but a scheme akin to buying a home on hire purchase. In essence, it consists of a contract for the sale of the property, with the buyer occupying the premises and paying the purchase price to the owner by instalments. Legal title to the property is conveyed to the borrower only on the final payment.

This form of credit is generally used in the context of low-quality, low-priced housing. The borrower is particularly vulnerable as he or she does not have the protection afforded by the law to the main-stream mortgagor. An occupier can be evicted for non-payment, losing both a home and the rental payments already made. The drip mortgage is often used by landlords to avoid statutory protection afforded to tenants of rented property and is, potentially, the source of much abuse. It should be treated with great caution.

Other variations

Other types of mortgage include the following:

- **Unit-linked endowment mortgages** The borrower pays interest along with regular monthly payments which are invested in unit trusts. At the end of the mortgage the idea is that the units are cashed in and the proceeds used to discharge the capital borrowed. This is a risky venture because unit values can go down as well as up and so it is possible that the units when cashed in do not discharge the mortgage debt.

- **Annuity mortgages** This is a scheme aimed at older borrowers who already own a home. The borrower mortgages the flat and with the proceeds purchases an annuity which provides an annual income for life. This is an expensive way of generating income, particularly if interest rates rise, and is generally not to be recommended.

Types of mortgage deals

Whichever method you use to repay your mortgage, you also need to choose the type of mortgage deal to go for.

- **Fixed-rate mortgages** These mortgages guarantee that interest rates will stay the same for a set period (for example, three or five years). After the set period has expired, you pay a variable rate. Fixed-rate offers have proved popular, but their value hinges on the economic climate that prevails through the period of guarantee. If interest rates are both low and stable, then the fixed-rate method can prove more expensive. If interest rates are unstable and likely to rise, a fixed rate can produce savings and security. Many lenders require an extra payment (an arrangement fee) to secure the availability of such a mortgage and charge a penalty (up to six months' interest) if you change mortgages within the fixed period.
- **Variable-rate mortgages** Most mortgages have a variable interest rate which can move upwards or downwards according to changes in the lender's current standard rate. All major lenders offer similar rates, which are based on the Bank of England's base rate, but away from the high street the amount of interest charged can differ sharply. For example, in one recent case a lender charged 12.9 per cent while, at the same time, a high-street lender was charging 6.9 per cent on a similar mortgage product. The borrower sought to challenge this for being an exorbitant credit arrangement under the Consumer Credit Act 1974. This challenge failed because, although the court held that the interest charged was unreasonably high, it was not exorbitant. In addition, the court recognised that variable-rate mortgages were not covered by the statutory provisions and that, provided that the lender did not act dishonestly or maliciously, it could vary the rate to whatever level it saw fit.

- **Capped-rate mortgages** These mortgages are a mixture of variable and fixed-rate mortgages. Essentially the lender guarantees that the interest rate will not *exceed* a set level for a set period but that it will *fall* in line with variable mortgage rates.

- **Base-rate trackers** A recent development, this sort of mortgage comes with an interest rate linked directly to the Bank of England's base rate (say, 1 percentage point higher than it). When the base rate falls or rises, the mortgage interest rate automatically moves with it: that is, the move is not at the discretion of the lender. Clearly this is advantageous when the base rate falls; however, when it rises the borrower has no cushion.

- **LIBOR-linked mortgages** The interest rate in this type of mortgage is linked to the London Inter-Bank Offered Rate (LIBOR), the rate at which banks offer to lend money to each other. Again, like base-rate trackers, here the interest rate is set at a certain percentage above LIBOR and it changes according to movements in LIBOR. This sort of mortgage is useful if the borrower wants the loan in foreign currency.

- **Flexible mortgages** These sorts of mortgages are useful for borrowers who can pay off their loans early or who might prefer to repay in differing amounts, within permitted limits. Most flexible mortgages count overpayments as made on the date made and this will bring about an immediate reduction in the interest outstanding. Being able to alter the monthly amount paid might benefit those who wish to take a 'mortgage break' or those whose income fluctuates, for example, the self-employed. Some of the newer flexible mortgages are linked to a current account; in such cases the lender supplies a cheque book which enables the borrower to borrow more money at mortgage rates – this can be a cheap way of borrowing for other large purchases, such as a car, or for home improvements. As the borrower's salary will be paid into the account, each month there will be an overpayment which reduces the balance of the loan and interest outstanding. The degree of flexibility may vary, so read the small print.

How to apply for a mortgage

Choosing a lender
If you want to buy a flat – and you need a mortgage – you will have to decide who to borrow from and find out how much you can get.

Building societies and banks are the two main kinds of mortgage lenders, and they account for nearly all new mortgages these days. However, a new style of lender is emerging. These lenders do not have high-street branches and instead work from a central location. They are often associated with an existing bank or insurance company, and much of their business is conducted over the telephone or via the Internet. Some supermarkets now offer mortgages in the same way. The advantage to you is that it allows you to sort out your mortgage from the comfort of your armchair – the loan can be approved in principle before you put the telephone down or leave your computer, and the application form will be forwarded for your signature. These direct mortgages are advertised widely and your mortgage broker will have the details.

Checklist: what to ask a lender

- Does it have fixed-rate, variable or capped interest rates?
- What interest rate does it charge for each different kind of mortgage?
- If you are a first-time buyer, does it offer you a special interest rate?
- What happens when interest rates change?
- What is the maximum it will lend you?
- What percentage of the valuation will it lend you? (This is technically referred to as the loan-to-value ratio.)
- How easy would it be to switch from one type of mortgage to another?
- What types of insurance (see Chapter 12) will you have to buy as a condition of the loan?
- Is the advice the lender gives completely independent: is the firm trying to sell you the products (say, insurance) of the company it is tied to or are you free to choose the best for yourself?
- Will there be a redemption charge or penalty (see page 54) if you pay off the mortgage early?
- Is there an administration fee for closing the account?

With the emergence of supermarkets and insurance companies into the mortgage market and the decline in the number of mortgage applications, competition has become fierce. Home-buyers not only have a wide choice of institutions from which to borrow, but also face a bewildering range of schemes, discounts, cash-back offers and other incentives to tempt them towards a particular lender. It is advisable to shop around and check out the various offers available. It is not surprising that 44 per cent of all borrowers go through a financial adviser to help them find the best deal. In addition, many estate agents are owned by building societies, banks or insurance companies and may offer to arrange a mortgage for you. *Which?* magazine frequently publishes reports dealing with mortgages. See above for a checklist of what to ask a lender.

How much can you borrow?

Most lenders have a formula for working out how much they will lend you. This calculation is usually based on your annual income before tax. If you are buying a flat on your own, you will probably be able to borrow up to 3½ times your annual income; if it is with a partner (no distinction is usually made between married and unmarried couples), the amount will be around 2½ times your joint incomes. However, some lenders are more generous than others in this calculation, so it is possible you could be offered different amounts by different lenders.

Although it may be possible to obtain a mortgage of 100 per cent, expect to pay a higher rate of interest. Most lenders will advance between 90 and 95 per cent of the purchase price, subject to valuation of the property. With such high advances the lender may require the borrower to take out insurance to guarantee payments (see Chapter 12 for details). If you need 'top-up' finance because the loan you can get is not sufficient, you may be able to get it from an insurance company or a bank. You may have to pay a higher interest rate on this top-up loan than on the mortgage itself, and may have to take out another insurance policy to cover it, so think very carefully before you do this.

It is important to realise that just because a lender will advance you a sum it does not necessarily mean that you can afford the repayments. From October 2004, most lenders will have to assure themselves that you can afford the loan from your income or other sources. Although this duty will be imposed under the Financial Services And Markets Act 2000, this safeguard does not offer a guarantee as to your future ability to pay. Moreover, if you have a 100-per-cent mortgage, and interest rates rise and property prices fall, you are immediately vulnerable to negative equity. Do not stretch yourself by borrowing the absolute maximum you can. You may well have other financial commitments – like children or elderly relatives – now or in the future. Bear in mind too that you will need money to equip and run the flat (buy furniture and curtains, pay the council tax, service charges, etc.) and for other stages of the conveyancing process (solicitor's fees, survey, etc.).

Getting a mortgage certificate

It is possible, in many cases, to obtain a so-called mortgage certificate, even before a property is found, which states how much the lender is willing to advance you (subject to the value of the flat you want to buy). It is estimated that one in seven buyers obtains such a certificate. The buyer will normally approach only one lender for a certificate, but there is nothing to stop a number of certificates being obtained from different lenders. Nevertheless, there is little advantage in approaching more than one lender unless you expect difficulties in obtaining a mortgage at all or for the amount sought.

You apply for such a certificate usually by filling in a form giving details of your income and commitments. The lender will almost certainly check with your employer (if you have one), bank and present landlord to find out whether you are a credit-worthy and reliable person before giving you a certificate. This could take some time, so make sure you allow for it when planning. A mortgage certificate is usually valid for a limited period, but it could be useful if you need to persuade a seller that you are a serious buyer who will have access to the finance required.

The certificate is not, however, an absolute guarantee that the lender will advance the money on the property you want to buy. Whether the money is forthcoming will depend on factors such as:

- the results of the survey (see page 105)
- the length of the lease on the flat (anything less than 60 years could be problematic)
- the age and location of the flat.

Arranging the mortgage

When you have found a suitable flat and have put in an offer on it you can apply formally for the mortgage. You have to provide the lender with information on the flat you want to buy, including the price. You will have to say how much you need to borrow, and probably also where the rest of the money (say, for the deposit) is coming from.

The lender will then arrange to have the flat valued, which you usually have to pay for. This is a basic mortgage valuation (see pages 80–1 for details), but most lenders will ask if you want a home-buyer's report or a full structural survey (see pages 81–2) done at the same time. If the lender decides not to give you a loan based on the valuation – or if you decide to pull out of the purchase – the fee you pay for having the valuation done will not be refunded.

Bear in mind too that the borrower has to pay the lender's legal expenses as well as his or her own fees in connection with the purchase of property. To keep costs down, the borrower's conveyancer will usually act for the lender as well.

Following approval of the application, the lender will issue a mortgage offer. It could take as long as three weeks from making an application to receiving an offer. The proposals put forward by the government to speed up the process of house-buying and -selling (see page 87 for details) may require buyers to obtain 'in principle' mortgage offers before they make an offer on a property.

A mortgage offer sets out the conditions on which the mortgage is to be given; the lender could insist, for instance, that you should take out mortgage payment protection insurance. Usually the offer is valid for between three and six months, but it can be withdrawn at any time. It must be read carefully because, once the mortgage is set up, the terms in the offer will be binding. Some lenders charge a reservation (or administration or booking) fee to secure the sums to be borrowed, which could be between £100 and £300. Such a charge is more common in offers of fixed-rate mortgages. The fee may be refundable if the money is not borrowed.

The government has announced proposals to ensure that 80 per cent of mortgage applications are dealt with by lenders within two working days of receiving all the relevant information. Research has shown that one-third of all buyers in England and Wales complain about delays by the lender and other problems connected with obtaining mortgage finance. The government also advocates the introduction of a new type of finance, the 'chain-breaking loan', which would be cheaper than a traditional bridging loan (one taken to tide a person over between the time when he or she has to pay the purchase price of a new property and the time when the proceeds of the sale of another and/or mortgage funds become available). This would enable a buyer to purchase a flat or house even though problems existed elsewhere in the chain of transactions. It still remains to be seen when these proposals will become reality.

Mortgage covenants

The lender imposes various obligations on the borrower in addition to the one repaying the loan. These will be listed in the mortgage deed, which will be kept in the custody of the lender throughout the mortgage. A copy of the deed will be provided to the borrower. The obligations may include:

- keeping the property in good and sufficient repair
- carrying out repairs and remedying defects as specified by the lender
- obtaining the consent of the lender before structural alterations and extensions are carried out
- sub-letting the premises only with the prior consent of the lender
- complying with all the provisions of the lease
- keeping the premises insured (see Chapter 12).

In the case of non-payment or breach of any other obligation, the lender may seek, and will have the right, to take possession of the flat. The court, however, may postpone repossession with conditions as to future payments/conduct.

The mortgage debt can be paid off prematurely only if written notice is given to the lender, who may then ask for a 'redemption fee'. Penalties for early redemption may be the equivalent of three or six months' interest, regardless of notice given, but such a fee is the exception rather than the norm: a usual redemption fee is in the order of £65.

Problems for existing borrowers

If you are an existing borrower on a variable rate, you might discover that you are paying a higher interest rate for the same product from the same lender than a new customer is paying. At the time of writing, it is a good time for new borrowers: interest rates are low and competition is fierce. While new custom is attracted by bargain offers, existing borrowers are being told by some leading high-street lenders that they are not eligible for the bargain rates. Recently, disgruntled borrowers have argued their case before the Financial Services Authority (FSA)* and won on the basis that the bargain rate represents the new variable rate. If you are in this situation, make a written complaint to the lender and, if not satisfied with the lender's response, after eight weeks you can complain to the Financial Ombudsman Service.* As always, keep copies of letters sent and the date and time of telephone calls made and received.

The borrower's rights

The borrower is given certain powers and rights in relation to the mortgaged property. These include the following.

Redemption

The right to redeem (repay in full) the mortgage at any time after the earliest possible date stipulated for redemption in the mortgage deed (normally six months after the date the mortgage is created) cannot be excluded, unreasonably postponed or unduly restricted by any other contractual terms. The lender may, however, impose an early redemption or penalty charge. This is common in the case of fixed-rate mortgages and mortgages which offer cash-back deals. The general rule is that the better the initial offer, the longer the tie-in period and the steeper the penalty if you seek to repay early.

Possession

Normally, borrowers wish to live in the property they have bought with the mortgage funds advanced. It is a historic right of the lender to take possession of the property at any time and without the borrower having defaulted (see pages 58–9); nevertheless, if you occupy the premises, and are not willing to leave voluntarily, you have some protection in the requirement that the lender must get a possession order from the court. The court has the discretion whether or not to grant possession to the lender.

Sale

The borrower has the right to sell the flat, but will need the consent of the lender before a sale can go ahead. If the borrower is in arrears with mortgage repayments, the lender has the right to seek to sell the flat, usually at auction and may object to any private sale going ahead; however, in such circumstances the borrower can go to court and ask the court to override the lender's objections to a private sale. This is so even if the flat is not worth the value of the outstanding loan (i.e. there is negative equity). This opportunity for the borrower to find a buyer is important, as a private sale will often command a higher price than a sale by the lender. But the borrower must make an application to court for an order of sale before the lender applies for a possession order, because afterwards the court will no longer entertain the borrower's claim for an order of sale.

Leasing

Subject to the lease, the borrower can sub-let and otherwise rent out the flat. Most mortgage contracts, however, will insist upon the borrower obtaining the prior permission of the lender. It is then likely that the interest rate will be increased. For example, so-called 'buy to let' mortgages carry higher interest rates than the conventional mortgage: this reflects the fact that the borrower is making a financial profit from the lender's money. The lender may also charge you an administrative fee for reading the lease and approving the letting.

Lender's remedies

The lender has a number of powerful remedies that can be used against a borrower in breach of the mortgage agreement. The costs involved will be added to the mortgage debt and a variety of fees will become payable as a result of the administrative work undertaken by the lender. This array of fees should be detailed in the information pack provided when you take out the mortgage. A code of conduct regulating the treatment of borrowers in financial difficulties has been drafted by the Council of Mortgage Lenders,★ a voluntary trade association to which most lenders will belong. The basic aim is that lenders should be sympathetic and treat borrowers in a fair manner. Copies of the code should be available from your bank or building society.

Breaches of the code are likely to influence a court in deciding whether or not a possession order should be granted and complaints will be subject to the Mortgage Code Arbitration Scheme run by the Mortgage Code Compliance Board.★ Compensation can be awarded under the scheme. Banks, building societies, insurance companies and the like are to be subject also to the wider jurisdiction of the Financial Services Authority (FSA).★

The current voluntary code

The Council of Mortgage Lenders' guidance imposes a code of practice on its members and the key obligations include:

- ensuring that borrowers are aware at the outset of the conse- quences of failing to keep up with their repayments
- encouraging customers to make contact as early as possible when difficulties arise
- responding sympathetically and positively to such approaches
- monitoring the accrual of default charges so that minor problems do not quickly become major ones
- exploring all possible avenues for dealing with cases of arrears, possession being a last resort
- providing information to customers regarding recognised advice sources and to work with these sources where acting for the borrower
- limiting the commencement of recovery action for any mortgage shortfall debt to a period of six years
- avoiding excessive or intimidatory practices in the collection of arrears.

Responsible lending: the way forward?

From October 2004, most mortgages will be caught by the Financial Services and Markets Act 2002. This will require most lenders to comply with new, compulsory rules and guidance issued by the FSA. A principle of 'responsible lending' will then be imposed on mortgagees which will require lenders to have regard to the interests of their customers and to treat them fairly. The idea is, as the FSA explained, '. . . that customers should not be exploited by lending in circumstances where they are self-evidently unable to repay through income and yet have no alternative repayment plans'. Although the rules are still being worked out, they are likely to include:

- a requirement that the lender shows that account was taken of the borrower's ability to pay
- a restriction on the level of charges that the lender can lawfully impose. As regards early redemption, the lender will be able only to charge a reasonable pre-estimate of the costs incurred by the lender. In relation to charges on arrears, again they will have to represent a reasonable estimate of the costs to the borrower. With reference to extortionate credit charges, the current Consumer Credit Act regulation will be replaced by a general obligation not to charge excessive sums which are contrary to the interests of the borrower. The lender will have to take note of the charges made by other institutions
- new measures are forthcoming which are intended to reduce the occurrence of arrears and repossessions. Clearer and more detailed information will be given to an intended borrower so as to allow the borrower to consider whether the repayments can be afforded, to tell the customer what risks exist if the repayments are not made and to direct the borrower to sources of advice if things go wrong. Lenders will also have to publish their own policy and procedures for dealing fairly with a borrower in arrears.

Breach of contract

The lender can sue the borrower for breach of contract to pay the money due or to perform any other covenant. Although the normal rule is that proceedings for breach of contract must be started within six years of the breach, with mortgages (classified as a 'specialty' contract) the period is 12 years. If, for example, there is a negative equity on the property sold, the lender can pursue the borrower for the outstanding balance. As regards mortgages regulated by the FSA

Policy and procedures

The draft lender's policy and procedures are more defined and extensive than the current Council of Mortgage Lenders' guidance and are likely to include:

- providing to the borrower, within five working days of the arrears becoming known, details of the missing payments, the amount of the arrears, the arrears charges likely to be incurred, the action that the lender can take, the willingness to discuss any proposals put forward by the borrower and organisations that provide free advice to those in arrears
- using reasonable efforts to negotiate a new structure of repayment with the borrower as an alternative to taking possession of the flat
- consulting with the borrower's adviser (e.g. Citizens Advice Bureau or other debt-counselling agency) regarding the arrears
- supplying to the borrower in arrears a monthly statement of payments due, arrears amassed and charges incurred
- taking a reasonable approach to the time within which the arrears are to be repaid and devising a plan which is tailored to the borrower's financial circumstances
- allowing the customer to change the repayment date of the mortgage instalments and the method by which payment is made
- taking possession of the flat only when all other reasonable attempts to recover payment have been taken
- before going to court for a possession order, providing the borrower with an update of the information already provided and some guidance as to obtaining local authority housing.

from October 2004 the borrower must be informed of any shortfall and the ability of the lender to sue will be limited to six years.

Taking possession

The lender has the right to take possession of (that is, repossess) the mortgaged property from the date the mortgage is entered into. In theory, this right exists even if the borrower has not defaulted on payments. In reality, however, lenders take possession only on default and as a means of obtaining vacant possession before exercising their power of sale. Many borrowers give up possession when they have defaulted on their payments, but if not, and if the flat is occupied, the lender must obtain a possession order from the county court. The court has the discretion over whether to grant this order. Generally speaking, if the borrower can devise a reasonable financial plan which will, over the remaining years of the mortgage, discharge both arrears and future payments, he or she could avoid repossession.

Sale

The lender has a right to sell, which can be exercised only if the following conditions are met:

- the borrower has failed to repay the loan following three months' notice to do so; or
- the borrower is in at least two months' arrears with the repayment of interest; or
- the borrower is in breach of any other covenant in the mortgage deed (for example, to insure or to repair).

Although the lender might need a court order for possession (see above), it does not need a court order to sell the flat. On sale, the purchaser will get a good title to the flat and the proceeds will be held on trust by the selling mortgagee and used, first, to discharge any prior mortgage; second, to discharge its own mortgage and costs; third, to discharge any inferior mortgages (for example, a later mortgage); and, finally, anything left will be paid to the borrower.

As regards mortgages regulated by the Financial Services Authority, the lender will have to market the flat as soon as possible. It will also have to obtain the best price reasonably attainable having regard to market conditions and the increasing indebtedness of the borrower.

Foreclosure

Foreclosure is an order of the court which terminates the mortgage and transfers the title to the lender. It requires a court order and is rarely granted. This is because foreclosure takes the flat away from the borrower even if it is worth more than the debt outstanding and disregards any capital repayments made while the mortgage was in operation. If applied for, the court will inevitably substitute an order for sale.

Staving off repossession

The most common reason for a lender wishing to obtain possession of a flat (or repossess it) is default on mortgage payments by the borrower. Although the number of repossessions was rather high in the 1990s, it does not mean that if you have difficulties in repaying your mortgage the flat will be repossessed immediately.

If you have mortgage payment protection insurance (see Chapter 12) and you become unemployed or fall ill, your insurance may help to make the mortgage repayments. Where no insurance is taken out, if you become unemployed, the Department for Work and Pensions (DWP, replacing the DSS) can make payments to cover interest due under a mortgage. In such circumstances the DWP will pay the mortgage interest, but not the costs of an endowment policy.

You could lessen the chances of a repossession order being granted by the court by:

- raising the necessary money and paying off the arrears
- requesting the lender to accept a short-term reduction in the monthly repayments
- sub-letting the flat (with the lender's permission) to generate some income to repay the mortgage debts
- persuading the lender to allow a switch from an endowment mortgage to a repayment mortgage if the monthly premiums for the latter are less. This would involve surrendering the endowment policy and using the proceeds to repay mortgage arrears
- asking for an extension of the term of the mortgage (for example, from 25 to 30 years) in the case of a repayment mortgage
- finding a buyer who can pay a more favourable price than would be obtained by the lender. If legal action is being undertaken at the time, the court may deny the lender possession and allow the sale to proceed.

Remortgaging the flat (that is, taking out another mortgage for the same or greater amount) is in these circumstances not advised. The risks in doing so are great – you may face higher interest rates, be forced into the clutches of non-high street credit agencies and end up owing more money than before. Although replacing your existing mortgage with another may appear to save money (for example, in lower interest rates, cash-back offers, etc.), such savings may be outweighed by the legal, administrative and valuation fees involved.

Benefits and mortgage payments

Income support and jobseeker's allowance are social security benefits to help people on low incomes. If you qualify for either benefit, you may get limited help to meet your mortgage payments, service charges and ground rent. As mentioned above, the government will pay only the interest, not the capital, repayments. Moreover, there is an upper limit of £100,000 on the size of the mortgage which is eligible. If the mortgage is larger than this, assistance may be given on only the first £100,000. The payments are made directly to your lender.

Restrictions may be imposed if your housing costs are considered to be excessive. One restriction is that the payment is limited to the average national interest rate. If you pay more than that, then the excess will not be covered by the state. Hence, you will face a growing mortgage debt. If you experience this shortfall, contact your mortgage lender immediately.

Rules that came into force in 1995 stipulate that if your mortgage was taken out *before 2 October 1995*, generally no help will be given with housing costs for the first eight weeks, 50 per cent of eligible interest will be paid for the next 18 weeks and 100 per cent thereafter. This does not apply to pensioners. If the mortgage was taken out *after 2 October 1995*, no help will be given for the first 39 weeks of a claim. After that time, the full amount of eligible interest (subject to the £100,000 ceiling) will be paid. The 39-week rule does not apply to pensioners. Other categories of claimants may receive special treatment. For further information contact your local Benefits Agency, housing centre or Citizens Advice Bureau.

In addition, a new mortgage-interest 'run-on' benefit has been introduced (imaginatively named the Extended Mortgage Interest Income Support Run-on!). This benefit operates when you or your partner have been claiming income support, incapacity benefit or jobseeker's allowance for 26 weeks, have been receiving help with mortgage payments and have started full-time work which is expected to last for five weeks or more. It continues the previous mortgage interest payments for a further four weeks. The idea is to overcome barriers to taking up work caused by the gap between pay day and repayment day.

Restrictions

You cannot claim for:

- premiums on mortgage protection insurance policies
- payments towards buildings insurance
- interest exceeding the national average rate
- interest payable during ineligibility periods (8 weeks or 39 weeks as appropriate)
- any amount relating to capital repayments (e.g. premiums of an endowment policy)
- interest relating to borrowings in excess of £100,000.

Chapter 5

A summary of the buying and selling process

There are normally distinct phases in the creation or transfer of a lease: preliminary negotiations and checks, followed by the formal contract after which the lease of the property is conveyed to the buyer. This chapter gives buyers and sellers an overview of the process, with some indication of how long the procedure takes and the types of costs that are involved. Chapters 6 and 7 go into the details of the pre-contract and post-contract phases respectively. See Chapter 6 for government proposals to speed up the process of flat-buying and -selling.

Different kinds of conveyancing

The process involved in buying/selling a flat ('conveyancing') varies according to whether the title to the land is registered or unregistered (see page 66). There are also some differences between the purchase of a new lease and that of an existing lease.

New lease, old lease?

The differences between the creation of a new lease and the transfer of an existing one are fairly minor. The buyer of a new lease can, at least, attempt to negotiate the terms of the lease, whereas the buyer of an existing lease has to be content with terms which have been negotiated by others. There is also a difference in terminology in the two situations: the sale of a new lease of a flat is normally called a 'grant' and the buyer may be termed a 'grantee', but the sale of an existing lease is described as an 'assignment' and the buyer referred to as an 'assignee'.

Getting to know the jargon

Several phrases and terms can cause confusion and need to be explained at this early stage.

- **Title** This is either the freehold or leasehold interest, which is being bought or sold.
- **Land** This is widely defined as including a plot of ground, buildings on the plot and fixtures attached to buildings. Although you may not think of it in these terms, even if you own an upper-floor flat with no garden you are still a land-owner.
- **Deed** A formal legal document that is signed, in the presence of a witness, by the parties to a transaction: e.g. a *title deed* on the grant of a lease or a *mortgage deed* on finalising a mortgage.
- **Conveyancer (legal adviser)** The person who carries out the legal work involved in the transfer of ownership: usually a solicitor, but can be a licensed conveyancer. There is nothing to stop d-i-y conveyancing (but see pages 75–6).
- **Contract** This is the document which makes the sale legally binding. It is usually in two identical parts, one signed by the buyer and the other by the seller, and has to be exchanged.
- **Lease** A lease is the document which transfers the title to the buyer and details the premises leased, the number of years for which they are let, the ground rent payable and all other conditions on which the lease is held (that is, the covenants).
- **Exchange of contracts** Most contracts will be drafted by conveyancers in two identical parts. One part will be left with the buyer and the other with the seller. Each will sign their own part and then swap them. This act of swapping parts is the exchange, and at that point the contract is binding.
- **Completion** This stage follows after the contracts are exchanged and is when the lease or assignment is 'engrossed' in deed form and signed by the parties. This completes the transaction.

Other terms can be found in the main Glossary at the end of the book.

In the granting of a (new) lease by a developer of flats, there is the normal contract stage followed by the final stage, completion. However, in most sales of new flats, the developer provides a comprehensive package, and the terms are largely non-negotiable. The lease is prepared and 'engrossed' (typed up) in deed form and completed by the developer's solicitors. The Law Society's★ protocol (see below) is not normally applied when the sale is by a developer. Usually, such a lease contains all the relevant clauses and the developer adopts a 'take it or leave it' attitude. In addition, National House Building Council (NHBC)★ cover (see page 106), planning permission and building regulations are far more important with a new flat than with a second-hand flat.

In contrast, selling an existing flat takes the normal conveyancing format and usually the Law Society's protocol is used, but the emphasis for the buyer is on matters such as service charges, insurance premiums and existing breaches of leasehold obligations.

The Law Society's protocol

The pre-contract conveyancing process, particularly for the sale of existing leases, has been simplified, since 1990, by the introduction of a standardised procedure. This procedure is known as the 'protocol'. The protocol includes a standard type of contract and a checklist of steps to be taken in order to ensure that the conveyancing goes ahead smoothly and quickly. A distinctive feature of this scheme is that as soon as the seller notifies a conveyancer that a potential buyer has been found, the conveyancer prepares a bundle of documents ('the package') to be sent to the buyer's conveyancer. These documents include a draft contract, 'office copy entries' (if registered land), outline of title deeds (if unregistered), property information form, a fixtures, fittings and contents form, and a copy of the lease with details of service charges and insurance. Although it is preferred practice, the protocol is not compulsory, and there remain many conveyancers who stick to their own tried-and-tested methods. It may be a good idea to ask your conveyancer to use the protocol because it should speed up the conveyancing process. The choice, however, usually rests with the seller's conveyancer. Those conveyancers who already use the protocol will normally show a TransAction sign and logo on their office windows.

Registered or unregistered land?

The system of conveyancing used also depends on whether or not the title to the land is registered. In practice, however, the distinction between registered and unregistered land crops up only in sales of existing flats. All new flats will have registered titles (the whole of England and Wales has been designated a compulsory area of registration). The main differences between registered and unregistered land lie in how the seller's title to the land is proved and the way in which the transfer occurs. (The detailed implications of the distinction between the two are examined in Chapter 7.)

First registration

As a result of England and Wales being areas of compulsory registration, new purchases of what was previously unregistered land will need to be registered for the first time. This does not apply to new leases of seven years or fewer, or to longer leases where on assignment the remaining term is seven years or fewer. It is thought that this figure will be reduced further in future years. First registration is triggered also on the next legal mortgage of the flat (unless a mortgage was already in existence) and following death of the existing owners. It is not triggered, however, if the lease is surrendered to the landlord or merges with the freehold estate (see Chapter 17). On first registration, all interests which were previously protected as land charges should become protected on the land register.

A typical transaction

The process

- An offer is made on a flat privately or through an estate agent.
- The buyer and seller instruct their respective legal advisers.
- The buyer arranges mortgage finance.
- The seller's legal adviser obtains proof of the seller's ownership of the flat. If the flat is unregistered, this will be a chart of how ownership passed to the seller (an 'epitome' of title). If the land is registered, this will be a copy of the Land Register (known as 'office copy entries'). A copy of the lease will also be obtained.

- The seller's legal adviser prepares a draft contract which describes the property to be sold and the rights and obligations that go with it.
- If the conveyancing protocol is used (see page 65), the seller will have conducted a local land charges search and forwarded (with the documents mentioned below) the certificate showing the buyer the results of that search. Otherwise, the buyer will have to conduct an official or personal search in the local land charges register maintained by the local authority.
- The contract, the draft lease, assignment or sub-lease, and proof of the seller's ownership are sent to the buyer's adviser.
- The draft contract is approved by the buyer's legal adviser.
- The buyer arranges for a survey of the property and obtains the mortgage offer.
- The buyer's legal adviser makes formal enquiries of the seller about the property; and traditionally either the buyer or his or her adviser makes enquiries of the local authority about the surroundings, as well as making a local land charges search.
- Both the buyer and the seller agree to the contract as drafted and are ready to enter into a legally binding written contract to buy and sell the flat.
- The contracts are exchanged and the buyer provides a deposit, equal to either 5 or 10 per cent of the price of the flat.
- If the title is unregistered, the buyer's legal adviser will examine recent conveyances of the property; if it is registered, the buyer's legal adviser inspects the Land Register.
- If anything needs clarification, the buyer's adviser makes enquiries of the seller.
- If there is a mortgage offer, the adviser for the lender (usually the same one as acting for the buyer) also investigates the seller's title documents.
- The buyer's legal adviser makes searches to discover any rights of third parties over the property. For unregistered land, a search is made of the Land Charges Register at the Land Charges Registry; if registered, a search is made of the Land Register at the district office of the Land Registry.
- The final version of the lease, sub-lease or assignment is drafted, embodying the relevant terms as agreed and, when approved by both parties, the final copy is typed up in deed form.

- If mortgage finance is involved, the lender prepares the mortgage deed to be signed by the borrower.
- Completion takes place. The buyer pays the balance of the purchase price and the seller provides the title deeds (if unregistered land) or the land certificate (if registered land). The lender takes the documents and the signed mortgage deed in return for providing the mortgage funds.
- In unregistered land conveyancing, the buyer used to acquire legal ownership of the flat on completion. For any new sale of unregistered land, the title must be converted to registered title (that is, registration must occur first). If the title is registered, the transaction has to be registered at the Land Registry before legal ownership passes to the buyer.
- The buyer notifies the Inland Revenue so that any necessary stamp duty land tax can be paid.

A rough timetable

Typically, from looking for a flat to completion often takes five to seven months. The conveyancing aspect of the transaction takes about two or three months. This is a rough and ready rule and can act merely as a guide: the exact period can be shorter or longer. There are many reasons why it takes this length of time:

- It can take up to a month to obtain the results of a local land charges search from the local authority.
- Obtaining a mortgage offer can be delayed by the time it takes to investigate the buyer's financial standing and to survey the flat to be bought. You can, and should, apply for a mortgage as soon as you find a flat. Contracts will not be exchanged before a mortgage offer is made. It can take several weeks (on average four) for a bank or building society to confirm the availability of funds for the transaction.
- It is common for there to be a chain of transactions, with each separate transaction needing to be synchronised with the others. For example, if John is buying Ted's flat, Ted is buying Diane's flat and Diane is buying Doris's house, Diane cannot proceed until everyone else in the chain is able to exchange contracts at the same time. Problems arising in one link of the chain (for example, if Ted cannot easily obtain a mortgage) can hold up all the other related transactions.

Costs involved

Buying and selling a flat can prove costly. The buyer will have to pay the following:

- **Legal adviser's fees** These can vary enormously and it is wise to shop around for the most attractive quote. A buyer will have to pay higher fees than a seller. As a rough guide, expect to pay conveyancer's fees of somewhere between ½ per cent and 1½ per cent of the value of the property.
- **Search fees** The buyer will have to pay for searches of the local land charges register maintained by the local authority (estimated to be between £35 and £75) and also the land charges register (for unregistered land) or the Land Register (for registered land).
- **Lender's legal costs** These will be kept down if the buyer's legal adviser acts also for the lender. The figures are prescribed by the individual building society or bank, but are likely to fall within the £100–£200 band. Your lender might refund this sum as part of your mortgage deal.
- **Costs of survey** The amount will vary according to the thoroughness of the survey commissioned (see page 80). The lender will also require a valuation report for which the buyer must normally pay.
- **Deposit** The buyer will have to pay a deposit (usually between 5 and 10 per cent of the value of the flat) when contracts are exchanged.
- **Stamp duty land tax** The buyer must pay a government tax of 1 per cent of the total value of the flat if it exceeds £60,000 (higher rates apply for flats valued at over £250,000 and £500,000; see page 96).
- **Land registration fee** If the land is registered, the buyer has to pay this fee, which is currently on a sliding scale of between £40 and £800.
- **Hidden costs** These include the costs of moving house, buying new furniture and appliances, and redecorating.

The seller will have to pay the following:

- **Estate agent's fees** These vary normally between 2 and 3 per cent of sale price. The costs of advertising the flat will also have to be met.

- **Legal adviser's fees** The seller will have to pay for the services of a legal adviser for selling the flat.
- **Hidden costs** These include removal expenses and, if buying another property, the expenses incurred as a buyer.

Common problems

In 1998 a consultation paper (*The Key to Easier Home Buying and Selling*) from the government identified the main problems experienced by buyers and sellers in England and Wales and showed how widespread they are:

- An estimated 28 per cent of offers made and accepted failed to make it to completion.
- One-third of all buyers ran into problems in the period between making an offer on a property and obtaining a mortgage. Typically these difficulties were caused by delays on the lender's part, valuation problems and conditions attached to mortgage offers.
- Half of all buyers and sellers experienced problems in the period between the mortgage offer being made and exchange of contracts. This is the time when most conveyancing problems are likely to arise. Delays on the part of the conveyancers, the need for an additional survey and organising completion (particularly when a chain exists) are the usual causes.
- One-quarter of all buyers and sellers had problems between exchange and completion; these concerned the arranging of a completion date and the handing over of the keys.

Interestingly, 30 per cent of buyers and sellers blamed each other for the problems that arose.

E-conveyancing: the future?

As yet, electronic conveyancing is not possible because of the general rule that a transfer of land needs to be completed by 'deed', which is a paper document. An exception to this rule already applies to the creation (but not assignment) of a lease not exceeding three years in duration. Such short-term leases can already be created by electronic means if the parties choose to do so. To enable the widespread use of e-conveyancing, therefore, the law will have to adapt and change its conceptions of what constitutes a deed and a land contract – electronic dispositions will need to have the same effect as those made on paper. In order that the entire conveyancing process can be conducted electronically, legal advisers will have to have a secure, Internet-based link with the Land Registry. This is currently known as a 'network access agreement'.

In addition, e-conveyancing would mean that, for example, searches are undertaken, contracts are drafted, seller's property-information forms are provided and funds are transferred in a dematerialised form. Stamp duty land tax provisions, which currently only extend to paper documents, will also need to be revamped. Mortgage lenders, estate agents and local authorities will have to make their systems compatible with e-conveyancing. A 'chain manager' at the Land Registry will have to monitor the progress of related transactions and provide up-to-date information to the parties involved. Those who want to carry out their own conveyancing will find it more difficult, but still possible to do so. The Land Registry will have to offer access to a computerised system at its nearest district office, and provide guidance.

Slowly, but surely, the ground is being laid to realise the grand design of a quick and efficient system of land transfer. The Land Registry has set up an e-conveyancing task force to develop this revolutionary system. The major advances are to be found in two new pieces of legislation:

- The Land Registration Act 2002 makes major changes primarily to allow for an electronic system of dealing with land. The Act attempts to make it possible to investigate title to land online, reliably and with the absolute minimum of additional enquiries and inspections. Unfortunately, the technology is not yet in existence, nor is the precise detail of a paperless scheme of conveyancing. The Land Registry has, however, a prototype system which it is taking around the country to show interested parties; but this is far from being complete or perfect. It is expected that online conveyancing will be with us within the next five to ten years, and the government is in the process of setting up a pilot scheme to see what practical difficulties emerge.
- The Electronic Communications Act 2000 has made general provision to facilitate electronic commerce. In particular, it deals with encryption and the legal recognition of electronic signatures.

In the hope of instilling public confidence in e-commerce, the Act imposes a voluntary code of control over businesses (known as trusted third parties) that provide cryptography services such as electronic signature and confidentiality services. Those that are approved will be registered.

E-conveyancing at a glance

The key features of the scheme will be:

- the conveyancing documentation will be in electronic form. This is known as 'dematerialisation' (e.g. land certificates and mortgagees' charge certificates will disappear)
- most conveyancing steps and communications between the parties will occur online
- there will be simultaneous completion and registration of title. At the moment, there is a 'registration gap' (of up to two months) between these stages
- the payment of fees and balance transfers will be coordinated by Electronic Funds Transfer
- there will be increased up-to-date information and transparency as to chain transactions
- mortgages will be the subject of immediate e-discharge on redemption.

Chapter 6

'Subject to contract': the first stages

Having found a suitable flat, a potential buyer has to embark upon the process of acquiring it. This may appear to be a rather daunting task, but it has to be remembered that the majority of leasehold transactions proceed smoothly to the reasonable satisfaction of both buyer and seller. Moreover, most of the legal work (and paperwork) is done by legal advisers and other professionals, so the buyer and seller do not have to be involved at every stage. This chapter starts at the point where a potential buyer is in a position to put in an offer on a flat and explains what happens at each stage until just before the contracts are exchanged. Owing to the sometimes drawn-out nature of negotiations, the wide range of enquiries that need to be made and the length and complexity of the standard lease, it is not unknown for errors, mistakes and misunderstandings to arise. Some of the more common pitfalls are dealt with in Chapter 8. Although both sellers and buyers of flats will find the current chapter useful, it is assumed that 'you', the reader, are a first-time buyer.

Agreeing terms

Further research before making an offer
Check that you know the answers to the points listed under 'Running costs' on page 36. Before making an offer on a flat you have seen and like, you must consider a few more practical details.

- Check that the seller is able and willing to move out when you want to move in. This is particularly important if either of you is in a chain and is waiting to buy/sell other property.
- Find out if there are any 'sitting tenants'; that is, if the flat or part of it has been sub-let to other people. If it has, you should get legal advice before you go any further.

- Check informally if there are any restrictions on the use of the flat – for example, can you keep pets? Although they will come to light in the draft contract, it may help to know before then.
- Ask the seller what the price includes in terms of fittings and fixtures. There may be some items that he or she is willing to leave (for example, cooker, fridge, washing machine) for which you have to pay separately. These details will be formalised in the contract later on.

Making an offer

When you have decided that you want to buy a flat, put in an offer for it without delay. If the seller is going through an estate agent, contact the agent to make the offer.

If you can, make the offer orally. It is still standard practice (although technically unnecessary) to make it clear that your offer is 'subject to contract' or 'subject to survey'. Until the contract is put into writing and signed, you are covered if:

- you are unable to obtain a mortgage or loan
- a survey advises you against going ahead with the purchase
- you change your mind for some other reason.

When making an offer remember that most sellers will expect some bargaining. A buyer can bring the asking price down a little unless there are other potential buyers who are likely to pay the full price. Once you have made an offer, either it will be accepted straight away or you will have to wait until other potential buyers have made their offers. Problems that could arise at this stage include 'gazumping' and 'gazundering', and these are dealt with in Chapter 8.

The seller will decide whether or not to accept the offer made and this decision will be influenced, for example, by how near it is to the asking price, the state of the housing market, the length of time the property has been up for sale and how desperate he or she is to move. Moreover, the problem of a 'negative equity' might put pressure on the seller to hold out for the advertised selling price for the flat. In other cases, it might be advantageous for a seller to get rid of the flat at a lower-than-expected price so as to be free of liabilities to meet mortgage repayments, service charges and other obligations under the lease (for example, to redecorate). Any 'loss' incurred because of a depressed market might balance out if the seller is then able to buy a new property at a reduced price.

Estate agents' deposit

Some estate agents request a deposit from you to demonstrate your commitment to buy. This is not the same as the deposit you will have to pay on the flat when contracts are exchanged (see Chapter 7). There is no legal significance in this payment to the estate agent and, if the transaction does not go ahead to contract, the deposit can be recovered. Under no circumstances should you pay more than a nominal sum (for example, £25) to indicate good faith. Make sure that you receive a signed receipt for any deposit you pay. If you refuse to pay any deposit, the estate agent will still be desperate for a sale and will probably not bother too greatly about the absence of a deposit. The agent does not have to pay interest on preliminary deposits of £500 or less. All such money has to be held in a separate client account and the agent must be covered by adequate insurance. The agent must be able to account immediately for all money held on behalf of clients. The agent cannot deduct costs or charges from clients' money unless given written authority to do so.

Instructing legal advisers

The term 'legal adviser' is used in this chapter to mean your solicitor or licensed conveyancer, whichever you instruct to do the conveyancing for you.

Do-it-yourself or use professionals?

There has never been anything to prevent 'do-it-yourself' conveyancing, but it is a difficult and risky business. At its most complicated, the process demands a knowledge of land law, trusts, planning and contract law. Moreover, although it is not beyond the abilities of the average person, leasehold conveyancing is more complicated than its freehold counterpart. The covenants concerning repair and maintenance, the rights of the tenant to use common areas, services provided and the liability to service charges, for example, are crucial matters that need to be considered extremely carefully. Once the transaction is completed, the parties are, to all intents and purposes, bound to it, so they have only one chance to get it right. Obviously, even professionals sometimes make mistakes, but at least they are insured and will be in a position to compensate for any loss that arises (see Chapter 8).

Who can do the conveyancing?

Until 1987 conveyancing for payment could be undertaken only by a qualified solicitor. It is now lawful for 'licensed conveyancers' to undertake conveyancing work on a professional basis. Licensed conveyancers can set up in business alone or work for solicitors' firms, estate agents, building societies and the like. This erosion of solicitors' monopoly on conveyancing (and the increased freedom of solicitors to advertise) has produced cut-price competition. It is worth shopping around for the best deal. It is reassuring to note that according to a government consultation paper in 1998, 80 per cent of buyers and sellers were satisfied with their legal advisers.

Legal advisers are obliged to charge only what is 'fair and reasonable', but this excludes stamp duty land tax and Land Registry and other unavoidable fees. It is prudent to ask about such 'hidden extras'. A mere estimate of costs does not bind the adviser to the figure quoted. The Law Society★ recommends that any estimate should be put in writing by the adviser (see Chapter 5 for a rough idea of costs).

The vast majority of purchases of residential flats will take place with the aid of a mortgage. This means that the lender (the building society or bank) will require a conveyancer to represent its interests. This may involve a third legal adviser, but often your legal adviser will be allowed to act for the lender as well. In any event, this will increase the overall cost to you.

To find a conveyancer, you could ask a legal firm you have used in the past if it has members specialising in conveyancing. If you are going through an estate agent, the agent may be able to suggest a legal adviser. Alternatively, ask friends, relatives and colleagues, check with your local Citizens Advice Bureau or look for an adver-tisement in your local paper or *Yellow Pages* or on the Internet.

Tell your legal adviser as soon as you wish to put in an offer on a flat and give him or her the name and address of the seller and that of the seller's legal adviser. The seller will provide the equivalent information to his or her legal adviser.

Arranging a mortgage

It is more than likely that you will need to borrow at least part of the cost of the flat you want to buy. Loans to people buying property are usually in the form of long-term mortgages, and are made by banks, building societies or other institutions like insurance companies, local authorities or finance houses. Chapter 4 explains in detail how and when to apply for a mortgage, what kinds of mortgages there are and what rights borrowers and lenders have.

The draft contract

At this stage in the process the seller's legal adviser prepares a draft contract which describes the property to be sold and the rights and obligations that go with it, which is approved by the buyer's legal adviser.

Preliminary documents

The buyer and seller are unlikely to become involved in preliminaries involving proof of title, but there will be a flurry of activity between their advisers and banks or building societies.

Before the contract is drafted, the seller's adviser will obtain title deeds to the property (if it is unregistered land) or an up-to-date copy of the Land Register (obtainable from the district office of the Land Registry) and a copy of the filed plan depicting the land to be bought (if it is registered land). See Chapter 7 for the distinction between unregistered and registered land, and its relevance to the flat-buyer/seller. The title deeds will normally be in the custody of the seller's bank or building society, who will release them to the legal adviser subject to certain conditions.

Preparing the contract

The contract, prepared by the seller's adviser, is commonly typed on a standard form (usually the Standard Conditions of Sale), which contains a large number of provisions. It incorporates both the **particulars** and **conditions** of sale. The particulars include a description of the property, the nature of the lease to be sold, and the rights which the owner may exercise over other land (benefits such as a right to use someone else's driveway) and rights which other people may exercise over the land to be sold (burdens such as the right of someone to use the driveway of the property to be bought; any charges on the land; and any freehold covenants which restrict the use of the land).

The conditions state the terms on which the property is to be sold, for example, provisions as to the deposit, covenants, vacant possession, the date for completion and insurance.

For the professional, it takes only a short time to fill in the details in these standard contracts, delete irrelevant provisions and add any special terms required for that particular transaction. In the case of a new lease (or sub-lease) being granted, the draft of that lease may be annexed to the contract. If the lease is being assigned, as well as a copy of the lease to be bought, there may be a draft deed of assignment attached.

Fixtures and fittings

One important issue the contract deals with is that of fixtures and fittings: it sets out what is included in the flat as part of the purchase price. Items often mentioned include fitted carpets, curtains, mantelpieces, gas fires and light fittings. Generally speaking, if the articles are attached to the building (substantially screwed in, nailed down or plumbed in) they will be regarded as *fixtures* and left in the property. This rule of thumb is not, however, conclusive, because if fixing an item to the building is the only way that it can be enjoyed (for example, a large painting or mirror), it will remain a moveable (a 'chattel' or *fitting*) and not become a fixture. Fittings may be taken away at will unless the contract specifically mentions them as being left behind.

In addition, the purpose for which an article is on the premises is a key factor in determining whether it is a mere fitting or a fixture. If it is intended to be an improvement of permanence, it is likely to be considered a fixture rather than a removable fitting. The only fixtures a tenant may remove during or at the end of the lease are those that, despite being attached to the building, are ornamental or domestic in nature. This category would normally include cookers and mantelpieces. If, however, an item is part of the architectural style of the room (for example, curtains specifically designed for a room) or if its removal would cause major damage to the fabric of the building, it must not be removed. When an article is removed, any damage caused to the property should be made good and this may involve some redecoration work. The seller may otherwise be liable to compensate either the buyer of the lease or the landlord.

The seller is rarely entitled to remove fitted wardrobes, kitchen units, showers and doors. Such items are clearly intended to be fixtures and cannot be classified as either ornamental or domestic. As a general rule, fitted carpets, light fittings, gas fires, attached towel rails, soap fittings and tap fittings also fall into this category, despite the term 'fitting'.

Unless the contract states otherwise, the fixtures are paid for in the purchase price of the flat. The seller can insert a contractual provision whereby the buyer pays an extra sum for items which the seller would be entitled to remove but is leaving behind.

Because the rules concerning what is and is not removable are confusing, it is important for both seller and buyer to know what is to be included in the purchase price, what will be removed and what will be left behind at extra cost. It is useful to have an inventory annexed to the contract detailing the items to be paid for by the buyer, and their prices. A well-drafted contract should mention any doubtful items (for example, fitted shelves, satellite dishes and wall lights) and not simply trust that they are covered by the term 'fixtures'. Under the conveyancing protocol (see page 65), there is a fixtures, fittings and contents form designed for this purpose.

Approval by the buyer's adviser

The draft is forwarded, with an identical copy, to the buyer's legal adviser for amendment or approval. The terms of the contract may be further negotiated at this stage, and it is not uncommon for the final agreed draft to be quite different from that originally proposed. There may be much 'to-ing and fro-ing' between the advisers to sort out such issues as the date of completion, the amount of deposit to be paid and, where it is a new lease or sub-lease that is being created, the wording of the covenants.

Once agreement has been reached, the buyer's adviser retains one copy of the draft and returns the other to the seller's adviser, who types out the contract in its final form and then sends one copy back to the buyer's adviser for checking.

Auction contracts

If the flat is being sold by public auction, the contract should be prepared by the seller's legal adviser in collaboration with the auctioneer. Although the law does not require this contract to be in writing, in practice the contract is drafted in written form. It is concluded on the fall of the auctioneer's hammer, and any documentation will be signed subsequently.

An auctioneer is in a somewhat odd position because he or she initially acts as the seller's agent and can sign a contract on the latter's behalf. On the fall of the hammer, however, the auctioneer becomes, through implication, the agent of the buyer and can sign the contract also on behalf of him or her. An estate agent does not have the authority to sign a contract on behalf of the seller, unless given instructions to do so.

The survey

As the seller gives no guarantee as to the condition of the property (the principle of *caveat emptor* – 'let the buyer beware' – applies), the buyer should commission a survey of the flat. The contract usually states that the buyer takes the premises in the condition they were in when the contract was entered into.

The Royal Institution of Chartered Surveyors★ can provide details of suitable surveyors and valuers, but it is easy to find one from looking in *Yellow Pages* or on the Internet. It is generally advisable to hire a surveyor who is independent of the estate agents who are selling the property. Some problems that could arise at this stage of the process are dealt with in Chapter 8.

A specialised search for any environmental hazards is advisable when a property is in a brownfield area. This extra protection costs about £40. It is also possible to have an energy audit carried out so as to test a property's energy efficiency: this usually costs about £25 and will be added on to a home-buyer's report or full survey.

Valuation

If part of the money needed to buy the flat is going to come from a bank or building society, the lender will insist on a surveyor's valuation of the property before agreeing to grant a mortgage. The fee for this valuation (£100 upwards, on a sliding scale) has normally to be paid by the borrower. This valuation is, however, carried out on behalf of the lender and is simply to find out whether the property is adequate security for the loan. It is based on a quick visual inspection and takes on board only the age, size and type of the property; the location and amenities; and the general state of repair of the premises. This type of valuation is not a structural survey and is, moreover, no guarantee that the property is worth the price asked for it. It will, however, determine the maximum amount the lender will advance.

Warning

It is estimated that 80 per cent of buyers rely on the valuation report alone. Remember, a valuation is not a survey – it is prepared for the mortgage lender's purposes, not yours, and is carried out to help the lender decide how much to lend you on the flat. It does not tell you whether the flat is worth the price you are paying for it.

Never rely on a valuation report because the property inspection will not pick up structural defects and disrepair. If you do rely on it and later discover defects, you will have no claim against the surveyor, the lender, or the seller.

Home-buyer's report

Most lenders allow the borrower to see a copy of the valuation report, but that is not the same as having your own structural survey carried out. Fortunately, the surveyor who carries out the valuation for the lender can be asked to produce a home-buyer's report (at a cost of about £300) or to carry out a full structural survey for you at the same visit. As the surveyor is going to visit the property anyway, this can save time and money.

The home-buyer's report is more extensive than a valuation. It is a mid-range survey. It should detect any subsidence and damp but it will cover only those areas that are reasonably accessible and visible. Essentially, it should confirm whether or not the building is in a reasonable condition.

Full structural survey

The full structural or building survey is more detailed than the home-buyer's report and will cover all the main features of the property. Such a survey costs between £400 and £600 and should be undertaken if the property is old, run down or unusual. As many flat-owners have to contribute (via a service charge) to the cost of repair and maintenance of the whole building, such a survey is the safest option. A ground-floor tenant may, for example, be expected to contribute to the replacement of the roof. The survey should, therefore, encompass as much of the building as is possible including the roof, foundations, gutters, and communal services such as water, gas and electricity supplies. If a serious defect emerges, you may be better advised not to proceed with the purchase because the cost of putting it right will usually be yours (perhaps shared with other tenants). The mortgage lender may also decline to make a full advance and retain sums until the repair work is carried out. If the survey identifies a potential defect, such as damp, it may be necessary to call in an expert company to confirm what remedial work will be required and at what cost. It may be useful to discuss the report with your surveyor for direct advice as to whether the flat is worth purchasing. The surveyor should also spot any 'planning blight' (that is, where the value of the property is affected by some construction or development in the area).

Making enquiries

Preliminary enquiries

The buyer's legal adviser makes what are normally described as 'preliminary enquiries' of the seller. This is done by sending a standard printed form containing a set of formal questions together with any additional queries that have arisen from an inspection of the property or the title documents. These enquiries are important because the seller is under only a limited duty to disclose defects in the property. Unfortunately, the questions are not always plainly worded and can be difficult for the lay person to understand.

If the Law Society's protocol is used by the seller, these enquiries are made via a Property Information Questionnaire. This form is divided into two sections: one is to be completed by the seller and the other by his or her legal adviser. The buyer may then make additional enquiries on an Additional Property Information Form.

As always, the responsibility of deciding whether any further enquiries are necessary rests with your adviser.

Examples of preliminary enquiries

The enquiries made at this stage usually cover matters concerning the ownership of boundary walls, rights of others to cross the land, planning problems, mains services and disputes involving the property, among other issues. In the case of a flat, several specific questions appear on the form (often called a Property Information questionnaire):

- Does the seller own the freehold of the land or a leasehold estate?
- What is the name and address of the landlord(s) and to whom is ground rent payable?
- Is the landlord's consent necessary for the sale and, if so, has it been obtained?
- Have any covenants been broken?
- What service charges are payable?
- Is there an insurance policy currently governing the property and, if so, what are the full details of the policy and coverage?

There is space on the form to allow extra questions to be asked (for example, concerning services provided, drainage, access to the flat and cost of past works on the premises).

Whether or not the protocol is used, the seller is not obliged to answer these preliminary enquiries, but responses that are deliberately untruthful may make him or her liable for misrepresentation and/or give rise to liability in negligence on the part of his or her legal adviser. It is, therefore, usually the case that the answers are not guaranteed to be accurate (in fact it is common for an exclusion of liability clause to be inserted), but some standard form contracts used by legal advisers expressly allow the buyer to rely on the replies. However, it is common for the answers to these important questions to be very circumspect and unhelpful: 'inspection will show', 'please search', 'we cannot say' and 'not to the seller's knowledge'. The whole point of the exercise can be defeated by non-committal answers.

In any event, mistakes and non-disclosures are unlikely to be discovered until after the lease or the assignment has been completed. Compensation may then be the only remedy for the disgruntled buyer (see Chapter 8).

Local searches

There are a number of matters that need to be clarified with the local authority before a contract is entered into. This is usually done by a search of the local Land Charges Register; for this you need to submit a standard form to the authority, pay a fee and ask for details of any local land charges entered against the land. A personal search may be made by calling at the offices of the local authority and, on the payment of the fee, conducting the search then and there. This does not, however, protect a buyer to the same degree as an official search, but it is a quicker alternative than waiting for the results of an official search. This search of the local Land Charges Register, which offers a view of the register only as it is on the day the search is carried out, is traditionally made by the buyer, but under the Law Society's conveyancing protocol (see page 65) the task falls on the seller. If the protocol is used, the seller sends the form to the local authority before finding a buyer. A document detailing the results of the search (the official search certificate) will be provided by the local authority. This speeds up the process and avoids delays. The cost of the search will be charged to the seller, but will normally be passed on to the buyer when contracts are entered into. The cost of a search varies between local authorities as does the time taken to complete the search.

Why a local search should be done

Matters which emerge from a search of the local land charges register include:

- planning enforcement notices
- conditional planning permissions
- tree preservation orders
- some compulsory purchase orders
- whether the property is a listed building
- financial charges for expenses incurred by the local authority (for example, for street works or repairs to a dangerous building).

Because the results of a local search are valid for only approximately three months, it may be that the search is out of date by the time the parties are ready to enter into a binding contract. Rather than wait the two or so weeks that it takes, on average, to obtain an official search certificate, it is possible to take out insurance (a search validation scheme) to cover the risks associated with the search being out of date. In conjunction with the protocol, the Law Society offers solicitors, on the payment of a small premium, insurance cover of up to £500,000 provided that the search is no more than six months old. As an alternative, some local authorities offer an updating service at a small charge.

Additional enquiries

The buyer's adviser also makes additional enquiries of the local authority for matters not covered by a local search. A standard form for enquiries was revised in 2000 and deals with a variety of issues including:

- any road works proposed within 200 metres of the property
- possible diversion or closure of roads or footpaths
- roads and paths maintained by a local authority
- public footpaths
- proceedings pending as regards an infringement of building regulations
- noise abatement orders
- sewers and drainage.

The replies will give the buyer information that the seller is under no duty to disclose and that would not be revealed in a survey. The local authority may be liable for any negligent replies.

Other searches

Other searches may be appropriate, depending on where the property is situated or whether you are purchasing the flat from a company. These may include:

- a Coal Authority search to check if the land is within an area of past, present or future mining
- enquiries of Railtrack if the property is near a railway line, to discover whether there are any adverse rights of way relevant to railway workings

- enquiries of planning authorities to discover whether the proposed development of other land might affect the flat to be bought
- a search at Companies House when the seller is a company; this will confirm if the company has the power to sell and show whether it is being wound up
- searches for limestone and tin-mine working
- a National Rivers Authority search if the flat is near a river; this will disclose who is responsible for the repair and maintenance of riverbanks
- a British Waterways Board search if the flat is near a canal; this will reveal whether you have a right of way over the tow path.

Agreeing the contract

The buyer and the seller will receive from their respective advisers a copy of the contract (which will be identical) in readiness to exchange them (see Chapter 7). The copy should be checked carefully to see whether it reflects the agreement actually reached between the parties (for example, price, extent of the premises, duration of lease and ground rent). Any changes must be negotiated and agreed between the parties and their advisers, and the copies altered accordingly.

Summary of initial steps to be taken

- Buyer selects a flat and makes offer 'subject to contract'.
- Buyer employs surveyor and obtains mortgage offer.
- Buyer receives draft contract and outline proof of seller's ownership.
- If Law Society's protocol is used, seller forwards Property Information Questionnaire and local land charges search certificate to buyer.
- If protocol is not used, buyer makes a local land charges search and preliminary enquiries of seller.
- If satisfactory survey and search are obtained and a mortgage advance is secured, the parties are ready to sign and exchange contracts.

A better way?

In October 1999 the government put forward proposals aimed at making the process of home-buying and -selling in England and Wales faster, more transparent and consumer-friendly. The measures, first described in the 1998 consultation paper (*The Key to Easier Home Buying and Selling*), propose that sellers should provide (or make available) an information pack to buyers. This will be provided by sellers or estate agents. These proposed reforms were set out in the Homes Bill 2001, which was set to become law. Unfortunately, the Bill was one of a number of items of legislation unable to complete their passage through Parliament before Parliament was dissolved for the 2001 general election. The government now intends to introduce this 'Home Information Pack' in 2004.

Reform

Under these proposed changes to the law, the Home Information Pack will contain standard documentation and information, including:

- copies of title documents
- replies to standard preliminary enquiries made by the buyer
- replies to searches made of a local authority
- copies of any planning, listed building and building regulations consents and approvals
- for new properties, copies of warranties and guarantees
- guarantees for any work carried out on the property
- a surveyor's 'home condition' report
- a draft contract and the lease
- recent service charge accounts and receipts
- building insurance policy and payment receipts
- any regulations made by the landlord or management company
- memorandum and articles of the landlord or management company.

Buyers would be encouraged to get a preliminary mortgage offer to ensure that the sale could be completed within a short period. They would also have to pay for a building society or bank valuation and might have to undertake a wider structural survey.

The cost to sellers under these new proposals is estimated to be £500; buyers would need to budget for over £500. Although it appears that the overall cost of the buying and selling process would therefore go up by an average of £500, it is hoped that legal and other fees would come down because of the reduction in the time taken.

All the professions and other bodies involved in the home-buying and -selling process (lenders, local authorities and other service providers) would be encouraged to take full advantage of advances in information technology to speed up the process. In addition, lenders would be called upon to examine the scope for developing 'chain-breaking' loans, which would be suitable for a wider range of people than current bridging loans. Insurers would be asked to develop further, and market more widely, insurance to protect buyers and sellers from gazumping, gazundering and other problems (see Chapter 8).

The above reforms are intended to:

- help the buyer commit to the transaction
- shorten the period of uncertainty between acceptance of offer and exchange of contracts, thereby reducing the likelihood of gazumping
- reduce the need for negotiations and the overall timescale of the transaction from three months to just over three weeks
- demonstrate the seller's seriousness and discourage time-wasting
- increase openness and transparency
- help the seller to determine a more accurate selling price
- enable the buyer to make a more informed decision as to whether to buy and what price to offer
- draw the buyer's attention to problems with the lease document
- reduce the number of factors which cause transactions to collapse after the terms have been initially agreed
- enable the Home Information Pack duties to be enforced by local Weights and Measures Authorities. Fixed penalties can be imposed and the seller sued by the prospective buyer.

Will Home Information Packs work?

The scheme was tested in Bristol at the government's expense. Although fewer than 200 people took part in the trial, it demonstrated the following.

- Nearly two-thirds of buyers consulted the surveyor's 'home condition report' whereas few buyers read the current technical legal documentation.
- Fewer transactions were threatened with problems after an offer had been made and, as a result, there was more consumer confidence that the transaction would progress smoothly.
- Only 5 per cent of buyers were dissatisfied with the new process, compared to 40 per cent under the current system.
- Packs could be assembled in an average of 11 working days. Half of the packs that took two weeks or more to assemble, however, concerned leasehold property.
- Legal advisers believed the system to be more efficient in that the crucial preparatory legal work took place in a matter of days, rather than being spread out over several weeks.
- Estate agents had mixed views: some thought the pack worked well whereas others felt that it delayed the marketing of properties and, in a fast-moving market, could result in the loss of prospective purchasers.
- The 'home condition report' was well received by buyers, over 50 per cent of them preferring this to other types of survey. Surveyors, however, were concerned with the level of inspection and the amount of detail to be included in the report. In particular, they felt that the 'home condition report' did not compare well with a conventional home-buyer's survey.

Over all, it was agreed that the pack could be improved. In particular, it was felt that the home condition report should be improved in both layout and content. Some legal advisers believed that the legal documentation should be translated into a consumer-friendly format. The government has now revamped the contents of the sellers' packs in conjunction with consumer representatives and the professional bodies. The precise form of the documentation has, however, yet to be published.

Chapter 7

Exchange of contracts and completion

The contract, which contains all the terms of the transaction and which is signed by or on behalf of both seller and buyer, is not normally binding until the exchange has taken place. Once that has happened, the conveyancing can proceed to completion. This chapter covers this final stage of the process, at the end of which the lease of the flat passes from the seller to the buyer.

Exchange of contracts

This stage in the process cannot proceed until the buyer's building society, bank or other lender (the mortgagee) has made a mortgage offer (see Chapter 4). This is because, on exchange of contracts, the buyer is committed to the contract and to pay the full purchase price to the seller.

There are three primary methods by which exchange can occur. With **personal exchange** there is a meeting of the legal advisers of buyer and seller in one office (usually that of the seller's adviser) and the signed contracts are physically passed between them. This type of exchange is suitable where the advisers work close to one another or where one of the parties does not have an adviser (which is not to be recommended).

Exchange by post is a common practice. This normally involves the buyer's adviser sending his or her client's part of the contract (accompanied by a cheque for the deposit – see pages 91–2) to the seller's adviser, who then posts back the seller's part. It is, however, uncertain when the precise moment of exchange arises. Some argue that the contract becomes binding when the seller's part is put into the post, whereas others contend that it is when the seller's part is received. It is better to have the position clearly spelt out in the contract as, for example, with the Standard Conditions (that is, the *pro forma* terms that advisers incorporate into most contracts), which stipulate that exchange occurs when the last part is posted.

Most exchanges, however, take place over the **telephone**. The contracts are approved over the phone and it is then deemed that the documents have been passed between the parties. This is not a foolproof method and the courts have expressed the wish that it be undertaken only by the partners within a firm of legal advisers and that clear and detailed notes of the telephone discussion be taken by (and agreed between) the conveyancers. The Law Society★ has produced formulae for use in exchange by telephone, fax and telex. Email exchange is now also possible.

If you are in a chain of transactions, it is necessary to synchronise all exchanges on the same date. It would be disastrous to exchange contracts for the purchase of a flat and then discover that the potential buyer of your present property is withdrawing from the transaction.

The effect of the contract

Once a valid contract is in existence (normally on exchange), the seller is usually regarded as holding the flat on trust for the buyer. Although the legal title remains with the seller until the lease is passed to the buyer on completion, the 'beneficial' or 'equitable' ownership (that is, real ownership, not merely paper title) is regarded as having passed to the buyer. The consequences of this somewhat mystifying notion are dealt with in Chapter 8.

Deposits

It is customary for the buyer to pay a deposit when the contracts are exchanged. (Note that this is different from the optional deposit paid by the buyer to the estate agents: see Chapter 6.) Traditionally, this is either 5 or 10 per cent of the purchase price (less any preliminary deposit paid to an estate agent). The deposit demonstrates that the buyer is committed to the transaction; it amounts to part-payment for the flat; it constitutes a guarantee to the seller; and it provides the buyer with an incentive to keep to the bargain. That the seller is not expected to pay a deposit so as to show goodwill is illogical and unfair, because if he or she withdraws the buyer could lose money (for example, what he or she has already spent on legal costs). See Chapter 8 for potential problems at this stage of the process and their effect on the deposit.

Deposits: stakeholder or agent?

Most deposits are held by the seller's legal adviser, as stakeholder or agent for the seller.

From the buyer's perspective, it is generally better to ensure that the deposit is held as **stakeholder** because then the deposit cannot be transferred to the seller prior to completion and the funds must be kept in a deposit account. Subject to agreement, however, the stakeholder will be able to keep the interest earned. If the money is held by the seller's adviser as **agent** for the seller, the deposit normally must be paid over to the seller on request. Any interest that accrues while the money is in the agent's hands must be paid to the buyer. The question as to whether the seller's adviser is to hold the deposit as stakeholder or as agent needs to be resolved during the drafting of the contract. The parties should be consulted on this matter, but they can, in any event, give their instructions to their advisers.

Most sellers prefer their adviser to hold the deposit as agent. One advantage of the agency system is that it makes it easier for a chain of purchases to be negotiated: a single deposit provided by the person at the bottom of the chain may be used as a deposit for all the other linked purchases in that chain. If the circumstances are such that the seller cannot recover the deposit passed on under a linked purchase, the first buyer can sue the seller personally for recovery of the initial deposit. The Law Society's protocol (see page 65) endorses the agency system.

However, a major disadvantage of the agency system for the buyer is that he or she may have difficulty recovering it if the seller becomes bankrupt before completion. A partial means of protection for the buyer is to get an undertaking, from the seller's adviser, that the deposit will be released only for the purpose of providing a deposit for the seller to buy a replacement property. The buyer will then have the security that the money is still 'in the system' and has not simply been paid over to the seller personally.

Transfer of ownership

As shown in Chapter 5, there are two systems of land transfer in operation, depending on whether the flat is on unregistered or registered land. You do not have to be personally involved in the process of land transfer, whether you are the buyer or the seller – your legal adviser will handle it for you.

If the Law Society's protocol is used, the package of documents forwarded initially to the buyer will include unverified details of the seller's title. The responsibility of finally establishing 'good title' lies with the seller and, subject to contrary agreement, this must be done within a reasonable time (for example, two weeks) of exchange of contracts. In practice, however, title is proved when the contracts are drafted.

Given that unregistered land is rapidly being phased out, it is almost certainly the case that the flat will be within an area where the registered system is either in operation or will become operational when the lease is bought. The main difference between the two systems lies in the way in which the seller's title to the property is proved. The actual mode of transferring legal ownership is also different. In unregistered land, the transfer is done by a traditional conveyance and the passing of title deeds to the buyer. In registered land, the title passes by a transfer certificate and the registration of the buyer as the new registered proprietor of the flat.

Unregistered land

In the unregistered system, the process of what is called deducing the seller's title is by an examination of the title deeds (that is, past conveyances) of the property. The prospective buyer should get from the seller evidence of the seller's title to the property. This will take the form of title deeds (either the freehold or leasehold title) which disclose all dealings with the property during, at least, the preceding 15 years. Legal advisers usually provide a summary of deeds (called an 'abstract of title' or 'epitome of title') and, in practice, this normally consists of copies of a few conveyances ending with the last conveyance to the seller. The buyer's mortgagee will also check the seller's title.

Registered land

The registered system is more efficient and straightforward: ownership is guaranteed when the seller's name appears on the official register of title. The Land Registry claims to process approximately £1 million worth of property every minute. The buyer's legal adviser needs only to make a search at the Land Registry and check that the seller's name is entered as registered proprietor. An office copy of the entry on the Register (and filed plan) should have already been forwarded to the buyer with the draft contract, but it is possible that it is out of date. A further inspection of the Register must, therefore, be made to ensure that there have been no changes since contracts were exchanged.

Since 1990, the Land Register has been open to public inspection, and the authority of the registered proprietor (for example, the landlord) is not required for the prospective buyer to inspect the registered title to the property. The Land Registration Act 2002 also allows for the inspection and copy of documents held at the Registry. This means that the buyer of a flat on registered land is in a much better position than if it were on unregistered land and can easily verify who has claim to the land.

The Land Register will offer the following information:

- a description of the property
- who owns the property
- details as to the mortgage lender (if any)
- if registered since April 2000, the price last paid for the property
- details of any private rights of way and any other restrictions affecting the property.

Warning

If the title is registered as 'absolute freehold' or 'absolute leasehold', the titles are guaranteed by the Land Registry to be perfect. If the title is 'good leasehold', the buyer should be wary because this does not offer a guarantee that the freeholder had the right to grant the lease; it is not an attractive proposition to mortgagees and does not reveal whether there are adverse rights affecting the freehold.

Checking previous owners

After contract, but before completion, the buyer's legal adviser will make a search of the land charges register (for unregistered land) against the names of all previous owners of the land or at the Land Registry (for registered land) against the title number of the land. This type of search is to discover whether there are any adverse rights (for example, undischarged mortgages, rights of way or restrictive covenants) affecting the property which are protected and which will bind the buyer following completion of the transaction. The search will also reveal whether there is any bankruptcy petition registered and a receiver appointed.

Completion

As described in Chapter 6, the new lease (or sub-lease) will have been drafted by the seller's adviser and approved by the buyer before contracts are exchanged. If it is a pre-existing lease that is being sold ('assigned'), the old lease will pass to the buyer and this will also have been examined before a contract is entered.

Prior to completion, a statement will be prepared by the seller's adviser and sent to the buyer's adviser. This will disclose the exact sums to be paid on completion. Service charges, ground rent and insurance premiums are matters that will be calculated up to and beyond the completion date and, if appropriate, liability will be apportioned accordingly between the seller and the buyer.

Completion (that is, the conveyance of the land) takes place when the buyer pays over the balance of the purchase money and the seller hands over the relevant title deeds (for unregistered property) or land certificate (for registered property) and the lease or assignment in deed form. Although the date of completion can be negotiated, it occurs normally within four weeks of exchange of contracts and takes place at the office of the seller's adviser. If keys are being held by an estate agent, the seller will authorise their release at this stage. Should the completion date be delayed by reason of default on the part of the buyer, the seller can claim interest on the balance of the purchase money.

If the land the flat is on is unregistered, the buyer becomes the legal owner of the flat at this time. In the registered system of conveyancing, the legal title passes to the buyer when his or her name replaces that of the seller's as registered proprietor on the Land Register. To do this, the buyer's adviser has to send to the Land Registry an application form with the relevant documents and fee.

Mortgagees and completion

Completion involves, essentially, the buyer paying the money for the flat and receiving in return the documents of title and the lease. Generally, however, the situation is complicated because the flat being sold will be subject to the seller's mortgage and the buyer will be assisted by a mortgage advance. The mortgage deed will be signed by the buyer prior to completion. The seller's mortgagee will have possession of the title documents and lease and will release them only when the existing mortgage is paid off. The buyer's mortgagee will hand over the money only on condition that it receives the title deeds or land certificate and the lease. At the end of the completion process, the following will usually occur:

- the seller's mortgagee receives a banker's draft to clear the seller's mortgage and has to give an undertaking to do so within a couple of weeks
- the seller's adviser receives a banker's draft for the balance of the sale price which will be paid over to the seller
- the buyer can move into the new flat
- after the formalities of the stamp duty land tax (see below) and registration have been attended to by the buyer's adviser, the buyer's mortgagee normally takes custody of the title deeds (or lodges the land certificate at the Land Registry), the lease and the mortgage deed.

Stamp duty land tax

Stamp duty (or as from December 2003 'Stamp duty land tax') is a tax payable to the government on some deeds and documents, including leases, assignments and other conveyances of land. A flat-buyer may, therefore, need to pay stamp duty land tax. The buyer must notify the Inland Revenue of any tax due within 30 days of completion. This is done by completing a Land Transaction Return. If the Return is not submitted for up to three months, a fixed penalty of £100 is payable; the fee goes up to £200 after that. Interest and further penalties may be imposed. The rate for stamp duty changes periodically – the figures given below were correct after the Budget in April 2003 but you will need to check whether they have changed: contact your legal adviser or the Inland Revenue for up-to-date rates. The amount of stamp duty land tax payable is always rounded up to the nearest £5.

Existing leases

The same rules apply as to the sale of freehold land.

- Sale of a flat up to (and including) the value of £60,000 is exempt from stamp duty land tax (unless annual rent exceeds £600, in which case 1 per cent applies). All assignments (regardless of duration) have to be notified to the Inland Revenue.
- On flats valued between £60,001 and £250,000, stamp duty land tax of 1 per cent has to be paid on the *whole* purchase price. For example, stamp duty land tax payable on a flat costing £125,000 will be £1,250.
- On flats valued between £250,001 and £500,000 the rate is 3 per cent of the total amount.
- On flats over £500,000 the rate is 4 per cent of the total price paid.

New leases

The rules for new leases are more complicated because, as well as the stamp duty land tax on the price paid for the flat, there is a duty also on the average ground rent payable. If no tax is payable, only new leases that are for a term of seven years or more need to be notified to the Inland Revenue.

Disadvantaged areas duty exemption

The government has introduced a scheme under which buyers of flats and houses within disadvantaged areas are exempt from stamp duty land tax up to a purchase price of £150,000. To discover whether or not the property falls within this type of area, contact the Inland Revenue and tell them the postcode. They will immediately be able to tell you whether that postcode is within the scope of the exemption or not.

Implied covenants of title

Unless excluded or modified explicitly, there are several covenants of title implied into every contract and conveyance. These differ slightly according to whether the lease was granted before or after 1 July 1995, but in general terms they are:

- a covenant for title known as quiet enjoyment. This guarantees to the tenant that possession will not be interrupted by any acts of the landlord or of persons acting on the landlord's behalf
- good right to convey. This does not guarantee that the seller has a sound title, but does guarantee that he or she has not done, nor omitted to do, any act which will prevent the buyer from getting a good title (for example, there remains an undischarged mortgage on the flat or there is an undisclosed right of way over the land on which the flat is situated)
- further assurance. This covenant imposes on the seller a duty to do anything which is necessary to vest the property in the buyer
- that the lease is valid and subsisting. This covenant guarantees that the lease being assigned has not been forfeited by a superior landlord
- that the rent has been paid and the covenants in the lease have been duly performed. Where, for example, the lease contains a covenant to keep the flat in good repair, the seller is impliedly covenanting with the buyer that the flat is in good repair.

Excluding fixtures

As fixtures (see page 78) are deemed to be part of the land itself and are therefore included in the price of the flat, it is possible to depress the value of the lease (for the purposes of stamp duty land tax) by the seller severing the fixtures from the land and selling them separately to the buyer. This could produce some saving on the duty payable (see the example opposite). However, the sale of fixtures needs to be genuine and not at an inflated price. The Inland Revenue might challenge the agreement and, if so, it could prove a somewhat unpredictable exercise. Any items which are not fixtures can also be sold separately and do not attract tax.

EXAMPLE

A flat is worth £62,000 and will attract stamp duty land tax on the whole amount at 1 per cent. The flat contains carpets, curtains, fire-places, etc. which in total are valued at £2,000. If the contract stip-ulates that the buyer is to purchase those items at £2,000, the value of the flat falls to £60,000 and is, therefore, exempt from stamp duty land tax. The buyer saves £620.

Chapter 8

Rights, wrongs and remedies

The great majority of leasehold transactions proceed reasonably smoothly to the satisfaction of both buyer and seller. However, given the nature of the conveyancing process, there is scope for errors, mistakes and misunderstandings to arise at virtually every stage. This chapter deals with some of the most common problems that you could come up against both during and just after the process, whether you are the buyer or the seller of a flat. It discusses the issues at stake and indicates where the law stands on them. Wherever possible, practical courses of action that you yourself could take are suggested. However, there are some issues that only your advisers are qualified to deal with. In such cases this chapter arms you with enough (jargon-free) information to understand what your advisers are saying and know what they should be doing on your behalf.

Before exchange of contracts

Gazumping and gazundering

In a buoyant property market it is common for a potential flat-buyer to discover that he or she has been out-bid by a rival buyer. It is estimated that this occurs in 2 per cent of transactions. As well as losing the desired flat, the unlucky victim of **gazumping** may have already incurred considerable professional expenses: surveying costs, legal fees and fees for preliminary enquiries and local authority searches. It is estimated that these could amount to over £600. You could, however, take out insurance for financial loss arising from gazumping (for details contact your legal adviser or an insurance broker). The government wants this type of insurance to be developed and promoted further.

Legal remedies

There is a variety of legal remedies which can be used when things go wrong.

- **Rescission** This remedy allows a party to withdraw from the contract if there is misrepresentation, a mistake or breach of a contractual term (see page 103).
- **Repudiation** This is where an important breach of contract is accepted by the other party as putting an end to the contract. This would be relevant where there had been a major misde-scription of the premises or the seller had a defective title to the flat.
- **Damages** Compensation is available for any breach of contract and is designed to put the aggrieved party into the same position he or she would have been in had the contract been fully performed.
- **Specific performance** This is an order of the court which compels a reluctant party to perform the contract as agreed.
- **Rectification** This is the power of the court to re-write the contract so as to give effect to the true agreement reached between the parties. It is particularly useful when there has been a typing error or mistranslation in the written contract of what was agreed.

There is nothing to prevent gazumping from happening, because until the contract is signed and exchanged there is only a 'gentleman's agreement', under which neither party need act as a 'gentleman' and from which either party can withdraw at will.

In a depressed property market, the danger lies with the buyer refusing at the last minute to go ahead with the purchase unless the price is reduced. This has been called **gazundering**, and is quite rare: the buyer may have found a more suitable property or had a change of heart. As with gazumping, there is nothing that the other party can do about it.

Proposals have been put forward that a pre-contract deposit should be taken from both parties and that this deposit should be forfeited if a party withdraws from the transaction without good cause. Another possibility is that the parties could enter into a written contract (a 'lockout' agreement) preventing the sale to anyone else for, say, 14 days. However, in the Homes Bill 2001 the government did not intend any reforms to prevent gazumping. It has concluded that the changes made to the conveyancing process – the introduction of the Home Information Pack, for instance (see Chapter 6) – should speed it up and therefore minimise the practice of gazumping.

In a so-called **contract race**, the seller's legal adviser sends a draft contract to the advisers of several would-be buyers and, simply, the first one to return it, signed and with the necessary deposit, gets the flat. The Law Society* has attempted to regulate this practice by obliging the seller's adviser to disclose the existence of other prospective buyers to all the contestants. Not all advisers fulfil this obligation and, in any event, it does not prevent gazumping, but it does give notice of the possibility to all the parties involved. The 'contract race' is generally limited to when there is a booming market.

Protecting yourself against gazumping

The following steps will reduce the likelihood of gazumping occurring:

- reducing the length of time between tentative agreement and the final contract. This can be done by pre-qualifying for a mortgage and appointing a conveyancer before the offer is accepted
- enquiring of the estate agent whether it has a policy on gazumping. Some agents ask their clients to sign an agreement stating that they will not gazump
- keeping the estate agent informed as to the progress in obtaining mortgage finance and a survey
- use of the proposed Home Information Pack which will, in due course, become mandatory in all residential sales (see Chapter 6).

Professionals and professional liability

Estate agents
Whether you are a buyer or a seller the chances are that you will be using the services of an estate agent. It is important that the agent acts

in your best interests right through the conveyancing process. If you feel you have a genuine grievance against the agent – say, he or she does not keep you informed of progress in your conveyancing, or has misled you about the property itself or the date of completion – there are various ways of seeking a remedy (see Chapter 3).

Other professionals

Professionals become involved at various stages in the process of buying and selling a flat. The price is worked out by a valuer, the structural soundness and state of the premises are assessed by a surveyor, and the title to the flat is checked and later conveyed by your legal adviser (solicitor or licensed conveyancer). You may even have dealings with the architect or builder of the flat, especially if it is new. If your professional gets it wrong, possible avenues for legal action are breach of contract and/or negligence.

When professionals get it wrong

Examples of problems with professionals could include:

- shoddy workmanship by the builder or architect of a new building
- over-valuing or under-valuing of the flat by the valuer
- failure by the surveyor to pick up major structural flaws (for example, dry rot, woodworm and death-watch beetle)
- failure by the legal adviser to discover a defect in the seller's title or a restrictive covenant inhibiting the use of the flat.

Breach of contract and negligence

Legal proceedings for **breach of contract** must, generally, be started within six years of the date of the contract. Subject to limited exceptions in the Contracts (Rights of Third Parties) Act 1999, only a party to that contract can sue. This means that only the people employed directly by, for example, the buyer can be sued by that buyer. A buyer will, therefore, be able to sue only his or her legal adviser, surveyor or valuer.

Negligence, however, is of wider scope and has developed to protect the rights of the consumer. The essence of negligence law is that a person must take reasonable care so as not to injure *anyone* who is a reasonably foreseeable victim of that person's actions. It covers victims who have no contractual relationship with the negligent party. For example, the seller's adviser will, therefore, owe a duty of care to the buyer; the lender's valuer will owe a similar duty to the buyer. The general rule is that action must be brought within three years (personal injury) or within six years (other damage) from the negligent act. Negligence occurs when a person who has a duty of care to someone (for example, a surveyor to a flat-buyer) breaches that duty and a loss results from the breach.

Your legal adviser will advise you about your rights to sue a professional, and you may be able to obtain funding for this from the Community Legal Service Fund, run by the Legal Services Commission.* (This funding has replaced legal aid.) Note, however, that if you win and recover compensation the funding may be clawed back from your winnings. If you wish to sue your solicitor, the Office for the Supervision of Solicitors* (run by the Law Society) will provide a list of solicitors in your area who would be willing to bring an action against another solicitor.

Fraud, misrepresentation and mistake

- **Fraud** A contract which is induced by fraud can be set aside (for example, where the contract purports to grant a lease of premises that are not owned by the grantor). However, the defrauded party is free to stick with the contract and then sue for damages. The contract can be set aside provided the parties can be restored to their original positions (for example, the buyer can recover the purchase money).
- **Misrepresentation** Either party can withdraw from the contract following a negligent (that is, careless) or innocent (that is, genuinely mistaken) misrepresentation or misleading statement. The court retains a discretion to award damages in lieu of withdrawal.
- **Mistake** When a mistake is discovered after completion, the aggrieved party may be able to withdraw from the contract (for example, if the premises had been damaged before contract or vacant possession of the flat cannot be obtained by the seller).

Latent defects

Of particular relevance to flat-owners is the Latent Defects Act 1986, because it tackles the problem of when time begins to run for the purposes of the time limit for bringing an action against someone for negligence. As a general rule, time begins to run from the date of the negligent act, but in some cases the damage does not arise until much later. In the case of a negligent construction, for example, there may be difficulties in deciding when the time limit starts. Is it the date when the damage appears? Is it the date that the plaintiff (the person bringing the legal action) acquires the flat? Is it the date when the plaintiff first discovers the damage? The Act provides that:

- as regards latent damage not involving personal injury, the relevant period is either six years from the negligent act or three years from the date on which the plaintiff knew, or ought to have known, of the damage, whichever is the later. There is, however, a ceiling of 15 years from the date of the negligence beyond which the action will be out of time
- where the building is acquired by successive owners, a fresh right of action arises and time starts to run from the date the property is bought
- similar time limits apply also where the plaintiff suffers financial loss by relying upon carelessly given advice (for example, from a solicitor).

Surveys and guarantees

When the survey detects a major defect

If during a survey a defect is discovered, the buyer is, at the very least, forewarned and, bearing in mind the cost of repair, can decide whether or not to proceed with the transaction. The surveyor's report should be read carefully and may also be used to negotiate a reduction in the asking price for the flat. However, clear surveys are not an absolute guarantee that the premises are without fault. If you are aware of a defect and still choose to proceed with the contract, you will not be able to sue the surveyor. The responsibility then rests at your door.

A negative report from the surveyor or an under-valuation of the property might mean that the mortgage lender will refuse to proceed, reduce the amount to be loaned or retain a sum from the advance until the remedial work has been completed.

Warranties offered on new flats

All new houses, flats and conversions should be insured against structural defects and, indeed, mortgage lenders will be reluctant to lend money on new properties without some scheme of insurance operating. The most popular one is that offered by the Buildmark scheme from the National Home Building Council (NHBC)*; an alternative scheme is offered by Zurich Municipal and is called Newbuild.

Buildmark scheme Builders of newly built properties may be registered with the NHBC, which is a non-profit-making body with a register of about 25,000 builders. NHBC inspectors view new properties and, if a property meets certain standards, issue a certificate of sound construction. If the builder is registered with the NHBC, the property will fall within its Buildmark insurance scheme, which provides protection for certain structural defects arising within ten years of the property's first sale and up to a maximum liability of the original purchase price (taking into account the effect of inflation). The cover includes common parts.

If you sell the flat, the insurance automatically passes to the buyer without the need for any formal transfer or notification to the NHBC. If you need to make a claim, contact the appropriate regional office of the NHBC.

Under the scheme the builder agrees to make good any defects (except for wear and tear, lifts and fences) within the initial two years. Central heating systems are covered for only one year. This is known as the initial guarantee period.

The NHBC gives separate warranties, as follows:

- to compensate for any loss arising from the builder becoming insolvent before the building work is complete. This is limited to 10 per cent of the contract sum or £10,000, whichever the greater
- to make good any failure of the builder to remedy defects arising within the first two years (the initial guarantee period)
- to cover the cost of major structural damage during the remaining eight years of the guarantee. This is known as the structural guarantee period. This does not extend to wiring and

plumbing, and the defect must be severe (for example, failure of double-glazing, damp proofing, dry rot and collapse). Minor defects, such as ill-fitting doors and defective gutters, are outside the guarantee. To claim, the cost of repair must exceed £500.

Guaranteed work on existing flats

In the case of an existing flat which has been treated for woodworm or damp, or has had some other kind of major repair in previous years, the firm that carried out the works may have given a long-term guarantee. The seller may be able to produce the relevant documentation, which should cover the buyer. If the documentation has been lost, however, it is unlikely that any claim would be entertained by the firm. It is also sometimes the case that the firm has subsequently ceased trading and that the guarantee is worthless. However, it is always worth asking the seller about guarantees if repair work has been undertaken.

The enquiries stage

As discussed in Chapter 6, the buyer has to make a search of the local Land Charges Register and make enquiries of the seller before contracts are exchanged. If the search produces a result which indicates, for example, proposed road works in the vicinity of the flat, then it is up to the buyer to decide whether to proceed. If the response to the enquiries is inaccurate, and the transaction goes ahead, it might be possible to sue the seller or the seller's adviser for misrepresentation or negligence. Some contracts, however, state that the buyer cannot rely on the replies given to such questions. Unless the reply was a deliberate lie, this clause will normally prevent a successful legal action. For example, sellers are legally obliged to tell you whether they have had disputes with their neighbours. If there has been a history of problems, the seller will be liable to compensate you for non-disclosure if he or she does not tell you.

Other pre-exchange complications

If the buyer is unhappy with the draft contract or the proposed lease, then it is up to the parties to negotiate further to resolve the problem.

If this cannot be done, then the seller's attitude will be to 'take it or leave it'. It should be remembered that prior to exchange of contracts either party can withdraw from the transaction at will. If a chain of transactions is involved, the withdrawal of one buyer before contract can frustrate all other sales and purchases in that chain.

After exchange of contracts

The parties are always liable to perform the contract or face being sued for compensation. The buyer should, however, take the precaution of protecting the contract against third parties (that is, to stop the seller granting or assigning the lease to someone else). Unless certain steps are taken, the contract will not be binding on that third party. The buyer can protect the contract by entering a land charge at the Land Charges Registry (if the title to the flat is unregistered) or a notice at the Land Registry (if the title is registered). If this is done, then the contract can be enforced directly against the intervening purchaser.

Once a valid contract is in existence (normally on exchange), the seller is usually regarded as holding the flat on trust for the buyer. Although legal title remains with the seller until the lease is granted or assigned, the 'beneficial' or 'equitable' ownership is regarded as having passed to the buyer. Lawyers call this the 'doctrine of conversion' and its consequences include the following.

- The seller must still manage and preserve the property and is liable to the buyer for any failure to carry out necessary repairs or maintenance. There is, however, no obligation to make improvements.
- The seller has the right to retain possession until the flat is conveyed to the buyer and remains liable for all running expenses until that time.
- Under the Standard Conditions (that is, the *pro forma* terms that legal advisers incorporate into most land contracts), the property should be conveyed in the same general condition as it was when contracts were exchanged. If not, either party is given the opportunity to withdraw.
- If the Standard Conditions are not used, and the flat is damaged or destroyed, the loss lies on the shoulders of the buyer and not

the seller. It is, therefore, crucial that the buyer insures the premises from the day that contracts are exchanged (see Chapter 12 for details).

- If the property is damaged by fire, an ancient piece of legislation called the Fires Prevention (Metropolis) Act 1774 might offer the buyer some protection. It allows a buyer to make a claim against the seller's insurers so as to have the building restored.
- Increases in the value of the flat after contract benefit the buyer. This could happen, for example, if there is a rise in house prices or an increase in the market value because planning permission has been obtained; or where the flat is bought at a depressed price because of a sitting tenant, who then dies unexpectedly between the stages of contract and completion.

Breaches of the contract between buyer and seller

Once contracts have been exchanged, either party may fail to meet his or her respective obligations under the contract: for example, the buyer may be unable to come up with the purchase money, the premises may have been misdescribed or the seller may fail to show a good title to the property. Breaches of contract can occur both before and after completion. Often breaches after completion will be breaches of the contractual covenants. General points to be understood about breaches of contract include:

- until a binding contract has been entered into, either party can withdraw from negotiations at will
- once the contract is entered into, both parties are bound by its terms
- if the buyer is in breach of contract before completion, the seller may forfeit the buyer's deposit and sell elsewhere (see 'Losing the deposit', overleaf)
- on the understanding that there is a breach of contract, there is a variety of remedies available to the innocent party (see page 101).

Bankruptcy or death

Sometimes, once the contract is entered into, either the seller or the buyer becomes bankrupt or dies. If it is the seller who becomes bankrupt, completion can and should still take place, though delays will undoubtedly occur. If it is the buyer who becomes bankrupt, it is likely that completion will not take place, though the deposit will be kept by the seller.

On the death of the seller, the personal representatives of the deceased can demand that the sale goes ahead or can themselves be forced to complete the transaction. (Any purchase money received will be held for those who inherit.) The contract can also be enforced if it is the buyer who dies, with the purchase money to come from the deceased's estate. Note that the estates of the deceased seller or buyer can, if necessary, be sued for breach of contract.

Losing the deposit

Generally, if, after paying a deposit on the flat, the buyer withdraws from the transaction without good reason, the seller may seize the deposit. Although there is a provision in the Law of Property Act 1925 which gives the court discretion, when it is fair and just, to order the repayment (only in full) of the cash deposit even if it is the buyer who is at fault, this is unlikely to occur in the context of a long residential lease. If it is the seller who is in default, the buyer can sue for return of the deposit. If the buyer withdraws because of a breach of contract on the part of the seller, the deposit can be recovered.

Problems found during the search of land titles

If there is a right of a third party protected on the Land Charges Register or the Land Register, the buyer may have to have it cleared before proceeding with the conveyance. Certainly, if a third party's right is discovered or if any defects in title emerge, the buyer will make further enquiries of the seller (known as 'requisitions'). The seller may not be able to solve the problem (for example, in the case of protected rights of third parties). Often the buyer may, in such a situation, be well advised to withdraw (that is, 'rescind') from the dealings and claim back any deposit paid.

Notices to complete

A delay in completion constitutes a breach of contract, and any loss incurred can be recovered from the defaulting party. Nevertheless, delay in itself does not allow the innocent party to withdraw from the contract. Such action can be taken only when the delay is unreasonable or when 'time is of the essence' to the contract. This will be so only if time is made of the essence expressly within the contract (it is rarely implied) or a notice to complete is served on the other party. The Standard Conditions provide that, if completion does not go ahead on the agreed date, the innocent party can serve such a notice any time after that date. It then becomes a term of the contract that completion will occur, say, within ten days of the notice and that time will be of the essence for both parties. The time limit does not have to be ten days; in fact, any reasonable period can be set by the notice.

If the notice is not complied with, and the delay is on the part of the buyer, the seller can seize the deposit and is free to sell elsewhere. Any loss on re-sale can be recovered from the delaying party. If it is the seller who does not comply with the notice, the buyer can recover the deposit (and interest) and sue the seller for loss. Where there is a delay in completion, the injured party can recover for bridging finance and extra legal and removal costs, for example.

Calculation of damages

The following points provide some guidance as to how damages are calculated:

- Where the seller refuses to honour the contract, the buyer can recover for the loss of the property. This includes the difference between the purchase price and its market value. If vacant possession of the premises cannot be obtained, the buyer could claim for the market-price difference in the value of the property; payments for temporary alternative accommodation; and, if relevant, the legal costs of buying another flat.
- If there is no loss of bargain (that is, the market value does not exceed the agreed purchase price), the buyer can recover the expenditure incurred by entering into the contract (for example, legal fees and surveyor's costs).
- The injured party is under a duty to take reasonable steps to minimise the loss: he or she cannot recover for more than the loss that would have been incurred had reasonable steps been taken to reduce or to avoid the loss.

Funds unavailable

If the buyer exchanges contracts, but does not obtain a mortgage offer and cannot then buy the lease, the seller can sue the buyer for breach of contract and/or seize the deposit. The seller will claim compensation, essentially, for the loss of profit on the transaction.

After completion

The following remedies can be used even after the flat has been bought.

- **Damages** Once the contract has merged with the lease, damages are not usually recoverable, but there are limited exceptions to this general rule: misrepresentation, breach of an assurance (for example, as to freedom of the premises from dry rot), and a breach of the covenants of title (see Chapter 7).
- **Rescission** In order to rescind the contract after completion, a court order is necessary. The court may make such an order only on limited grounds: fraud, misrepresentation or mistake (see the box on page 104). If the purchase has been financed by a mortgage, then rescission is unlikely to be granted because it would prejudicially affect the building society or bank. It would be considered unfair to remove the security for the loan. Therefore, if the term to give vacant possession has been broken, then the buyer will have to be content with compensation which will be measured to reflect the difference in value between the value of the flat with vacant possession and its value with a sitting tenant.
- **Rectification** Subject to any obvious and minor corrections being made to the lease by judges, when a mistake occurs in the final version then the lease as drafted (with the inaccuracy) will stand. An important exception to this applies where the lease fails to state accurately the terms of the real agreement between the parties (for example, the lease omits to mention certain covenants which were agreed). In such a case, the court can rewrite the lease so as to reflect the true bargain struck. This remedy is, however, at the discretion of the court. In addition, it really only covers the situation where both parties make the same mistake (for example, where both intended a term to be

included in the contract or lease but it was omitted by mistake). A mistake made by only one of the parties will not usually suffice.

Noisy neighbours

One of the major drawbacks with owning a flat is the risk of noisy neighbours. Over 118,000 complaints concerning noise have been made to Environmental Health Departments. This issue has prompted the government to impose stricter building regulations which increase soundproofing standards on new buildings. The Anti-social Behaviour Bill 2003 intends to place certain duties on public-sector landlords requiring them to devise (and publish) policies and procedures for dealing with problem neighbours. A tenant might be able to compel the landlord to take action against a noisy neighbour under the leasehold covenants. If the lease was created on or after 11 May 2000, the tenant may be able to sue another tenant directly for breach of covenant not to cause nuisance or annoyance to other tenants. This will, however, cost money and effort. Some tenants will prefer instead to engage the support and services of the local authority.

The Environmental Protection Act 1990 gives a local authority's Environmental Health Officers (EHOs) the power to act on complaints of noise emanating, for example, from dogs, raised voices and stereos. The 1990 Act is valuable as regards continuous noise emanating from a factory, for example, but is not much use against intermittent, domestic noise. The procedure is also complex and time-consuming. The complainant will normally be required to complete a diary in order to demonstrate exactly what the problem is, how often it is happening and what effect it is having. The EHO will then investigate and, where appropriate, serve a noise abatement order on the offenders. If the noise is not abated, criminal proceedings may be brought by the authority. In 1993–4, only 0.3 per cent of complaints led to criminal convictions; however, the law has been extended by the Noise Act 1996 which introduced a new night noise offence and a new procedure for the seizure and forfeiture of noise-making equipment. The 1996 Act applies to England, Wales and Northern Ireland and extends the protection previously offered by the 1990 Act. Unfortunately, until recently only 30 of 500 councils had signed up to the scheme. The government had insisted upon each council having a 24-hour manned service. This has now been relaxed and more local authorities are adopting the statutory scheme.

The night noise offence is intended to provide an effective remedy to problems of disturbance caused by excessive noise from dwellings (including gardens, yards, outhouses and so on) caused between 11pm and 7am. For the first time, a legal standard has been set for noise within a person's home, although the maximum permitted noise level is specified in technical terms. It is up to each local authority whether or not to implement the new offence within its area. On arrival at the scene, the local authority must take reasonable steps to investigate the complaint. The authority's officer must then decide whether the noise exceeds the permitted level; if so, a warning notice must be given to the person responsible for the noise and at least ten minutes must be given for the disturbance to be ended. If the noise continues then a criminal offence has been committed. A person guilty of a night noise offence may be fined up to £1,000. In addition, the authority may obtain a warrant to enter the property by force and to seize the noise-making equipment. The property taken may be kept for up to 28 days or, if later, until the trial proceedings are disposed of. The magistrates' court may, however, make a forfeiture order which deprives the owner of the equipment and allows the local authority to sell it.

The Anti-social Behaviour Bill 2003 is to allow the local authority the power to make a closure order in relation to licensed premises. The order will be appropriate where there is (or otherwise would be) a statutory nuisance caused by noise. The closure may be for a specified period not exceeding 24 hours. If the order is ignored, a fine and/or imprisonment may follow.

Chapter 9

The lease

It is sometimes said that lawyers have two major failings: one is that they do not write well and the other is that they think they do. Nowhere is this clearer than in conveyancing documentation. A lease is a highly technical document littered with expressions which are carefully chosen but which are often unintelligible to the lay person. The tradition of not using punctuation adds to the confusion. It is, therefore, full of traps for an unwary buyer.

The lease is important because it states the rights of the landlord (the freeholder) and the tenant (the buyer) at the start of the tenancy and governs the future relationship between them. The clearer the terms of the lease, the less is the scope for disagreement. The tenant needs to be sure that the premises can be used as intended and that the obligations imposed by the lease will not outweigh the enjoyment of living in the flat. The landlord needs to make sure that the tenant will not cause any nuisance or annoyance and will look after the premises. It is not surprising, therefore, that the lease is often a long document, containing clauses designed to cater for all foreseeable eventualities.

The creation of a lease or of a sub-lease, and the assignment of an existing lease, all follow a similar format.

The drafting of a lease

Although in limited circumstances leases can be created in the form of an ordinary written document or even orally, all legal leases for a fixed term exceeding three years must be created or assigned by deed (that is, a formal document which makes clear on its face that it is a deed). Since 1989, the need for a seal has been abolished, but it is necessary that the following conditions are satisfied.

- The deed must be delivered, which means that the person signing it must, by an act or statement, adopt the deed as being finally executed. Physical or actual delivery is not necessary.
- It must be signed by the individual in the presence of a witness who attests the signature; or, if signed by another but at the individual's direction, the signature must be made in the presence of the individual and two attesting witnesses.

The lease, sub-lease or assignment is initially drafted by the seller's legal advisers and will follow one of the many standard formats available, but will be tailored to the individual case. This means that, unless the flats are in the same block, one lease is rarely identical to another. The draft lease is submitted to the buyer's adviser for approval, comment and negotiation. Amendments will be made (traditionally in red ink by the buyer and green by the seller) to the draft if appropriate (about rent, covenants and other terms of the trans-action) and, after a certain to-ing and fro-ing between the parties, the final form will be agreed. The lease or assignment will then be put into deed form ('engrossed'), duplicated and provided to each party. Once signed, the deed has legal validity and the transaction is completed.

The wording of a lease

Although the language used in most leases is archaic and not easily comprehensible, some recommendations have, however, been made to make them more modern.

- A lease should be clearly expressed in straightforward language and be structured in an accessible and logical fashion.
- It should include a section of definitions which explain the precise meanings of key words and expressions employed.
- Punctuation should be used properly, bearing in mind that misplaced punctuation can give a sentence a meaning that was not intended.
- Each section of the lease should be as short and to the point as possible. Each clause should deal with a distinct issue – the use of numbered paragraphs and sub-paragraphs is recommended.
- The lease should include a schedule or list at the end in which the lengthy and complex provisions regarding covenants can be set out.

- It should state the basic terms of the agreement right at the beginning: the parties, commencement date, duration, permitted user and ground rent, for example.

Rules of construction

'Rules of construction' are used to resolve difficulties arising from ambiguities and uncertainties in leases. The main rules are described below.

If there is a dispute over what the parties intended, the actual words employed in the lease and the circumstances in which it was made are looked at (for example, nature of the property, background to the transaction, market considerations and purpose of the lease).

Ordinary words, such as 'fire', 'repair' and 'damage', are given their general and ordinary meaning. Technical terms, like 'covenants' and 'provisos', are interpreted in a technical, narrow sense.

Some words used in leases have a statutory definition. For example, month means calendar month; person includes a company; the singular includes the plural (and *vice versa*); and the masculine includes the feminine (and *vice versa*). The definitions of many other words used have been determined by Parliament.

It is important that the lease is read as a whole. Any uncertain expressions or clauses should be interpreted in the context of the rest of the lease and the purposes for which it was granted. Because the meaning of a word or phrase used in one part of the lease may govern the intention expressed in other parts, the need for consistency of expression is crucial.

If a covenant is ambiguous, the *contra proferentem* rule is used, whereby the covenant is interpreted in a manner unfavourable to the party who inserted it (usually the landlord) or, with respect to other terms, to the party who benefits from them. This is an arbitrary way of dispelling ambiguity and is a measure of last resort.

Certain terms will, in the absence of expressions to the contrary, be implied by law. The most important of these is the covenant for quiet enjoyment, which allows the tenant to occupy the premises without unlawful interruption by the landlord.

The structure of a lease

A lease normally spans several pages and traditionally consists of five sections: premises, habendum, reddendum, covenants, and provisos and options. At the end of many modern leases, schedules or lists will appear and set out in detail provisions relating to, for example, service charges and other covenants.

Owing to the length and complexity of the standard lease, it is inappropriate here to set out a specimen lease in its entirety. Even the standard schedules to the lease (normally describing covenants in detail, giving particulars of the rights and obligations that go with the flat) are too long to reproduce. Throughout this chapter, therefore, the extracts from a specimen lease look at only the most important features of a typical lease.

'**The Lease** made the 4th day of January 2003 **Between** Janet Clarke of 37 Lenton Road Newcastle (hereafter called 'the landlord' which expression shall where the context so admits include the person for the time being entitled to the reversion immediately expectant on the determination of the term hereby granted) and Zoe Rogers of 19 Poolfield Road Newcastle (hereafter called 'the tenant' which expression shall where the context so admits include her successors in title)

Witnesseth as follows:

In consideration of the sum of £75,000 paid by the tenant to the landlord (the receipt thereof the landlord hereby acknowledges) the rent reserved and the tenants' covenants hereinafter contained the landlord **Hereby Demises** unto the tenant **All Those** premises known as Flat 3, 44 The Covert Newcastle **To Hold** unto the tenant from the 4th day of January 2003 for a term of 99 years **Yielding and Paying** thereafter during the said term the yearly rent of £160 by equal quarterly payments in advance on the usual quarter days the first of such payments being due proportion thereof to be made on the date hereof for the period to the 25th day of March next.'

The premises

The premises part of the lease will include the following details:

Parties to the lease
This will provide the names and addresses of the parties and a short description of their respective roles (for example, 'landlord' and 'tenant' or 'lessor' and 'lessee').

Date on which the tenancy starts
The commencement date of the lease may be earlier, later or at the same time as the date of the deed which creates the lease.

Price paid for the lease and the ground rent
The expression 'Yielding and Paying' in the specimen lease signifies that it is the responsibility of the tenant to seek out the landlord to ensure that the ground rent (here £160) is paid.

Intention of the parties to create a lease
There is no set formula to be used, but the more commonly found expressions are 'demise', 'lease', 'let' and 'grant'. They all mean the same thing and demonstrate the necessary intention. They are called 'operative words'.

Brief description of the property
This is known as the 'parcels' clause and defines what property is being leased. For the lease of a flat, the precise boundaries of the flat should be stated. This will involve mention of which walls, floors and ceilings are to be included. A scale plan prepared by an architect or a surveyor is frequently attached. The lease should make clear whether the plan or the verbal description is to prevail if conflict arises between the buyer and the seller. A more detailed verbal description is often to be found in a schedule to the lease and may read something like this:

> 'All that flat known as Flat 3, 44 The Covert Newcastle **Together** with the ceilings and floors of the said flat and the joists and beams on which the floors are laid but not the joists and beams to which the ceilings are attached unless those joists and beams also support a floor of the said flat **And Together**

with all cisterns tanks sewers drains pipes wires ducts and conduits used solely for the purposes of the said flat but no others **Excepting and Reserving** from the demise the main structural parts of the building of which the said flat forms part including the roof foundations and external parts thereof but not the glass of the windows or the window frames of the said flat nor the interior faces of such of the external walls as bound the said flat.

All Internal Walls separating the Premises from any other part of the building shall be party walls and shall be used and repaired as such.'

The description states exactly what the buyer is getting and is relevant in connection with the tenant's obligations to repair.

Boundaries

Boundaries are often a source of contention for flat-owners. Where the lease does not say anything specific about boundaries, there are certain rules of thumb. First, the lease of the top flat carries with it the air space and roof space above it. This means that the tenant is responsible for the repair of an entire roof of a building and can extend upwards into it. Second, the tenant acquires the space between the floor of the flat and the underside of the floor of the flat above and so is allowed to run cables and wires through the ceiling space. Third, where the flat has an outside wall, the tenant has both sides of that wall, and so can attach objects to the outside wall.

Exceptions and reservations

These are appropriate where the landlord seeks to exclude some part of the building from the lease (stairways and passage, say) or to reserve a right of way over some part of the premises leased (say, a garden or path). These exceptions and reservations may be contained in a separate schedule in the lease and might read as follows:

'All those gardens drives paths and forecourts and the halls staircases landings and other parts of the building which are used in common by the owners or occupiers of any two or more of the flats … All those main structural parts of the building including roof foundations and external parts thereof … cisterns tanks sewers drains pipes not used solely for the purpose of one flat.'

Other rights and obligations

The lease might also grant to the flat-owner various rights known as 'easements' over other flat-owners' properties in the same block. These could include, for example, rights of access, support and entry to carry out repairs. Correspondingly, the lease will give similar rights over the tenant's property to the other flat-owners. Generally speaking, and as there is no contractual relationship between the flat-owners themselves, these rights can be enforced only via the landlord and not by the other tenants. If the lease is granted on or after 11 May 2000, however, the Contracts (Rights of Third Parties) Act 1999 changes this rule and, in certain circumstances, will allow one tenant to sue another.

These rights are often set out in separate schedules within the lease along the following lines:

'Rights included in the demise
1) The right in common with the lessor and occupiers of other flats and all others having the like right to use for purposes only of access to and egress from the premises all such parts of the reserved property as afford access thereto.
2) The right of passage and running of gas electricity water and soil from and to the premises through the sewers drains wires pipes ducts and conduits forming part of the reserved property.
3) The benefit of any covenants entered into by the owners of other flats with the landlord so far as such covenants are intended to benefit the premises of the tenant.
4) All rights of support and other easements and all quasi-easements rights and benefits of a similar nature now enjoyed or intended to be enjoyed by the premises.
5) The right to use in common with the owners and occupiers of all other flats and their visitors the gardens drives paths and forecourts forming part of the reserved property.
6) Such rights of access to and entry upon the reserved property and the other flats as are necessary for the proper performance of the tenant's obligations hereunder.'

The tenant will also be subject to certain obligations imposed by the lease, for example:

'Rights to which the demise is subject
1) All rights of support and other easements and all quasi-easements rights and benefits of a similar nature now enjoyed or intended to be enjoyed by any other part of the building over the premises.
2) Such rights of access to and entry upon the premises by the landlord and the owners of the other flats as are necessary for the proper performance of their obligations hereunder or under covenants relating to other flats and similar to those herein contained.
3) The burden of any covenants entered into by the landlord with the owners of other flats so far as such covenants are intended to bind the premises or the tenant.'

The habendum

This part of the lease states the length of the tenancy (in the specimen it is 99 years). It is common for the term and the commencement date of the lease to be stated in the introduction to the lease and then repeated in the habendum. In the specimen lease the habendum begins with '**To Hold** unto the tenant from …'. The term normally starts at midnight after the commencement date stated (in the specimen this is at midnight between 4 and 5 January) and will expire at midnight on the last day of the period specified (in the specimen, at midnight between 3 and 4 January 2102). It is necessary that the beginning of the term is set out with certainty and that the end is specified or can be calculated.

The reddendum

The habendum is usually followed by the reddendum clause, which states the rent to be paid by the tenant. In the example, the reddendum starts with the words '**Yielding and Paying** thereafter …'. As regards a long residential lease, only an annual ground rent is payable. Ground rent is a rent for the 'bare site' of the land (£160 in the specimen lease) and is substantially lower than the full market rent for the premises. The ground rent is in addition to the purchase price of the lease (in the specimen £75,000) and is traditionally payable in instalments on each 'quarter day'. The quarter days are 25 March, 24 June, 29 September and 25 December. The lease will make it clear whether the rent is payable in advance or not. If not, the presumption is that rent is payable in arrears.

The covenants

The covenants strike at the core of the landlord–tenant relationship. They state the rights and obligations of the parties under the lease. Covenants can be positive in nature (that is, they can compel one party to do something, for example, to pay rent or to insure) or negative (that is, they can restrict one party from doing something, for example, using the premises for certain purposes).

Both parties usually enter into a series of **express** (that is, explicitly stated) covenants, with the heavier burden normally falling upon the tenant. Certain covenants may also be **implied** by law and these are not normally stated explicitly in the lease. Examples of covenants commonly found in leases are illustrated below. The covenants relating to insurance, repairs, alterations and service charges are considered in more detail in separate chapters.

A tenant's covenants

It is the tenant who agrees to perform the majority of the covenants found in a typical lease. The most commonly found covenants are given below.

Against assignment and sub-letting

In the absence of any explicit restrictions to the contrary in the lease, a tenant can assign, sub-let, part with possession of, or share possession of the premises. It is uncommon for long residential leases to impose restraints upon this freedom. Nevertheless, sometimes such restrictions do appear (for example, where the freehold is owned by a common employer of the tenants). The lease may also require the tenant to give notice to the landlord of any dealings with the premises so that the landlord will always know in whom the lease is vested and whether any sub-lease has been created. The landlord is then likely to charge an administration fee, payable by the selling tenant.

To pay the ground rent
This might appear in the lease as:

> 'The tenant shall pay the reserved rent on the days and in the manner above specified.'

To repair
An example of such a covenant is:

> 'The tenant shall to the satisfaction in all respects of the landlord keep the premises and all parts thereof and all fixtures and fittings therein and all additions thereto in a good and tenantable state of repair decoration and condition throughout the continuance of the lease including the renewal and replacement of all worn or damaged parts and shall maintain and uphold and whenever necessary for whatever reason rebuild reconstruct and replace the same and shall yield up the same at the determination of the lease in such good and tenantable state of repair decoration and condition and in accordance with the terms of this covenant in all respects.'

Against alterations
This covenant prohibits alterations without the landlord's consent and covers work such as knocking down internal walls, making extensions or loft conversions, and inserting windows in the roof. It could be drafted thus:

> 'The tenant shall not make any alterations in the premises without the approval in writing of the landlord to the plans and specifications and shall make those alterations only in accordance with those plans and specifications when approved.'

To insure
Such a covenant might be worded:

> 'Insure and keep insured the premises against loss or damage by fire [other perils] in the full value thereof in the names of the landlord and the tenant through such agency as the landlord shall from time to time specify and whenever required produce to the landlord the policy of such insurance and the receipt for the last

premium for the same and in the event of the premises being damaged or destroyed by fire [or other insured risk] as soon as reasonably practicable lay out the insurance moneys in the repair rebuilding or reinstatement of the premises.'

On the use of the flat

A covenant will normally be included which obliges the tenant to use the premises as a private residence only. This will not normally prevent people working at home, but is aimed at stopping the premises being used, for example, as a hotel or shop. Such a covenant might read:

'The tenant shall not use the premises for any purpose other than a residence.'

An additional express covenant will normally be that the tenant must not do, or permit to be done, on the premises anything which may become a nuisance or annoyance to other occupiers or the landlord. This might read:

'That no act matter or thing which shall or may become or grow to be a public or private nuisance or a damage annoyance grievance or inconvenience to the landlord or any occupier of adjoining neighbouring or other land or buildings or which may lessen the value of any such land or buildings shall be carried on or done or suffered on the demised premises.'

There may be specific prohibitions (for example, no pets). Sometimes there is a whole list of regulations about use and behaviour with which the tenant must comply.

To permit the landlord to enter and view

Because the tenant is granted exclusive possession of the flat (which means that, subject to provisions to the contrary, the landlord can be excluded from the premises) this covenant is often included so that the landlord can inspect the state of repair of the property. This might be drafted as:

'The tenant shall permit the landlord to have access to and enter upon the premises as often as may be reasonably necessary for the landlord to do so in fulfilment of the landlord's obligations hereunder or under covenants relating to other flats and similar to those herein contained.'

To leave the premises

The tenant will undertake to quit the premises at the end of the lease, for example:

'That the tenant will at the expiration or sooner determination of the term hereby granted surrender and deliver up to the landlord or successors in title peaceable and quiet possession of the demised premises.'

This does not, however, prevent the tenant from taking advantage of any rights afforded by Parliament to stay in the flat (see Chapter 17 for details).

A landlord's covenants

The landlord will give comparatively few covenants to the tenant. The following do, however, regularly find their way into a lease.

Quiet enjoyment

This is always implied into a lease, but often it will be stated explicitly that the tenant will be granted the quiet enjoyment of the premises. This means that the landlord has good title and will allow the tenant possession and peaceful enjoyment of the premises. This prevents the landlord (or agents) from interfering with the tenant's possession of the flat. This covenant might appear as:

'The landlord covenants with the tenant that the tenant shall have quiet enjoyment of the property as against the landlord and all persons claiming through the landlord.'

To enforce covenants against other tenants

This could be, for example, to prevent one tenant causing a nuisance to another. Such a convenant could be drafted as:

'If so required by the tenant, to enforce the covenants on the part of the tenant entered into by any other tenants of any other part of the building of which the demised premises form part

provided always that the tenant making this request should do so in writing and shall indemnify the landlord against all costs, claims and expenses in respect of such enforcement.'

To repair and decorate

Although the burden of repair will fall heavily upon the tenant, the landlord might undertake to repair and decorate the outside of the premises and common parts (that is, the parts reserved by the landlord). An example might be:

'The landlord shall keep the reserved property and all fixtures and fittings therein and additions thereto in a good and tenantable state of repair decoration and condition including the renewal and replacement of all worn and damaged parts.'

Maintenance of common parts

The common parts of the building (lifts, stairways and passages, for instance) will usually be in the control and under the responsibility of the landlord. This obligation might be expressed as:

'The landlord shall keep the halls stairs landings and passages forming part of the reserved property properly carpeted cleaned and in good order and shall keep adequately lighted all such reserved parts of the property as are normally lighted or as should be lighted.'

Implied covenants

In addition to express covenants in the lease, there are a few obligations imposed by law. These include the covenants:

- for quiet enjoyment given by the landlord (see page 126);
- not to derogate from the grant. This imposes upon the landlord an obligation, at the same time as granting to the tenant a lease, not to do anything which is inconsistent with that grant. The covenant would be breached if, for example, the landlord did something which would make the premises less fit for habitation; interfered with light which reached the tenant's windows; or created an excessive noise
- not to disclaim the landlord's title. This is a covenant by the tenant not to deny the landlord's title or act in a way inconsistent

with being a tenant. This prevents the tenant from doing something which prejudices the landlord's title (for example, by claiming to be the freeholder)

- not to commit waste. This is a covenant by the tenant not to alter the physical character of the premises through any action or inaction. Waste may be voluntary, that is, a positive act which diminishes the value of the property. It can also be permissive, which covers failures of maintenance and repair, leading to dilapidation of the premises. Due to this implied obligation, even if there is no express provision for repair, the tenant is still required to undertake basic repair and maintenance of the flat.

For other implied covenants relating to repair see Chapter 15.

The 'usual covenants'

A lease may, instead of containing a long list of covenants, expressly be made subject to the 'usual covenants' without detailing what they are. This is rare, but the 'usual covenants' include:

- covenant by the tenant to keep and deliver up the premises in repair and to allow the landlord to enter and view the state of repair of the flat
- covenant by the landlord for quiet enjoyment
- covenant for re-entry (technically called a 'proviso') which allows the landlord to forfeit the lease on the non-payment of ground rent or breach of other covenant. This will, however, normally be spelled out in the lease.

What other covenants are to be included in the description 'usual' depends on the nature of the premises, their location and the purpose for which they are being let. In cases of dispute, it might be up to a court to decide what covenants are 'usual' in the circumstances.

Provisos and options

The **provisos** part of the lease will usually consist of the explicitly stated right of the landlord to end the lease if the tenant fails to observe any of the covenants. This is called a right of re-entry or a forfeiture clause. Forfeiture is considered in Chapter 10. A forfeiture clause will read something like this:

'**Provided Always** and it is hereby agreed that if the rents hereby reserved or any part thereof shall be unpaid for twenty one days after becoming payable (whether formally demanded or not) or if any covenant on the part of the tenant herein contained shall not be performed or observed then and in any such case it shall be lawful for the landlord at any time thereafter to re-enter upon the demised premises or any part thereof in the name of the whole and thereupon this demise shall absolutely determine but without prejudice to any right action or remedy of the landlord in respect of any antecedent breach of any of the tenant's covenants.'

In the case of a residential lease, a clause permitting forfeiture for bankruptcy would not normally be found. This is because lenders will not advance mortgage funds on the security of a lease containing such a clause.

The lease may give the tenant an **option** to purchase the freehold or a right of pre-emption (which offers the tenant first refusal if the landlord wishes to sell the freehold). As discussed in Chapter 18, both can be made available for a specified period or remain open throughout the lease. The option may extend only to a named tenant or be available to subsequent tenants. Similarly, it may be exercisable on the payment of a stated sum or at a price to be determined. Much depends upon the clear drafting of the clauses.

Assignments, sub-leases and sales of freehold

Assignment

When an existing lease is assigned, the tenant sells the whole of the interest in the flat. It is similar to creating a new lease, but instead of opening with 'The Lease made ...' it will begin: 'The Assignment made ...'. There is normally an account of the original lease: its date, the parties, the term, the rent and the property involved. This shows how the present seller came to own the lease. If the original lease contains a covenant against assignment without the landlord's consent, the assignment will state that the consent has been duly obtained.

The operative part of the deed of assignment will be like this:

'... the seller as beneficial owner **Hereby Assigns** unto the buyer **ALL THAT** property described in the schedule hereto and comprised in and demised by the Lease **To Hold** unto the buyer for all the residue now unexpired of the term of years created by the lease **Subject** henceforth to the rent reserved by and to the lessee's covenants and conditions contained in the Lease.'

The property is usually identified in the schedule by reference to the original lease:

'The property is more fully described in a lease dated 4 January 2003 and made between Janet Clarke and Zoe Rogers.'

Normally no new covenants are introduced: the assignee (the buyer) is bound automatically by the existing covenants on a 'take it or leave it' basis. The original tenant of a lease granted before 1 January 1996 remains liable, even after the lease is sold on, for the fulfilment of existing covenants. Accordingly, an indemnity covenant is implied (it does not have to be spelled out in the assignment) that the assignee will reimburse the seller for any non-payment of rent or breach of the other covenants and conditions. There is also an implied covenant that the seller has complied with the terms of the lease. As regards leases created after 1 January 1996, under the Landlord and Tenant (Covenants) Act 1995 the original tenant ceases to be liable on the covenants following the assignment of the lease, and the indemnity covenants have no application. See Chapter 10 for more details.

Grant of a sub-lease

The grant of a sub-lease (also known as an underlease) is not an assignment of the tenant's whole interest in the property. Sub-leases of residential property are common in the case of new housing estates in some parts of the country. In such instances, the free-holder leases the land to the developer for, say, 999 years at an annual rent of £500. On the land the developer builds five blocks of flats, for example, and sub-lets each individual flat for a term of, say, 990 years at a capital premium (the purchase price) plus a ground rent of £50 per year. This practice is known as a 'building' or 'letting' scheme.

The conveyance is similar to the grant of a lease, as described earlier. It is important to ensure that the sub-lease imposes an obligation to observe covenants at least as onerous as those contained in the head-lease. In order to achieve this, the sub-lease normally states verbatim the relevant covenants appearing in the head-lease or incorporates them by reference.

A sub-lease too should contain an indemnity covenant. This is not implied by law and must, therefore, be expressly stated. This would read along these lines:

> '... by way of indemnity only to perform and observe such covenants and restrictions contained in the head-lease as are still effective and relate to the property and to indemnify the sub-lessor against any liability resulting from their breach or non-observance.'

Sale of freehold

If the freeholder sells the reversionary interest (that is, the freehold, sometimes described also as a 'fee simple'), the buyer of that freehold acquires the landlord's title subject to the existing lease(s). The conveyance will normally read:

> **'To Hold** unto the purchaser in fee simple subject to but with the benefit of the before recited lease.'

This means that the buyer of the freehold can enforce the tenant's covenants contained in the lease and, similarly, will be bound by the landlord's covenants contained in that lease. The original landlord will, if the lease was created before 1 January 1996, remain liable on the original covenants. If the lease is granted after that date, the original landlord can apply to the court (if necessary) to be released from the original covenants.

If the buyer of the reversion is the existing tenant (see Chapter 17), a term that the lease will **merge** with, and be extinguished by, the freehold will usually be incorporated into the conveyance. This will avoid questions being raised subsequently when the property is next sold on. A specimen of such a term is:

'The purchaser as the owner of the fee simple estate and of the leasehold estate in the property declares that from the date of this deed the lease shall no longer continue in force but shall be merged in the fee simple.'

Under the Landlord and Tenant Act 1985, tenants have the right to be informed by written notice when the landlord sells the freehold reversion and must be given the name and address of the new owner. This notice must be provided either within two months of the sale or by the day after the next payment of ground rent is due. Failure to give such notice is a criminal offence. The incentive for a landlord to observe this requirement is that, whether or not the Landlord and Tenant (Covenants) Act 1995 applies, he or she remains liable (jointly or otherwise with the new buyer) on the covenants until the notice is served. The Landlord and Tenant Act 1987 offers 'qualifying tenants' the limited right of first refusal when the freeholder decides to sell the freehold (see Chapter 18).

Certificate of value

On every grant or assignment of a lease or sub-lease, and on every freehold sale, the transfer will contain a certificate of value. Traditionally, this was essential for stamp duty purposes. Although since December 2003 it is no longer strictly necessary, a lease is still likely to contain a certificate of value. Such a certificate will read:

'It is hereby certified that the transaction hereby effected does not form part of a larger transaction or of a series of transactions in respect of which the amount or the value or the aggregate amount or value of the consideration other than rent exceeds £★.'

£★ will be the lowest amount of £60,000, £250,000 or £500,000 as appropriate (see page 97).

Chapter 10

Breaches of covenant

Most people who buy flats appreciate that they are acquiring a temporary ownership of a property during the life of the lease. It is also generally understood that the lease represents a contract between the landlord (owner of the freehold) and the tenant (buyer) and that the terms and covenants of the lease must be complied with. The covenants remain enforceable throughout the existence of the lease.

The traditional rule is that only the parties to a contract can sue on that contract, but this rule may be modified somewhat by the Contracts (Rights of Third Parties) Act 1999. In limited circumstances, this allows third parties to a contract to sue landlords, builders and developers, for example. The contract must, however, expressly provide for such third-party enforcement or intend to confer a benefit on the third party. So it all turns on the wording of the particular term of the contract. In principle, this means that tenant covenants could be mutually enforceable without the involvement of the landlord. In addition, sub-tenants might be able to enforce covenants in the head-lease against the superior landlord and *vice versa*. Subsequent assignees of a lease might use the new law to sue, say, an architect or builder with whom the assignee had no contractual tie. Nevertheless, the law can be side-stepped by writing the contract to exclude third-party rights entirely.

What constitutes a breach of covenant?

Covenants impose obligations on both landlord and tenant either to do something or not to do something. Examples of breach of a tenant's covenant are:

- not paying ground rent promptly (breach of the covenant to pay rent)

- using the flat for bed-and-breakfast purposes (breach of the user covenant).

Examples of breach of a landlord's covenants are:

- letting the premises fall into disrepair (breach of the covenant to repair)
- attempting unlawfully to evict a tenant (breach of the covenant of quiet enjoyment).

Parties bound by covenants

The issue of who can enforce a covenant and against whom is of particular importance when a tenant assigns the lease (that is, sells the flat to someone else) or creates a sub-lease (that is, creates a lease for a lesser duration than that of the tenant), and when a landlord sells the freehold. Following the Landlord and Tenant (Covenants) Act 1995, how this issue is settled in assignments of leases and land-lords' freeholds depends on whether the lease was granted before or after 1 January 1996. The Act, however, leaves largely unaffected the law relating to sub-leases: the minor differences are explained below.

The landlord can easily discover who the current tenant is, but it is not always as easy for the tenant to discover the identity of a new landlord. Nevertheless, it is crucial for the tenant to be able to identify the landlord in order to enforce the latter's covenants. To overcome this problem, and unless it is obvious from the lease, the tenant must receive notification of the landlord's name and address. If the freehold is subsequently sold, the old landlord must furnish the name and address of the new landlord by the date the next ground rent falls due or, if later, within two months of the sale.

Pre-1996 leases

Privity of contract and estate
It is important to realise that the original parties to the lease will, even if they sell the freehold or leasehold, remain liable on their covenants for the duration of the lease. This is because '**privity of contract**' exists between them. So when the lease or the freehold is sold on or a sub-lease is created, there is no contractual relationship

between the original landlord and the new tenant; or the new landlord and the original tenant; or the head landlord and the sub-tenant. Accordingly, in those situations the covenants cannot be enforced by or against the newcomer simply because of the contractual relationship between the original parties. This rule is subject to potential variation under the Contracts (Rights of Third Parties) Act 1999 (see above).

Otherwise, the only means by which the new party can sue or be sued is if the covenants run with the lease. If so, the benefit and burden of the leasehold covenant will pass to each person who buys the title from successive landlords or tenants.

The mechanism by which this is done is known as '**privity of estate**'. The idea here is that the covenants become imprinted on the estate and run with the lease. Privity of estate exists between those who currently stand in the position of landlord and tenant. Accordingly, once the original tenant assigns the lease, he or she no longer has privity of estate with the landlord. Privity of estate will now be between the landlord and the assignee (the buyer). Thus the buyer becomes automatically liable on the original covenants for as long as he or she has the lease. When the lease is again assigned, the seller's liability ceases (except as to indemnity or covenants breached while he or she was in possession) and passes on to the new buyer.

Similarly, when the original landlord parts with the freehold, the successor is responsible for complying with the landlord's covenants. Usually, this liability persists only while he or she remains the freeholder. However, as mentioned above, the original landlord is still bound by contract to the original tenant. It is the new landlord who stands in privity of estate with the current tenant.

Sub-letting

If the original tenant does not wish to dispose of the flat outright and, as an alternative, sub-lets the property, the sub-tenant has no relationship with the freeholder. There is privity neither of estate nor of contract between them. This is subject to the Contracts (Rights of Third Parties) Act 1999, but otherwise the freeholder and the sub-tenant cannot sue one another. The contractual tie is between the sub-tenant and the tenant, and privity of estate exists between them. The tenant will, therefore, ensure that the sub-lease contains exactly the same covenants as the head-lease from which it was carved.

Indemnity

It is necessary in a sub-lease to include an express **indemnity** covenant under which the sub-tenant will compensate the tenant for any breaches of covenant he or she commits.

In the case of pre-1996 leases, on assignment the original tenant will seek protection against being sued for a breach of covenant committed by an assignee. It is usual practice for an express indemnity covenant to be inserted into the assignment whereby the assignee will indemnify the original tenant against such claims. This should be clearly worded and could read: 'to pay the future rent and observe the covenants on the part of the lessee contained in the lease ...'.

EXAMPLES

Assignment of the lease

In 1961, Joan was granted a 99-year lease of a flat. The lease imposed extensive and onerous repair covenants on the tenant. In 1972, she assigned the lease to Betty who, in 1997, assigned the lease to Doris. Doris has allowed the property to fall into severe disrepair.

The landlord has a choice whether to sue Doris (privity of estate) or Joan (privity of contract), but cannot sue Betty because neither type of privity exists between them. Generally, the landlord would prefer to sue Doris.

Doris is, however, now poor, so there is no point in suing her because she has insufficient assets to meet the claim. The landlord will, therefore, sue Joan for compensation. Some 30 years after selling the flat, Joan is faced with liability for something which she has not done and over which she has no control.

Fortunately for Joan, she has a right of indemnity (whether expressed or implied into the assignment) against Betty. Accordingly, Joan will pass on responsibility to Betty and it will be Betty who carries ultimate responsibility. Betty's right of indemnity against Doris is

Post-1996 leases

The major purpose of the Landlord and Tenant (Covenants) Act 1995 is to overcome the above problems associated with the original tenant remaining liable for breach of covenant by a subsequent assignee. The new law is much simpler to state and understand.

The Act also offers the landlord the opportunity to escape from future liability after he or she has sold the freehold. It achieves this by abolishing the privity of contract relationship, after the sale, between the original parties. However, this operates only if the sale is not in breach of a covenant restricting such transactions.

As regards the tenant, this release occurs automatically, but for the landlord to be released an application must be made and agreed by the tenant or approved by the court. Clearly, once the tenant or landlord is released, neither can sue nor be sued on the covenants.

---

worthless because of the latter's poverty. There is nothing that Betty can do.

Sub-letting

In 1995, landlord Brian grants a lease to Tony who, in turn, sub-lets the flat to Ray. Ray is in breach of a covenant contained in the head-lease. Brian cannot sue Ray, but he can claim against Tony. Tony can recover compensation from Ray only if the sub-lease contained both the covenant which has been breached and an express indemnity covenant. Otherwise, Tony will have to foot the bill.

Selling the freehold

Brian sells the freehold to Liz. Liz is in breach of one of the landlord's covenants. Tony can sue either Brian (contract) or Liz (estate). If there is an explicit indemnity covenant in the sale of the freehold, Brian (if sued) could claim indemnity from Liz. Even without such a covenant, Brian would still be able to sue Liz at common law under an ancient rule of general application that allows a party to recover from the assignee money paid under legal compulsion to satisfy another's debts.

As this marks the end of original tenant liability, the implied indemnity covenants do not apply.

The Landlord and Tenant (Covenants) Act 1995

Although the major changes affect only leases granted after 1 January 1996, the Act does contain several provisions which apply equally to new or old leases. Consult your legal adviser if you need to know how it affects your liability.

Examples reworked

If the leases in the Examples had been granted after 1 January 1996, the change in the law would have produced the following effects.

Assignment:

- on her assignment of the lease to Betty, Joan would no longer have any liability
- on Betty later assigning the lease to Doris, the landlord would have to sue Doris
- on Doris becoming too poor to pay for repairs, the landlord would have to bear the loss.

Selling the freehold:

- when the freehold is sold to Liz, Brian could apply to the court to be released from liability on the covenants he entered into with Tony. If he is released, then he could no longer be sued on those covenants. If release is refused, then the old rules would apply as stated above.

Sub-letting

The Act focuses on assignments and leaves largely untouched the rules which apply to sub-tenants. The only exception to this relates to covenants to do with how the premises are used, where the Act allows the covenant to be enforced directly against any owner or occupier of the leased premises (that is, including a sub-tenant).

Accordingly, the landlord will not (with the exception of the user covenant) be able to enforce tenants' covenants directly against the sub-tenant. The tenant will remain liable for the sub-tenant's breaches.

Remedies for breach

Not surprisingly, both the landlord and the tenant have a number of ways of dealing with a breach of any express or implied covenant within the lease. The normal remedies for breach of contract (see Chapter 8) are available for breaches of covenant. Some of the remedies benefit the landlord alone, while others are open to both parties. The general remedies open to both are an action for damages, specific performance or injunction.

Remedies for both landlord and tenant

Damages
When there is a breach of covenant (for example, if the tenant sub-lets when he or she is not allowed to), the aggrieved party (in this case, the landlord) can sue for compensation. It can, however, be years before the case is resolved by the courts. The case will go before either the County Court or the High Court, depending normally on the amount claimed in damages. It is possible to represent oneself, but usually a solicitor will be employed both to pursue and to defend a claim. Damages are an attractive remedy where the breach is substantial and where monetary compensation is what the person suing wants. The amount of damages awarded is based on the position the aggrieved party would have been in had the covenant been observed. This means that the court must estimate the amount of loss that the injured party has suffered. As regards a claim by the landlord for disrepair, however, the compensation that is awarded cannot exceed the amount by which the value of the freehold has diminished. There is no such limit in the case of other breaches and it does not affect the tenant's claim for disrepair.

Specific performance
The party who seeks to enforce a covenant can apply to the court for the discretionary remedy of specific performance. This means asking the court to order the other party to perform the agreed contractual terms. If the court does this and the order is not

complied with, it becomes a contempt of court. The court can then act on behalf of the defaulting party and execute any documents necessary to carry out the contract.

As the remedy is discretionary, it is not always available and will usually be declined if monetary compensation would be an adequate remedy. If declined, the court will award damages to the claimant. In practice, it is unlikely that the landlord would be granted specific performance against the tenant; the tenant does not face the same difficulty. It would be granted where the judge feels that it is fair and just to do so (for example, where the landlord has failed to maintain common parts).

Injunction

It is necessary to go to court for an injunction, but (unlike the length of time involved in getting compensation) a temporary injunction can be obtained within days and will operate until the matter is heard formally by the court. An injunction can be positive (that is, ordering someone to do something) or negative (restraining someone from doing something). This remedy is particularly useful with respect to the landlord's covenant of quiet enjoyment and tenant's covenants relating to use of the premises or not assigning the lease without consent, for example. It is, however, a discretionary remedy and is not available as of right. There is no injunction to compel the landlord or tenant to carry out repairs. Such a breach is better dealt with by damages or specific performance. In basic terms, whereas specific performance makes a party honour (that is, perform) the contract, an injunction is designed to stop breaches of the contract occurring or continuing.

Remedies for tenants

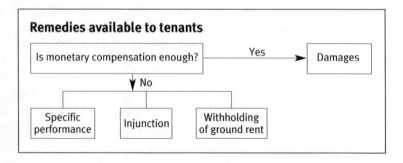

Remedies available to tenants

Is monetary compensation enough? — Yes → Damages

↓ No

Specific performance | Injunction | Withholding of ground rent

Withholding of ground rent

Where, for example, the landlord has failed to comply with a repairing covenant, the tenant can use the self-help remedy of carrying out the works and deducting the cost from future payments of ground rent. The right has been extended to allowing the tenant to deduct the costs from rent arrears (that is, rent already owed to the landlord). It allows the tenant to withhold ground rent so as to accumulate the capital sum to carry out necessary repairs which the landlord refuses to undertake. Although this remedy of self-help does not cover service charges, it is now possible to withhold such charges until the landlord complies with certain statutory obligations (see Chapter 13).

Several conditions must be met for the withholding of rent (in order for repair work to be carried out) to be lawful:

- The landlord must be in breach of a repairing covenant. There is no room for errors here and the tenant has to be absolutely sure that this is the case.
- The tenant must have given the landlord written notice of the need for repair and warned him or her (in writing) of the possible action to be taken.
- The tenant's expenditure must be reasonable and proper. It is advisable to obtain at least two estimates regarding the work proposed and, obviously, to choose the lower.

The tenant's right to withhold ground rent is not lost if there is a change of landlord.

An alternative strategy is to withhold rent and, rather than carry out the repairs, wait for the landlord to sue for the rent arrears. By making a cross-claim, the tenant might be able to obtain compensation for breach of the landlord's covenant to repair. The tenant would thus recover for loss arising from the disrepair and not be limited merely to the cost of effecting reasonable repairs.

The advantage of these forms of self-help is that the tenant does not have to initiate court proceedings and can sit back and wait for the landlord to decide what action to take. The disadvantage is that it all takes a great deal of time during which the repairs remain outstanding. Moreover, the landlord might attempt to forfeit the lease for non-payment of rent, but the court would grant the tenant relief and the landlord would be unsuccessful.

Statutory help

Where the landlord is in breach of a covenant to repair, the Landlord and Tenant Act 1987 allows the tenant(s) to apply to the court for an order appointing a manager of the building to take over responsibility from the landlord and for a compulsory purchase order so that the tenant(s) can buy out the landlord's freehold. This right is to be extended by the Commonhold and Leasehold Reform Act 2002. These remedies are discussed further in Chapter 15.

Remedies for landlords

The covenant to pay ground rent is treated differently from all other covenants given by the tenant. In long residential leases, it is common for there to be a ground rent payable. Rent becomes due on the day stipulated for payment and is in arrears from the following day. Several sanctions can be employed by the landlord against a tenant in arrears.

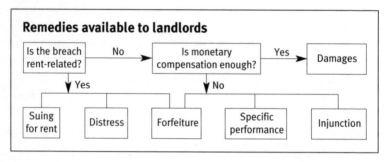

Remedies available to landlords

Suing for rent

Rent is a debt, and arrears are recoverable for up to six years by way of an action for breach of covenant. Once judgment has been given in favour of the landlord, then, if the tenant either cannot or will not pay, it will need to be enforced. There are two methods of enforcement: obtaining an attachment of earnings order and sending out the court bailiffs under a warrant of execution.

Distress

Distress is a simple remedy of self-help which the landlord can employ against a tenant without, generally, going to court. This ancient (and some would say outmoded) remedy allows the landlord, subject to certain restrictions, to enter the tenant's flat (but not by force) and seize and later sell goods found there. Because a long lease involves only a small ground rent, it is unlikely that the amount of arrears will justify the use of distress. Nevertheless, distress is sometimes used as a means of intimidating tenants (that is, by sending in the bailiffs and seizing the tenant's goods) so that they quit the premises at the end of the lease. Distress does not terminate the lease.

The remedy is hedged with restrictions:

- Distress applies only to rent arrears (or payments expressly reserved as rent in the lease; for example, service charges). It is not suitable when the amount of rent is in dispute.
- There has to be a lease. The remedy does not cover any relationship other than that between landlord and tenant.
- The remedy is not available where the landlord has sued the tenant for the debt (that is, rent arrears) or set in motion proceedings to forfeit the lease (see pages 144–50).
- The remedy cannot be exercised between sunset and sunrise and never on a Sunday.
- Entry to the flat must not be made by breaking an outer door, but it can be through an open (but not closed) window. Once inside, however, internal doors can be forced.
- Certain goods are immune from seizure: clothes and bedding (up to £100 in value); tools of the trade (up to £150); perishable foods; tenant's fixtures; and things in actual use when the distress is levied.

The landlord may exercise this remedy in person, but normally he or she uses a bailiff certified by the county court as being qualified to do the job. If distress occurs, the landlord or bailiff must give or leave for the tenant a notice which states the reason for the distress and the place of intended sale of the goods seized. No sooner than five days later, the goods can be sold and the landlord can discharge the rent arrears (and recover expenses) from the proceeds. Any balance must be paid to the tenant.

A danger for the landlord is that wrongful distress gives the tenant the right to seek substantial damages for consequential loss.

Two final points about distress: first, the landlord does not need to physically remove the goods from the flat. There is a concept known as 'walking possession', which allows the goods to stay on the premises, but which entails that legally they are impounded and cannot be removed or used by the tenant. Second, the landlord can remove and sell the goods of a third party found on the premises if it is reasonably believed that they belong to the tenant. Once they have been sold, there is nothing that the third party can do.

Forfeiture

Forfeiture for breach of covenant is the most powerful weapon in the armoury of the landlord. It allows the landlord to 're-enter' the tenant's flat and put a premature end to the lease (see Chapter 17). The landlord can, if forfeiture is successful, then sell a new lease of the flat to a new buyer. It is of particular relevance to a long lease which, unlike other types of tenancy, cannot be ended by a notice to quit. The rules governing forfeiture differ according to whether the breach complained of concerns the covenant to pay rent or some other type of covenant.

In practice, however, forfeiture is difficult for the landlord to achieve. This is because of existing safeguards designed to protect tenants: if the premises are occupied as a dwelling, the landlord must obtain a court order and the court will normally not allow the

---

Abuses of forfeiture

The remedy of forfeiture is subject to abuse by landlords and is often criticised.

- It can be invoked in relation to minor defaults and, therefore, can be a disproportionate response.
- The mere threat of forfeiture can be used to obtain substantial sums from leaseholders: for example, excessive administrative charges for processing consents and the like.
- The landlord can threaten forfeiture for non-payment of ground rent unless the tenant pays a very high additional charge.
- The mere threat of physical re-entry can be an easy way to intimidate tenants into paying excessive sums or to encourage them not to challenge the amounts claimed.
- There is no equivalent remedy for a tenant when the landlord is in breach of covenant.

landlord's claim to succeed if, for example, the tenant can show that the breach of covenant will be remedied. Further restrictions are currently imposed upon the landlord's ability to forfeit for disrepair or non-payment of service charges. The provisions of the Commonhold and Leasehold Reform Act 2002 have increased the restrictions on the landlord's ability to forfeit in relation to ground rent and administrative charges.

All well-drafted long leases will contain a forfeiture clause, and expressly give to the landlord the right to re-take possession. Forfeiture is not usually available unless there is such a clause; exceptions to this are where the premises are used as a brothel or when the tenant denies the landlord's title (for example, by claiming to be the freeholder). It is the landlord who has the option whether to terminate or to continue with the lease. There is no equivalent of forfeiture which allows the tenant to end the lease. Accordingly, even if the landlord is in flagrant breach of the covenants, the tenant is still bound to the lease and cannot escape it.

A forfeiture clause should be drafted so as to make clear whether the clause is to cover breaches of both negative (that is, 'do not') and positive (that is, 'do') covenants. This can be done either expressly or by inserting the words 'breach' and 'non-observance' into the clause which will then cover both aspects and allow forfeiture to be used for breach of any covenant.

Example of a forfeiture clause

A typical forfeiture clause would read as follows. Note that the wording 'performed or observed' means that it covers both positive and negative covenants.

'If the rent hereby reserved or any part thereof shall be unpaid for 21 days after becoming payable (whether formally demanded or not) or if any covenant on the tenant's part herein contained shall not be performed or observed then and in any of the said cases it shall be lawful for the landlord at any time thereafter to re-enter upon the demised premises or any part thereof in the name of the whole and thereupon the demise shall absolutely determine but without prejudice to any right of action of the landlord in respect of any breach of the tenant's covenants herein contained.'

Methods of forfeiture

There are two basic ways in which the landlord may forfeit and re-enter. The first is by actual, physical, re-entry; the second is by starting court proceedings for possession.

Taking physical possession for the non-payment of rent is a risky tactic unless the premises are unoccupied. The Criminal Law Act 1977 prohibits the threat or use of violence in order to enter when any person is present on the premises. The Protection from Eviction Act 1977 provides that an eviction is lawful only with the support of a court order for possession. Accordingly, physical re-entry will often be unlawful and is not common as regards residential property. The formal means of effecting re-entry is by serving a court claim form on the tenant that contains an unambiguous demand for possession. This demand should not be coupled with any other claim from the landlord. The procedure for forfeiture is both awkward and complex. Due to its far-reaching effects, the remedy is the subject of major safeguards.

Forfeiture for non-payment of ground rent

Most long leases require the payment of ground rent on a particular date whether or not it is demanded by the landlord. This is, however, misleading as in reality the rent cannot be lawfully recovered unless the landlord has formally demanded it (see below). Some landlords have demanded additional charges if the ground rent is paid late, to cover alleged 'administrative charges'. These can sometimes be in the region of £100 to £200 and, as such, utterly disproportionate to the real costs of sending a letter of reminder. A tenant will not usually be prepared to go to court over such an amount and will often pay the additional amount claimed. The landlord's reminder might also contain bullying threats about forfeiture and further legal action if the delay in payment is repeated.

The Commonhold and Leasehold Reform Act 2002 protects tenants against such abuses.

- The tenant will only be liable for any ground rent once the landlord has issued a written demand for payment.
- The landlord will be prevented from levying any additional charge if the rent is paid within 30 days of the demand, and any administrative charges that are levied should be reasonable. As with service charges (see Chapter 13), the tenant can apply to

the Leasehold Valuation Tribunal (LVT) to challenge the reasonableness of the administration charge. If the charge is fixed or produced by a formula set out in the lease, the tenant can apply to the LVT for the lease to be varied (see Chapter 15).

- The landlord will be unable to begin forfeiture proceedings for non-payment of ground rent unless the demand has been made and at least 30 days have since lapsed without the ground rent being paid. The demand must state the amount due and the date on which it is (or was) payable. The notice must also contain a summary of the tenant's rights and obligations.
- No forfeiture can occur when the sum of money claimed is below £350. This rule gives way when the sum has been owed for more than three years.

Forfeiture for non-rent-related breaches

Forfeiture for breach of a covenant other than non-payment of rent is governed by different procedures. New restrictions have, however, been placed on landlords' ability to forfeit for non-payment of service charges (see page 148). Before forfeiture can take place, a special notice has to be served on the tenant. This has to be done regardless of whether physical re-entry or court action is the method of forfeiture adopted by the landlord. The notice is a device whereby the tenant is given a last chance to make amends and perform the covenant. The notice must specify:

- the breach of covenant complained of
- where appropriate, how the breach can be remedied (for example, by repair)
- if relevant, that compensation be paid to the landlord as a result of the breach.

Any notice that does not comply with these requirements is void, and forfeiture cannot lawfully take place. Where the notice is valid and the breach is capable of remedy, the landlord cannot proceed until the tenant fails to remedy or to pay compensation within a reasonable time. If the breach is not capable of remedy (for example, where a stigma is attached to the premises because of illegal or immoral use), the landlord may proceed with the forfeiture after a reasonable interval (for example, four weeks). Sometimes it is uncertain whether or not the court will regard a particular breach as being capable of remedy. To avoid doubt and invalidity, the landlord should require the tenant to remedy the breach 'so far as the same is capable of remedy'.

The tenant may be able to stop the forfeiture by making a counter-claim or by separate summons before the landlord recovers possession. After possession has been taken, and unlike in the case of a breach of rental covenant (see page 142), no relief can be granted. Relief is regulated by a flexible discretion, but is unlikely to be granted if the tenant's breach was wilful or if the breach is incapable of remedy.

Forfeiture for non-payment of service charges or administrative charges

The non-payment of service charge is the most common reason why a landlord would seek to forfeit the lease of a flat. The Housing Act 1996 introduced restrictions on the landlord's ability to forfeit on this ground. It provides that the forfeiture cannot proceed unless the amount claimed has been agreed, admitted or determined by a Leasehold Valuation Tribunal as reasonable and due. After the amount is determined the landlord must allow the tenant 14 days in which to pay before starting proceedings.

Until recently, it was permissible to serve a forfeiture notice on the tenant before the amount was determined. Although the notice had to warn the tenant of his or her rights, this notice was sometimes used as a means of intimidating a tenant. Consequently, the Commonhold and Leasehold Reform Act 2002 prevents a forfeiture notice being served in relation to service charges or 'administrative charges' until after the amount outstanding is determined. 'Administrative charges' are defined as those charges that are required to be paid for approvals, for the provision of information, as a result of a failure to pay rent or other charges on time, or as a result of a breach of the lease.

Forfeiture for disrepair

This merits special attention because further limitations are imposed by the Leasehold Property (Repairs) Act 1938. This Act applies to leases granted initially for longer than seven years and which still have at least three years remaining unexpired. In certain circumstances, the Act makes it necessary for the landlord to obtain the approval of the court before pursuing the remedy of forfeiture or damages. The landlord must inform the tenant of the right to claim the protection of the 1938 Act and to serve a counter-notice. If such counter-notice is served within 28 days, the court may allow the landlord to proceed only if the landlord can show that:

- the value of the freehold has been substantially diminished
- the breach needs to be remedied immediately to prevent substantial diminution; to comply with statute; to protect the interests of other occupiers; or to avoid heavier repair costs in the future
- there exist special circumstances which make it just and equitable for permission to be given.

Losing the right to forfeit

The landlord can lose the right to forfeit the lease if by any action he or she waives the particular breach complained of. This can arise from any act on the landlord's part which is inconsistent with the intention to end the lease. Once waiver of a breach has occurred, it is irrevocable.

Waiver is decided by the courts and not by what the parties actually intended. It is the act (not the motives) of the landlord which the court will examine. Waiver can arise from ignorance, clerical error or by a careless expression in correspondence. Acts which could amount to waiver include, for example, the landlord's acceptance of, or demand for, rent for periods after the breach of covenant; and negotiations to grant a new lease at the end of the current one. The breach of covenant may be a 'once and for all' breach (for example, of covenant against sub-letting) or it may be a continuous breach (for example, of repair or user covenant or increasing arrears of rent). However, even if the landlord waives a continuing breach on one occasion, the lease can be forfeited on the recurrence of the breach.

Effect of forfeiture

There are a number of consequences arising from the forfeiture of a lease. First, once re-entry has lawfully occurred, the former tenant becomes a trespasser. Reasonable force can be used to evict him or her and to remove his or her goods. The lease is at an end and the former tenant no longer has to observe the covenants (for example, is no longer liable to pay ground rent).

Second, the forfeiture of the head-lease automatically destroys any sub-lease granted by the former tenant. As explained in the next section, the sub-tenant has the right to apply to the court for relief.

Third, a mortgage lender who holds the lease as security can seek relief against the forfeiture of that lease.

Protection for the tenant

In addition to the statutory help given to tenants against the landlord's claim for forfeiture for disrepair or non-payment of ground rent or administrative charges, the courts themselves can come to the help of the tenant. In the case of a breach of the covenant to pay ground rent, in the County Court the tenant can get automatic **relief** (that is, the court halting the forfeiture proceedings), by paying in to the court all arrears and costs not later than five days before the return date specified on the landlord's summons. In the High Court, the proceedings are automatically halted where at least six months' rent is in arrears and the arrears are paid (with costs) at any time prior to the trial. In other cases, relief can also be granted by the court to the tenant on such terms (normally to make good the breach of covenant) as the court thinks appropriate. If relief is granted, the lease will continue in existence. The scope for relief depends upon which court the proceedings are brought before, as explained below.

In the County Court, forfeiture will be averted if the tenant pays all arrears and costs within four weeks of the possession order or within such period as the court deems fit. If the tenant fails to do this, the possession order is likely to be enforced and further relief will not normally be available. It is possible, however, for the tenant to apply for an extension at any time before the landlord recovers possession. Once the landlord has taken possession, the tenant can still apply to the court for relief within six months of that recovery of possession. This, however, is unlikely to succeed.

In the High Court, there is a general discretion to grant relief against forfeiture, and it is likely to be granted unless the tenant's conduct has been extreme or the breach is unlikely to be remedied. The tenant can make an application at any time before trial which will, provided that all arrears and costs are discharged, normally be granted. Alternatively, the application can be made within six months of possession being granted to the landlord, but relief will not be granted if it would cause hardship to a third party (for example, a new tenant) or the landlord.

If forfeiture is allowed, third parties, for example, a sub-tenant and the tenant's mortgage lender, may be disadvantaged. Such persons also have a right to apply to the court for relief. The court usually favours the request of such third parties. Accordingly, the forfeiture becomes final only once the court order has been issued and all claims for relief denied.

Forfeiture is rare when the breach of covenant is remedied (for example, if the arrears and costs are paid by the tenant, sub-tenant or mortgage lender). Because of this, forfeiture is not commonly achieved for breach of a rental covenant in a residential lease. Nevertheless, the threat of forfeiture can be exploited to the landlord's advantage: for example, writing to the tenant's mortgage lender may persuade the lender to perform the tenant's covenants and to add the cost to the mortgage debt. The lender will be allowed to do this under the mortgage agreement and will normally prefer this route to applying for relief before the court.

Chapter 11

Co-ownership

It is common for a person to buy a flat (or a house) jointly with a spouse, friend or relative. The number of people who can co-own a single flat is not, however, limited to two. Unfortunately, English law is not renowned for its simplicity, and the recognition and enforcement of the property rights of individuals living together are complicated matters. The same rules apply irrespective of whether the property is a flat or a house.

Joint tenancy and tenancy in common

There are two recognised and distinct types of co-ownership: the joint tenancy and the tenancy in common.

Where there is a **joint tenancy**, the co-owners own the whole of the property together and on the death of one, the other(s) acquires the property automatically regardless of the terms of any will or the rules that apply on dying intestate (that is, without a will). This continues until there is only one owner remaining, and is known as the right of survivorship. It is advisable to declare on the lease whether the owners are to hold as joint tenants or not.

Conversely, if the co-owners are **tenants in common**, each owns a share in the property which they can deal with as they wish. On death, the share of the co-owner can be left by will to someone or passed to next of kin by virtue of intestacy. The shares of tenants in common do not have to be equal. If, for example, one party provides 75 per cent of the purchase price and the other contributes 25 per cent, it would be sensible to have a three-quarters and one-quarter share respectively. It is best to have this expressly declared on the lease, but it is likely to be presumed by the courts if dispute arises.

It is up to the buyers to decide what type of arrangement suits them. The nature of the relationship between them and the amount of the financial contributions each has made to the purchase will be the key factors.

EXAMPLES

Jan and John are married and buy a flat together, with Jan financing one-third of the purchase price, John the other two-thirds. The couple are not overly concerned about the commercial aspect of the transaction. They both make sure that their names are on the lease and expressly declare themselves to be joint tenants. If one of them dies, the other will own the entire flat absolutely and automatically. There is no need to process a will.

Sally and Kenneth, who are not married, buy a flat to live in together. Although they love each other, it is not their intention that, on the death of Kenneth, Sally will acquire his share and *vice versa*. Kenneth has children by a previous relationship and wants to ensure that they are provided for. This security is offered by the lease expressly stating that they are tenants in common.

If Kenneth had provided only one-third of the purchase price, Sally might feel justified in making sure that he has only a one-third interest in the flat (and, thus, one-third share in the proceeds of any subsequent sale). Provided their respective shares are made clear in the lease or assignment, if the relationship ends, the situation is uncomplicated. If Sally and Kenneth had jointly taken out a mortgage together to buy the flat, then, despite the difference in their shares, they are still equally liable to repay the mortgage. This remains so even if they split up and one of them lives elsewhere.

Ingredients of a joint tenancy

If the title to the flat is taken in joint names then the co-owners must be joint tenants of the legal estate (that is, the paper title). The important issue is what happens to the real ownership (that is, the entitlement to any proceeds of sale if the flat is sold). This is grandly called 'a beneficial interest under a trust'. This will become clearer in meaning as the chapter progresses.

This is why it is crucial to declare on the lease whether the parties' real ownership is as joint tenants or as tenants in common.

If the legal adviser omits to state how the parties are to hold the lease, assignment or sub-lease, then he or she has been negligent and can be sued for any loss.

The four unities

Under a joint tenancy the co-owners have a single ownership of the flat (that is, they together own the whole and do not own distinct shares). For a joint tenancy to exist, all of the so-called four unities must be present.

- **The unity of possession** This means that each joint tenant is as much entitled to possession of any part of the property as the others.
- **The unity of interest** The interest of all the joint tenants must be identical; that is, for example, they must all have the same leasehold estate.
- **The unity of title** Each joint tenant must claim title from the same conveyance.
- **The unity of time** The title to the flat must be conveyed in the joint tenants at the same time.

For a tenancy in common to exist there need only be the unity of possession (interest, title and time being irrelevant). Without unity of possession, there would be no co-ownership at all.

Telling the two types of co-ownership apart

Many co-owners are unaware of what type of co-ownership was created when they bought their flat. If a dispute arises or one of the co-owners dies or wants to move out, however, they will need to know what the legal situation is. The first document to check is the lease. If this expressly declares the co-owners to be joint tenants or to be tenants in common, then the declaration is usually decisive. If the lease is silent on the issue, the court will be left to determine what relationship has been created. In order to do so, the court will adopt the following approach:

- It will look to see if the four unities are present. If they are, a joint tenancy could exist; if not, it must be a tenancy in common. This means that the four unities are a necessary, but not sufficient, condition for the existence of a joint tenancy.

- If the unities are present, the court will look for words of severance that indicate a tenancy in common. Such words include 'equally', 'share', 'between' and 'to be divided amongst'. If such words are present, a tenancy in common will be created.
- If the unities are present and no words of severance exist, the court will have to consider certain presumptions that apply. A joint tenancy will be favoured, except where the purchase money was provided in unequal shares or the property is part of a business partnership.

Common terms, uncommon meanings?

A **trust** arises in all cases of co-ownership. Accordingly, the legal estate (the paper title) is held by trustees (the legal owners) on trust for the beneficiaries (who may also be the legal owners).

- A **beneficiary** is the true or equitable owner of the property.
- **Beneficial/equitable interest** is the interest that the beneficiary has under the trust. This may also be known as **equitable estate**.
- The **beneficial ownership** (also known as the **ownership in equity**) dictates who benefits and in what proportion, on the sale of the property.

Converting a joint tenancy

It is possible to sever (end) a joint tenancy of the equitable estate and create a tenancy in common. There are a variety of ways in which this can be achieved. The simplest method is by serving a written notice on the other joint tenant making clear that severance has occurred. In addition, any serious attempt by one joint tenant to sell, lease or mortgage part of the property would also sever the joint tenancy (even if without the knowledge or agreement of the other joint tenants). On the other hand, oral statements, commencement of divorce proceedings and the leaving of a will do not have any effect.

If there are more than two joint tenants, the party who severs affects only his or her share. The other co-owners remain joint tenants among themselves.

Example reworked

Jan and John are considering divorce. The joint tenancy does not now suit either partner, if only because neither wishes to benefit the other on death. Jan seeks to remain in the property until the flat is sold. They will now seek to sever their joint tenancy and convert it into a tenancy in common. Following severance, they will hold the property as tenants in common and the right of survivorship is ended. When Jan dies, her 50-per-cent interest in the flat could be left by will to whoever she pleases. (She has a 50-per-cent share because she and John were previously joint tenants; the fact that she paid less of the original purchase price than John is immaterial.) The same rule applies in the case of John.

Converting a tenancy in common

Just as it is possible to change a joint tenancy into a tenancy in common, the reverse can be achieved. This will require a written agreement (perhaps formally drafted in a deed) converting the tenancy in common.

Example reworked

Sally and Kenneth have a child together and wish to convert their tenancy in common into a joint tenancy and activate the right of survivorship. This can be done by creating a 'trust' in writing. There is no formula or special way of doing so but a deed is preferable. Their names already appear on the lease or assignment as legal owners. Once the tenancy has been converted, Kenneth would no longer be regarded as having only a one-third share in the flat and both he and Sally would now together own the flat in its entirety.

Trust of land

In every case of co-ownership, the law employs a device known as a 'trust'. This artificial and somewhat confusing notion requires that the co-owners hold the legal ownership (the paper title) of the flat on trust for themselves (usually) as beneficiaries. The legal estate is always considered to be held by the co-owners as joint tenants. Behind this paper title, what really counts is the ownership in equity (that is, who benefits and in what proportions if the flat is sold) and this is where the distinction between a joint tenancy and a tenancy in common bites.

The purpose of using a trust is to make the procedure for selling the flat easier and to ensure that the co-owners obtain their proper share of the proceeds of sale.

When the flat is conveyed into more than one name, the trust will arise automatically. Nevertheless, it is preferable for the conveyance to make express reference to the trust.

A lease may, for example, expressly state that Bill and Ben hold the legal estate on trust for themselves beneficially. If they are to be tenants in common, the lease might read: 'The purchasers agree that they are in equity tenants in common in the following shares: Bill two-thirds and Ben one-third.' If the lease fails to mention the trust, the existence of a trust is implied by law.

Right to occupy

The Trusts of Land and Appointment of Trustees Act 1996 gives a beneficiary the right to occupy a jointly owned flat. This is subject to the flat being available and suitable for the beneficiary. Where two or more beneficiaries have a right to occupy, the trustees can exclude or restrict such a right in relation to some, but not all, of them. The trustees must act reasonably in exercising this power. In addition, reasonable conditions may be imposed on the beneficiary in occupation. These will normally concern the payment of outgoings and the payment of 'rent' to the non-occupying beneficiary.

Dispute

Obviously if the beneficiaries are also the trustees (as with Sally and Kenneth in the previous example), one will not necessarily move out simply because the other wants to live in the flat alone. It might be necessary to go to court for an order declaring who is to occupy and on what conditions. The 1996 Act guides the court by providing a list of matters which are relevant. These include:

* the welfare of any minor
* the interests of any secured creditor
* the intentions of the co-owners when the property was bought (normally to live together)

- the purposes for which the property is held on trust (normally to provide a home for both of them).

These guidelines apply also where one trustee wants to sell the property against the wishes of the other(s).

Co-owners' decision to sell

If all the co-owners of a flat consent to its sale, there is no problem. The difficulties arise when there is a dispute between the co-owners, for example during the breakdown of a relationship. The general rule is that the sale of the flat cannot proceed unless all the co-owners agree.

In circumstances where one co-owner refuses, the other(s) may, as shown, apply to the court for an order compelling the reluctant party to join in the conveyance. Due to the nature of the 'trust', the court will usually grant the order. Nevertheless, the court enjoys a wide discretion to make such orders as it thinks fit and it sometimes orders that the sale should not take place. There are two main situations in which the sale may not be enforced:

- when a formal agreement has been made by the co-owners not to sell the flat without the consent of all
- when the co-owners bought the property in order to provide a family home. The court will be unwilling to allow the property to be sold against the wishes of one co-owner while there are dependent children in the property. In such a case, the court is likely to postpone sale until the children are of school-leaving age. If this involves the other spouse or partner moving out of the co-owned property, the court might stipulate that the person remaining in the flat pays a rent for the continued occupation. If the parties are married, then such matters will normally be resolved under the wide-ranging matrimonial jurisdiction of the court.

If creditors are involved

If a co-owner becomes bankrupt and his or her 'trustee in bankruptcy' (the person appointed by the court on bankruptcy to take charge of the bankrupt's affairs) seeks an order for sale, other considerations are brought into play. The court retains its discretion as to whether or not to order the sale, but it now has different conflicting issues to balance. Here, however, the tug of money will generally prevail over the interests of the family, and an order of sale will usually be granted. The Insolvency Act 1986 provides that, unless the circumstances of the case are exceptional, the interests of the creditors outweigh those of anyone else. The Act does, however, show some temporary compassion to the family and offers a limited opportunity to preserve – essentially for one year – the family home.

There are two ways in which the Act can delay, but not cancel, the rights of creditors and postpone the prospect of the family being made homeless:

- The bankrupt is offered limited rights of occupation, but only when the flat is also occupied by a person under the age of 18 years. The bankrupt cannot be evicted from the flat without the authorisation of the bankruptcy court. In reaching a decision the court must take on board all the circumstances of the case and, if it does order a stay of possession, this is unlikely to keep the bankrupt in occupation for longer than one year following bankruptcy.
- The bankrupt's spouse (but not cohabitant) is given certain rights of occupation. Such rights will also indirectly benefit the bankrupt. The spouse's right of occupation can be terminated only by order of the bankruptcy court. The court must take into account all the circumstances but, even if the spouse's right is upheld, the protection is effective only for one year following bankruptcy. It should be noted that the spouse's statutory right of occupation given under the Family Law Act 1996 (see pages 163–4) does not bind a trustee in bankruptcy.

Co-ownership by implication

It is possible that the name on the title deeds or registered at the Land Registry is that of one party only. As a general rule, the law presumes that the person whose name appears there is the only owner of the flat. Nevertheless, as regards married couples and cohabitants it is possible that, for example, by contributions to the purchase price or the mortgage repayments, a non-named party has acquired some ownership of the flat in equity. This will not be reflected in the lease and such contributions can be made either on the purchase of the lease or subsequently. A married person is in a stronger position than an unmarried one because, on divorce, the court has a wide discretion to redistribute ownership between the couple.

There are two broad ways in which a person not named on the title deeds or entered as registered proprietor can acquire what is termed 'beneficial ownership' and become, through implication, a co-owner.

The first is where there has been an informal agreement or understanding between the parties as to beneficial ownership and the non-owner has, as a result, done some act of reliance on the strength of that conversation. Usually, this kind of understanding arises from something the owner has said during a discussion about the flat (for example, 'this flat is as much yours as mine'). This shows the intention to give the non-owner a share in the property, but the problem with this is that it might be a phantom intention which the person making it never really intended to implement. Whatever spoken agreement was reached (for example, a 50:50 split) will normally determine who has what interest in the flat. In other circumstances, the court will order what it deems to be fair and just according to what was said and the reliance placed on it. A notion of 'proportionality' applies here.

The second means by which implied co-ownership can arise is by an inferred agreement. Here the court looks to the conduct of the parties and from that may infer a common intention to share ownership. If it finds that the non-owning partner has made monetary payments (for example, financial contributions to the deposit, purchase price or mortgage repayments) the court will readily imply the intention to share ownership.

It should be noted that certain contributions, like looking after the home and family (for example, financing improvements, rearing children, decorating, and doing housework) are not, in themselves, sufficient. The situation changes, however, if the non-owning partner looks after the children and thus frees the legal owner to go to work and earn the money that pays for the mortgage. Although an indirect contribution, it can generate a co-ownership of the flat.

A co-owner who obtains an interest by the inference of a common intention will, invariably, be a tenant in common. The share will be calculated with reference either to the value of the contributions made or to what the court assumes the intention of the parties had been. Indirect contributions are also relevant when working out the shares between the parties once co-ownership has been established.

EXAMPLE

Grant has owned a flat for the last 20 years. He has paid off the mortgage and the title is registered solely in his name. He meets Eve and falls in love. Eve moves into the flat and lives with Grant.

After two years, Eve feels insecure and asks Grant about their long-term future. She says that she will move out unless the title to the flat is registered in her name too. Grant does not want the relationship to end, but most certainly does not want Eve to have co-ownership of the flat that he had spent many years acquiring. He decides to blur the issue and says: 'Don't worry. It's your flat as much as mine.' Eve stays.

What Grant fails to appreciate is that (if the discussion can be proved, perhaps because someone witnessed it, or because it is referred to in a letter) he has, contrary to his real intention, given Eve half-ownership of the flat. If Eve had not enquired, then she would have had nothing.

Avoiding unwanted co-ownership by implication

The easiest means of avoiding a phantom intention being relied upon is not to have any such discussion in the first place. If the discussion is unavoidable, then it is wise to tell the truth and not make up palatable excuses.

In the context of an inferred agreement arising from something one or other party has done, the trust is dependent upon there being a financial contribution towards the initial or on-going purchase of the flat, rather than the use of the flat. So to prevent a co-ownership by implication, you should avoid getting direct contributions to the purchase price and mortgage repayments. Any monetary payments should be classified as 'rent'. If money belonging to someone else is to be spent in the acquisition of the flat, then the safest course is to have a signed agreement between the parties that the money is merely a loan or gift and is not designed to give that party a share in the ownership of the property. Any form of words will suffice provided that the intention not to give an interest in the flat is clearly spelled out. An example might be:

> 'The parties agree that the legal and beneficial title to the property is vested solely in Jim and that Jules does not acquire any interest whatsoever in the property by reason of his contributions.'

Subject to any express discussion to the contrary, this should prevent a co-ownership situation arising.

Advancement

Sometimes the presumption of a trust is displaced by an outmoded concept known as 'advancement'. This presumption arises where there is a special relationship between the parties under which it is natural for one party to provide for the other. Curiously, the rule applies only to 'gifts' by husbands or fathers (not cohabitants) to wives or children, respectively. It does not apply to wives advancing money to their husbands. Any payments made by a husband to the purchase price, for example, might be regarded as a gift and, if so, would not give the husband a beneficial ownership of the flat. Not surprisingly, the courts do not like the presumption of advancement and try to avoid its application. It can readily be rebutted by some clear understanding to the contrary between the parties.

Married and non-married partners

Although as yet no legislation governs the property rights of cohabitants, the situation of married couples is different. Acts of Parliament, such as the Matrimonial Causes Act 1973, are in force which protect the property rights of married couples. The issue of implied ownership (see pages 159–61) is not relevant because, on divorce, the courts have the flexible jurisdiction to redistribute property rights. Issues of property law and ownership are given less weight than the higher demands of relating the means of both parties to the needs of each. The court, therefore, looks to the future (in contrast to cohabitation where it analyses events in detailed hindsight). Prior to divorce, the wife can apply for a declaration of property rights under the Married Women's Property Act 1882. This may result, for example, in the court ordering the conveyance of the property into joint names.

Further information about the situation for married couples can be found in *The Which? Guide to Divorce* and for unmarried couples in *The Which? Guide to Living Together*, both published by Which? Books.

Improvements

Between cohabitants, paying for improvements does not in itself give rise to co-ownership. In relation to married couples, however, the Matrimonial Proceedings and Property Act 1970 expressly provides that if a husband or wife makes a substantial contribution to improvements to property, the contributing spouse will receive a share (or, if already a co-owning tenant in common, an increased share) in the improved property. This does not apply, however, if there is agreement to the contrary.

Family home rights

The Family Law Act 1996 offers spouses, provided they qualify (see below), rights concerning the occupation of the matrimonial home. No rights exist in relation to a flat bought by either spouse after separation, but property which was intended to be the matrimonial home, whether or not they both lived there at the break-up, is caught by the provisions. These rights to the matrimonial home are sex-neutral, that is, they can be relied upon by either husband or wife. There are no automatic rights of occupation benefiting other members of the family. The rights are available only to a spouse who does not own the legal estate, so they extend to spouses who have no ownership rights and to those who co-own only in equity (that is, have a beneficial ownership). The rights afforded to qualifying spouses are:

- if they occupy the flat, a right not to be evicted or excluded without a court order
- it they are not in occupation, a right (with the permission of the court) to enter and occupy.

Both rights continue until divorce and extend not only to the flat itself, but also to any garden, garage and outbuilding. The matrimonial rights will bind a buyer of a flat only if he or she is protected on the Land Charges Register (unregistered land) or the Land Register (registered land). For unregistered land, this will involve the entry of a Class F land charge; for registered land, as these rights cannot exist as 'overriding interests', the entry of a notice on the Charges Register. You do not need the consent of your spouse to take these steps. If you are buying a flat from a married couple who are separating, then providing your legal adviser checks that no matrimonial rights have been entered, you will not find the previous owner's spouse presenting you with an occupation order when you try to move in.

When one spouse has rights over the matrimonial home, it is open for either spouse to apply to court seeking an order declaring, enforcing, restricting or terminating the rights, and the court can make such order as it considers fair. The 1996 Act sets out the types of order that the court can make and identifies the factors that must be taken into account. These factors include the housing needs and resources of each party, the likely impact on any child and the conduct of the parties in relation to each other.

Although unmarried cohabitants do not have matrimonial rights to the home, they are not totally ignored by the 1996 Act. The Act allows cohabitants and former cohabitants to apply for a court order protecting their occupation of the flat in which they and the other party have lived as husband and wife or intended so to live. The reference to husband and wife excludes same-sex relationships. The occupation order, if made, will be only temporary and of limited duration. It is also personal to the parties and, unlike a spouse's rights, cannot bind a third-party purchaser of the flat.

Domestic violence

The Family Law Act 1996 covers domestic violence and allows for an order to be made removing the violent partner from the home. This can be accompanied by a non-molestation order with a power of arrest attached. In cases of violence, the court must balance the harm to the applicant and any child against the harm to the other partner caused by exclusion. If the couple are married, or were married, the court *must* make an exclusion order where more harm will be caused by allowing the violent partner to continue in occupation. If they are unmarried, the court has a power to exclude the violent partner, but is under no obligation to do so.

Property re-adjustment

On divorce, the court has the power to order the transfer of specific property from one spouse to the other. Any such order will take effect when the decree absolute is made. In deciding how to exercise its power, the court must take account of the welfare of any children; both spouses' financial resources (for example, income, earning capacity and personal property); the loss to each that will arise on divorce (this also takes into account the standard of living, needs, obligations and responsibilities of each spouse); the age and health of the parties; the duration of the marriage; the conduct of the parties; and any contributions made by looking after children and the home.

The matrimonial home is often the key asset of the family. It is the task of the court to ensure that both spouses and their children are suitably housed. Unfortunately, it is usually the case that there will not be enough funds to maintain two distinct homes without a drastic drop in the standard of living of one or both parties. If there are children involved, the court will normally prefer the option of keeping them in the family home.

The court may make the following orders:

- the sale of the matrimonial home, which can be made immediate or postponed, for example, until the children of the marriage reach a certain age (say, 16 years). The court may order that the proceeds of the eventual sale be distributed in equal shares between the parties. Meanwhile, the parent with custody is allowed to live in the flat and is obliged to meet all the outgoings
- an outright transfer whereby the entire ownership of the flat is transferred to one spouse. This could be in lieu of a maintenance order or on condition that the other spouse receives a lump-sum payment or a financial charge on the property
- permission for a spouse to occupy the flat for life or for a defined period. If the latter type of order is adopted, it is common for the resident spouse to pay an occupational rent.

Buying with friends

Particularly in London, buying with friends may be the only way you can afford a flat. The advantages are obvious: the costs of buying the property are spread, additional salaries may be taken into account in the calculation of how much you can borrow, and running expenses are shared. There are, however, potential pitfalls, and you will need to make arrangements, where possible, to avoid them:

- Mortgage lenders may be more wary of lending to a group of friends because the scope for default is greater the more purchasers there are.

- Often a lender will only look at the two highest salaries when deciding how much to lend. (Some lenders, however, will take into account other salaries; as always, shop around for a deal which suits you.)

- In order to establish what will happen if one friend dies, or to calculate what share each friend is entitled to if the property is sold, a trust should be declared on the lease. It is best that friends own as tenants in common.

- Agree in advance what is to happen if one friend decides to leave and sell his or her share in the flat, and put this in a written agreement signed by all the friends, each of whom should keep a copy. For example, it would be wise to require the person leaving to offer his or her share to the others before putting it on the open market. If one of you sells to someone outside the group, it might be necessary to remortgage the flat in order to reflect the change in ownership.

- Even if you leave the flat, you are still liable to make mortgage payments until your name is taken off the mortgage deed or the flat is remortgaged.

- Consider what is to happen if one friend becomes ill or redundant. As welfare benefits are limited in what they will contribute towards mortgage repayments (see Chapter 4), it might be wise for all of you to take out permanent health insurance and/or critical illness cover and mortgage payment protection insurance (see Chapter 12). Remember, as you are all jointly and individually liable under the mortgage, arrears will give you all a bad credit rating.

- Agree in advance how contributions to running expenses and maintenance costs are going to be paid for. These could form part of the written agreement mentioned above.

Buying from co-owners

The existence of a trust (always present when there is more than one legal owner) ensures that when the flat is sold, at whatever distant date, the process of transfer to the new buyer is simplified. The buyer will be able to obtain an absolute title without worrying about the beneficial interests of, say, Bill and Ben. To be sure that the transaction proceeds smoothly, the buyer should:

- take the lease, assignment or sub-lease from all the legal owners (the trustees) as stated on the lease or assignment
- pay the purchase money collectively to at least two trustees (that is, make the cheque or banker's draft payable to both Bill and Ben).

The buyer is then not liable for any misappropriation of the purchase money. If, for example, Bill absconds, having withdrawn the funds from a joint bank account, then Ben cannot look to the buyer for satisfaction.

Problems for buyers of co-owned flats

The major difficulty facing a buyer is discovering whether or not the flat is impliedly co-owned. If such a trust exists, it will not be disclosed by the conveyancing documentation and will not appear on any register. Therefore, the buyer will often be unaware that there is anyone other than the seller with an interest in the property and will be paying the purchase money only to the sole seller. The danger exists that the buyer could be bound by such an undisclosed interest.

The issue of whether the beneficial interest of a non-legal owner of the flat will bind the buyer depends largely upon whether the land is unregistered or registered. If unregistered, a buyer will be bound by that equitable interest if he or she has actual, constructive or imputed notice of the co-owner's rights. This means that the right will bind if the buyer or the buyer's legal adviser either knew or should have known of the co-owner's interest. If the buyer (or legal adviser) could not have known, then the buyer will not be bound by the co-owner's interest. There is no land charge that can be registered here. The concept of 'overreaching' (see below) applies equally to unregistered land as it does to registered land.

In the case of registered land, the general rule is that a buyer will be bound only by an interest which is protected by an entry on the Land Register. A massive exception to this rule applies, however, to the rights of a person in actual, physical occupation of the property. Any rights that such person has over the land will bind the buyer because they are protected as an 'overriding interest'. This means that a co-owner through implication has only to maintain occupation of the flat for his or her rights to bind a buyer. The protection will be lost, however, if the occupation is not readily discoverable. Of course, if the occupier is directly asked by the buyer whether he or she has any rights in the property, and either lies or fails to disclose the rights, the buyer will not be bound by those rights; otherwise, it would amount to fraud by the occupier on the buyer.

Solutions for buyers

To avoid being bound by an undisclosed co-owner's interest in the flat, the buyer should inspect the property to see if anyone else is living there and, if suspicious, search the electoral roll and make enquiries of neighbours. If the presence of someone other than the seller is detected, the buyer should obtain (before completion) that person's signature on a release form. This will normally be effective to defeat that occupier's interest. If no one else lives there, then the buyer will not be bound by the interests of the co-owner.

A final solution for the buyer is via the legal mechanism known as 'overreaching'. This means that, even if someone is in actual occupation and has an overriding interest, on the purchase money being paid to two trustees the interest of the co-owner will be overreached and will not bind the buyer. It does not matter that the buyer knew of the co-owner's rights. Overreaching would be relevant where there are two legal owners (for example, husband and wife), but a third party (for example, a parent) has a beneficial interest in the flat. Thus the buyer will be forced to pay the purchase money to the two spouses/trustees (as legal owners) and, on doing so, will overreach the parent's interest. The parent, in this example, will have to follow the proceeds of sale and make a claim against the sellers.

Implications for lenders

Where mortgage money is used to purchase the flat, the mortgage will normally take priority over the co-owner's rights in the property. Although technically the conveyance takes place moments before the creation of the mortgage, the co-owner will not have the opportunity to move into occupation before the lender's interest has been created. Therefore, in registered land there will be no scope usually for a claim by someone in actual occupation, because the flat would need to be occupied when the mortgage was created.

In addition, it is presumed that any other co-owner is impliedly consenting to the mortgage and to the relegation of his or her interest behind that of the lender. Accordingly, with first mortgages the lender will be protected from the claims of a co-owner.

The situation is more difficult with second mortgages (which may be raised to finance a business project, buy a car or extend or improve the flat, for example). The major difference here is that the co-owner will now be in occupation of the flat and the lender might be stuck with notice of the rights of the co-owner (unregistered land) or be bound by an overriding interest (registered land). The lender is, therefore, more vulnerable than with first-mortgage transactions. There are, however, two ways in which the lender can protect itself.

- First, if there are two legal owners and the mortgage money is advanced to them, the interest of any other co-owner will be overreached. The interest ceases from that point to be an interest in the land and does not bind the lender.
- Second, where the lender discovers that there is an adult other than the legal owner living on the premises, the lender will make it a condition of the advance that the adult sign a release or a disclaimer of rights document. This generally will give the lender priority, but it is not watertight.

A defence against the lender

It is an accepted feature of commercial life that the family home is used as ('charged as') security for a business loan or overdraft facility. The commonplace scenario is where the property, while jointly owned by husband and wife, is used to provide security for the payment of the husband's business debts. In such cases, the wife is putting at risk her interest in the matrimonial home without acquiring any direct benefit from the transaction – in short, she is acting as a surety for her husband. Because marriages usually involve a high degree of trust and confidence, many cases have come before the court in which one partner (usually the wife) has been unduly influenced, or induced by misrepresentation, to consent to the transaction by the other partner. The law offers the wronged partner some defence against the lender's claims:

- Where it is evident to the lender that the transaction does not benefit both parties, the lender should be alert to the risk of potential wrongdoing: that is, the lender should be put 'on inquiry'. (This does not happen if the transaction appears to be a normal joint transaction: for example, where it is to buy a holiday home or car.)
- If the lender is put on inquiry, it must take reasonable steps (see below) to ensure that the consenting partner's (the surety's) agreement has been properly obtained and that the surety is aware of the risks before entering the transaction.
- If such steps are *not* taken, the lender will be deemed to have notice of any wrongdoing that has occurred and will be bound by the surety's right to have the transaction set aside. If tainted, the charge will, at best, attach only to any beneficial interest in the property held by the wrongdoer.

Reasonable steps

Standard banking practice is that lenders shift the responsibility on to the shoulders of solicitors. If the solicitor certifies that the transaction has been explained to the surety, the lender will normally be protected from any claims later made by the surety. Recently, the law has changed to afford more protection to the surety. To be safe from claims, the **lender** must now:

- enter into direct communication (preferably have a meeting) with the surety to explain that the requirement to see a solicitor means that afterwards the surety cannot dispute that he or she is legally bound by the documents that will have been signed

- ask the surety to nominate a solicitor that he or she is willing to instruct to provide advice and to give the necessary confirmation to the lender. The surety should be told that, if he or she wishes, the solicitor may be the same person as is acting for the other partner. The lender should not proceed with the transaction until it receives an appropriate response directly from the surety
- provide details of the principal debtor's (e.g. the husband's) financial affairs to the surety's solicitor. This will include information about the purpose for which the proposed new loan has been requested, the current amount of his or her indebtedness, the amount of his or her current overdraft facility, and the amount and terms of the new loan
- obtain from the solicitor written confirmation that the necessary information has, indeed, been provided.

Legal advice

Unfortunately, the legal advice offered to a surety is often so perfunctory that it does not in fact act as a safeguard. In order to prevent this, the law now specifies what solicitors should do; if these steps are not followed, the solicitor is liable to be sued for negligence. The **solicitor** must now:

- explain, in non-technical language and at a face-to-face meeting, the purpose of his or her involvement, and inform the surety that the lender will rely upon the advice given to protect itself
- explain the documents and their legal consequence, provide details of the proposed loan and guarantee, and ask about the surety's financial means. Where relevant, there will be discussion of the principal debtor's existing debts and current overdraft facility, and the surety must be reminded that he or she has a choice as to whether or not to enter the transaction. The solicitor must ask whether the surety wishes him or her to negotiate with the lender on the terms of the transaction
- not give any confirmation to the lender without the surety's express authorisation.

Chapter 12

Insurance

Buying and owning a flat are major commitments and it is wise to take precautions in case things go horribly wrong. Different types of insurance are bound to crop up during the process of buying a flat: you may be asked to insure your life, your ability to make mortgage repayments, the contents of your flat and the flat (and the building it is in) itself. The last of these – insuring the premises of the flat – is something the lender of a mortgage will absolutely insist on, because the flat is the only security the lender has if the borrower defaults and it therefore needs to be maintained in good condition throughout the term of the mortgage. As a general rule, do not take out contents and building insurance with the lender because often the premium rates are not competitive. If you are initially tied to the lender because of some special mortgage deal, it might be advisable to change insurers at the earliest opportunity. One company covering both contents and buildings might prove cheaper and more convenient than having policies with different insurers. Insurance of the premises is the subject of one of the main covenants between a landlord and a tenant (see Chapter 9), so is dealt with in more detail here than other kinds of insurance.

Life insurance

All investment-linked mortgages and many repayment mortgages may require you to take out life insurance or term insurance so that if you should die during the term of the mortgage the amount of the loan outstanding will be repaid by the insurer to the lender (see Chapter 4 for details). If you are buying a flat with someone else, both (or all) of you may be asked by the lender to take out insurance. Premiums on these policies can vary substantially, so it is wise to shop around.

Mortgage payment protection insurance

It is normally recommended and advisable practice for the borrower to take out an insurance policy to cover mortgage repayments if he or she becomes unemployed or falls ill. The insurance is designed to cover the gap in welfare benefits for those who become entitled to income support or jobseeker's allowance. Indeed, government policy expects that you take out such insurance. In 1997, some 75,000 claims were made from the 2.5 million policies issued. There are three types: insurance to cover unemployment only; to cover accident and sickness; and – most comprehensive of all – to cover accident, sickness and unemployment. This cover is obviously an attractive proposition for many borrowers, but it adds to the monthly cost of the mortgage. Moreover, it has become clear that many claims by borrowers have been defeated because of the small print and hidden clauses within insurance agreements. To make matters worse for the insured, the government has announced the possibility of taxing payments made by the insurance company under such policies.

Pitfalls?

Although taking out mortgage payment protection insurance (MMPI) is advisable, it is no guarantee of financial security. Recent research has shown that:

- some 12 per cent of borrowers experience some difficulty with mortgage repayments, but only 1 per cent make an MPPI claim
- 30 per cent of claims are rejected (e.g. because of pre-existing medical conditions or because the claimant has been sacked or resigned from work). Appeals are rarely successful
- 20 per cent of successful claimants still managed to fall into mortgage arrears due to the time lapse between making the claim and payment out under the policy
- with the rise in house prices, premiums are becoming prohibitively expensive
- the claim process can be delayed by the slowness of former employers to provide evidence and the inefficiency of the insurance company's administrative staff.

The policies are not cheap. Premiums are worked out per £100 of cover. The largest building societies currently charge between £6 and £8 per £100; premiums may also reflect changes in interest rates. The benefits of such policies are also limited. For example, some unemployment policies cover the person insured for a period of 12 months following unemployment, whereas others extend protection for two years. Following ill-health, cover might extend for three years, but all policies exclude pre-existing medical conditions from protection. Another problem is that it might take months before any insurance payments are received by the borrower. Clearly, such policies need to be read and understood thoroughly before any cover is bought.

Normally, your mortgage lender will offer you this type of insurance cover, but you can arrange it privately through any insurance broker. The Council of Mortgage Lenders★ and the Association of British Insurers★ have devised a minimum benchmark standard for mortgage payment protection insurance (MPPI).

Home contents insurance

Home contents insurance is a must for all home-owners. Lenders will not insist upon this type of cover (unlike premises insurance: see pages 175–9), but in this age of rising burglaries and with the traditional risk of flooding from burst pipes and so on, it would be tempting fate not to take out such insurance.

The policy will cover clothes, jewellery, furniture and other personal possessions. Most insurers will require a valuation certificate for single items worth over £1,000. Always keep receipts for expensive items. Although such policies will not normally cover accidental damage, this extra coverage can be bought at an additional premium. The cost of the premiums reflects the amount of cover that you desire and also the area in which your flat is situated. If the area is noted for a high number of burglaries, the premiums will tend to be higher than in a 'safe' area. Some insurers will refuse to issue a policy if the flat has no window locks and does not have a good security lock on the outside doors. Reductions on premiums may be obtained if the flat is within a Neighbourhood Watch scheme and/or if a burglar alarm is fitted, or if a combined contents and premises policy is bought from the same insurer. Contents insurance should be taken out from the time your goods are moved into the flat. As with all policies, you should check carefully the conditions and exclusions set out by the insurer.

You should check the following:

- whether you will have to pay an excess towards the cost of each claim (for example, £50 or £100)
- whether it is an index-linked policy – if it is, the amount of cover and the premiums due will change automatically at each renewal, in line with inflation
- whether it is a new-for-old policy, that is, one which makes no deduction for age, wear and tear – if it is, any damaged or stolen items can be replaced with new ones
- that the policy covers accidental damage so that if, for example, your pet damages your expensive sofa, you can make a claim
- that the coverage is sufficient (the average contents coverage is £30,000). If you are under-insured your rights under the policy will be jeopardised
- whether you can accept the exclusions that are listed in your policy as *not* covered by the insurance. Read these exclusions carefully.

Most policies cover sheds and outbuildings as being part of the home, provided that they are locked. The extent of cover, however, can vary widely. Items left in the garden (furniture, gnomes and statues, for example) are often covered for theft up to a limit of £500. The coverage, of course, can be increased at an additional premium and can be extended to include shrubs, fish, etc. In all cases, watch for any excess you have to pay.

Special policies are available to cover, for example, council tenants and the very wealthy.

Premises insurance

It is usual for the lease to make provisions for the insurance of the premises, by either the landlord or the tenant, against damage or destruction. Such insurance will cover the fabric of the building, including walls, roof, windows, outbuildings and garage. Limits are normally imposed on wooden sheds. Fixtures and fittings will be insured as well as underground cables and pipes. Often the covenants in the lease will state who is responsible for the insurance, ensure that there is adequate coverage and deal with what will happen if catastrophe strikes. Perils to be covered should include fire, explosion, storm, flooding, earthquake and lightning. Some policies will also cover accidental damage (for example, breaking a window with a step-ladder). Subsidence coverage will normally carry a large excess (for example, £1,000) which the insured will have to meet personally and which will not be paid for by the insurer. If the property has already been underpinned, it may be difficult to find an insurer willing to issue a premises policy.

The burden of showing that damage arose from an insured peril rests on the flat-owner. In disputed claims, much depends upon the view of the loss adjuster hired by the insurer. A recognised arbitration system is run by the Financial Ombudsman Service*.

Who should do the insuring?

The lease may contain a covenant obliging the landlord to do the insuring and may allow him or her to recover this expenditure from the tenant by way of what is called 'insurance rent' or, as is more common, under the service charge provision (see pages 179–80 and Chapter 13). Occasionally, the tenant may be responsible for insuring the premises.

The decision as to who will insure will be governed largely by the structure of the building. If the building is a block of flats in multiple occupation with common parts and facilities, the landlord will normally insure the whole property under a single policy. It is easier for the landlord to assess the amount of cover required. The tenant may have some say over the risks against which the landlord insures but, as is emphasised below, none at all as far as the choice of insurer and cost of insurance (and hence the premiums) go. If the policy is in the sole name of the landlord, the tenant and the lender should insist on their interests being noted on the policy so that they can themselves make a claim against the insurer if necessary.

As regards a building divided into two self-contained flats, the burden may fall on each flat-owner. The landlord may, however, exert some control by specifying the risks to be covered by the policies. Each tenant's mortgage lender will also influence the policy taken out by the tenant.

Proof of insurance

Where one party is to insure the premises, the other will need to know that an adequate policy has been taken out and, moreover, is still in existence. There are several ways in which this can be ensured.

- The lease could insist that the policy is taken out in the joint names of the landlord and the tenant.

- A covenant can be inserted into the lease which requires the party who is supposed to take out insurance cover to produce the policy, and the last receipt for payment of the premium, either on request, or on specified events (for example, when the lease is being assigned) or at stated intervals.

- As the landlord who insures a whole building may not wish a tenant to see the policy in its entirety because it deals with all the other flats in the building, a covenant can be inserted whereby the landlord will produce evidence (for example, extracts from the policy) to confirm that insurance has been taken out. If the premiums are passed on to the tenant by way of the service charge, the Landlord and Tenant Act 1987 gives the tenant the right to inspect the policy (see page 180).

A specified insurer?

Both parties will try to ensure that the policy taken out is with a reputable insurer. The landlord might seek to use a company that pays monetary commission for putting the business its way, whereas the tenant may want the cheapest quote to be accepted. The lease may guide the parties:

If the tenant is to insure

The covenant relating to insurance may specify a named insurance company or one nominated by the landlord. This can be financially disadvantageous for the tenant, but the expense can be minimised by a provision in the lease allowing insurance by 'any company approved in writing by the landlord, such approval not to be unreasonably withheld'. If the landlord nominates an insurer, the Housing Act 1996 may come to the assistance of the tenant, because it allows the landlord's choice of insurer to be challenged. The tenant (or, indeed, the landlord) can apply to the Leasehold Valuation Tribunal (LVT)★ for a determination as to whether or not the insurance cover provided is unsatisfactory in any respect or whether the premiums charged are excessive. The LVT may make an order requiring the landlord to nominate a different insurer. If cover is deficient, the order could be for a policy to be taken out which is satisfactory in terms of cover and/or premiums. No application can be made, however, if the matter has already been formally agreed between the parties or has been determined by a court. Similarly, the LVT does not have jurisdiction if the lease requires the matter to be referred to private arbitration.

Note that this procedure does not apply where the landlord arranges the insurance and recovers the cost as part of the service charge.

If the landlord is to insure

In blocks of flats, the landlord is generally responsible for insurance of the building. Where the landlord is to insure, the lease often limits the choice to a reputable company. The tenant, however, has no direct control over the choice or the cost of insurance. Although for most people this is not problematic, tenants at the mercy of unscrupulous landlords could find that they are being exploited over this issue. One common scam is for the landlord to insure the premises – often based on higher-than-warranted valuations – through companies owned by his or her family or friends. Then he or she can charge high premiums for the insurance, and the tenants have to either pay up or go to court to have the lease varied or to challenge the reasonableness of the service charge.

Taking over from the landlord

The lease can be varied so as to replace the landlord's choice of insurer with that of the tenants. The insurance arranged by the tenants must be with an authorised insurance company, cover the interests of both tenants and landlord, provide cover of not less than the amount required by the lease and extend to all the risks specified in the lease.

The tenants must then serve a notice of cover on the landlord within 14 days of having insured. The notice must:

- name the insurer
- state the risks covered
- stipulate the amount and period of the cover.

Amount of cover and risks

Under-insurance (that is, where deliberately or not the premises are under-valued so that a lower premium is paid) can constitute a major problem for both parties. If a claim is made, the insurance company will simply scale down the amount to be paid out. It is also possible to over-insure, which will entail higher premium costs than is necessary. Therefore, the lease will attempt to specify the degree of cover sought by using one of several expressions. 'Adequate' coverage means that the extent of cover is as recommended by the insurance company. 'Full value' cover means that the policy covers the full market value of the premises, but might be considerably less than the cost of actually reinstating (that is, rebuilding) the flat. Coverage 'for the full cost of reinstatement' requires extensive cover to include the actual cost of repairing or rebuilding the premises from scratch. The landlord will prefer this last form of insurance cover. The Association of British Insurers★ has produced a guide to calculating rebuilding costs.

The lease may specify, either in a definitions section or in the covenant itself, certain risks against which the premises must be insured. It is impractical to spell out each and every potential risk and, accordingly, the clause will be comprehensive and flexible. For the tenant, it is important that the insurance cover at least matches the extent of his or her obligations to repair the flat if it is damaged. The amount for which the flat is insured should be reviewed periodically and especially when improvements to the flat have been carried out.

In practice, a major difficulty is in assessing the value of a block of flats for the purposes of insurance cover. The insurers themselves, and also surveyors, are sometimes unable to suggest a figure. The danger, of course, is that the block will be under-insured. This may encourage individual flat-owners to take out further insurance and this might be required by a mortgage lender who will be keen to ensure that the total insurance coverage is sufficient to protect its security for the loan. In the event of a claim, however, the tenant cannot claim for the same loss twice.

Insurance and the service charge

Although service charges are discussed in Chapter 13, special provisions apply when the service charge includes a payment for insurance. Under the Landlord and Tenant Act 1987, the tenant is afforded rights to information about insurance. In addition, a tenant can challenge the cost, as a service charge item, before the Leasehold Valuation Tribunal. Remember that these rights exist only where you pay a variable service charge which includes an element for insurance:

- You (or, if there is one, a recognised tenants' association) can ask the landlord for a written summary of the present insurance cover, which should specify the sum for which the property is insured, the insurance company and the risks covered. Instead, the landlord could provide you with a copy of every relevant insurance policy. The landlord has 21 days in which to respond.
- Having read the summary or the copy, you have six months within which to examine the original policy and any supporting accounts, receipts or other documents showing evidence of payment of the premiums both for the current period and the previous period.
- You may take copies of the documents, but the landlord may charge you a fee for copying or providing copying facilities.
- If there is a time limit in the policy within which a claim must be made, you can write to the insurance company to inform them of a possible claim under the policy.

Chapter 13

Service charges

In addition to having to pay ground rent, a tenant may be obliged by a covenant in the lease to pay an annual service charge to the landlord, his or her agent or a management company (see Chapter 14). On blocks of flats with large common areas and state-of-the-art facilities, service charges can run into thousands of pounds each year. Not surprisingly, service charges are a principal cause of dispute between landlord and tenant. It is thought that in London service charges have increased by 12 per cent per year over the last three years; the average charge is now £6,000 p.a. The question of service charges is also important with retirement or sheltered flats where the charge may include, for example, the services of a warden and domestic help. It is not unknown for the service charge on such properties to exceed £10,000 a year.

It is clearly in the landlord's interests to place the financial burden for repair and maintenance of the structure and common parts of the building upon the shoulders of the tenants. If the building is let to a small number of tenants (for example, a small conversion let out to four tenants), this can be done by imposing a comprehensive repair covenant upon each tenant; when parts of the building are leased to many tenants a different method must be adopted – so the landlord inserts into the leases a service charge provision. Such schemes are particularly common with blocks of flats. The amount of the service charge will reflect the cost to the landlord of performing his or her obligations under the lease. The principle behind a service charge provision is that the landlord retains responsibility for repair, maintenance and general running costs of the building, but passes on the costs to the tenants. By doing this he or she achieves what is known as a 'clear lease', and this makes the freehold more marketable.

Service charges and the lease

What is a service charge?

A service charge is the amount payable, directly or indirectly, for services (porterage and cleaning, upkeep of garden and lifts, for example), repairs, maintenance, insurance and other overheads incurred in the management of the property. Such charges are based upon a combination of actual and estimated costs and, accordingly, can vary from year to year. Charges can rise or fall. Some leases do not contain a list of services which can be billed for in the service charge, but instead contain a general and wide-ranging clause. The general rule, however, is that the landlord is not obliged to provide, and the tenant does not have to pay for, anything not covered by the service charge clause.

The key issues which should be clearly defined in the lease include:

- what services are to be provided by the landlord and what he or she can charge for (e.g. legal costs and management costs)
- the method of payment and collection of the service charge (normally yearly or half-yearly)
- the apportionment of the charge as between the tenants
- the procedure for certifying the expenditure
- the provision of a reserve fund (sinking fund). This represents advance payments to build up money for irregular and major works.

A specimen clause

The service charge provision might be drafted along the following lines:

'i) The tenant hereby covenants with the landlord to contribute and pay parts [a formula or percentage will be stated] of the costs, expenses, outgoings and matters mentioned in the schedule hereto

ii) the contribution under paragraph (i) of this clause for each year shall be estimated by the managing agents for the time being of the landlord (hereinafter referred to as 'the managing agents') or if none the landlord (whose decision shall be final) as soon as practicable after the beginning of the year and the tenant shall pay the estimated contribution by two equal instalments on 25 March and 29 September in that year.

The landlord hereby covenants with the tenant to supply to the tenant not less frequently than once every year a summary of the costs expenses outgoings and matters mentioned in the schedule hereto for the previous calendar year which summary shall also incorporate statements of the amount (if any) standing to the credit of the tenant.'

The nuts and bolts of the charge will then follow in a schedule to the lease which gives the details of what the tenant is liable to contribute towards. Although the precise catalogue of the services to be provided by the landlord and to be paid for by the tenant will depend upon the particular building, the schedule might mention:

- the cost of the landlord insuring the premises
- the expenses of the landlord in carrying out the obligations under the lease regarding repairs, cleaning, painting and lighting of common parts, for example. There might be provision to cater for any future, additional running costs arising from the development or extension of the building. It is in the tenant's interests that the clause does not cover 'improvements' and 'rebuilding'. Repairs could be limited to 'necessary' repairs and the landlord might seek the flexibility of carrying out repairs and maintenance 'as often as in the opinion of the landlord is reasonably necessary'. The tenant, if possible, should exclude from the clause remedial work done on the building owing to a defect in design, workmanship or materials
- the costs incurred by the landlord for the repair and maintenance of a lift
- the expense of decorating the exterior and the interior common parts of the building
- the fees and costs paid to any managing agent appointed. The tenant should ensure that management costs are reasonable. Where the landlord acts as the management agent, the fees should be limited to services actually performed by him or her. A provision which allows him or her remuneration equivalent to a percentage of the general administrative overheads should be avoided

- the fees and costs paid to any accountant, solicitor or other professional in relation to the audit and the certification of accounts. The clause might also allow for the payment of wages and salaries of employees
- all other expenses (if any) incurred by the landlord in relation to any arbitration or court action concerning the charges
- that the landlord can employ contractors to carry out his or her obligations under the lease or, if he or she carries them out personally, claim the normal charges (including profit) for the work
- that provisional assessments and demands may be made
- that a sinking fund be set up to cover the future replacement of major items such as lifts and boilers or the undertaking of major repairs and maintenance (for example, decorating the exterior of the building). This will help spread the expenditure for these costs over a few years
- that the landlord may charge interest on money borrowed from the bank to carry out the repair and maintenance obligations.

Qualifications

The landlord may seek to qualify the obligation to perform services. This can be done in several ways. First, the covenant might require him or her only to use 'reasonable' or 'best' efforts to provide the services or to provide them 'only so far as is practicable'. Liability might also be excluded for such things as shortages of fuel and workers, mechanical breakdown and the replacement of equipment.

Second, the lease may reserve for the landlord the right to change, add or withdraw services. The tenant should be wary of such provisions and argue that the lease should allow variation only on the grounds of good estate management (that is, only if a reasonable landlord would make the changes).

Third, the covenant might prescribe the standard of services as being 'such standard as the landlord considers adequate'. This is not in the interests of the tenant because, apart from the right to a management audit and to appoint a surveyor (see pages 187–8), there is no effective way of challenging the adequacy of the services provided. Recent reforms do, however, allow the tenant to challenge the amount claimed for inadequate works. Some assistance is also afforded by the Supply of Goods and Services Act 1982, which implies that the services are to be performed with reasonable care and skill and (subject to the lease) within a reasonable time. It is better practice for the lease to expressly require the services to be provided to a reasonable standard, but in relation to certain items more detail should be required: the provision of heating might, say, be connected to specific dates and times when it is turned on; service periods might be set; and minimum temperature levels might be established.

A fair share?

The landlord will seek to be fully reimbursed for the services provided. The lease should, therefore, ensure that his or her obligations to perform and the tenant's obligation to pay correspond. Once more, everything hinges upon the wording of the lease. Few tenants would object to the landlord being properly refunded for the cost of providing the service obligations.

Each flat-owner has a covenant to pay, as the service charge, a proportion of the expenses incurred by the landlord in the provision of the services (the total of the proportions paid by all the tenants should add up to 100 per cent). Sometimes certain items of expenditure are shared among only some of the flat-owners (for example, some flats may have a garage while others do not; and a ground-floor tenant may not have to pay for the upkeep of a lift). In other cases the apportionment may be calculated in a broad sense, that is, each flat-owner may have to pay the same proportion regardless of the size and position of the flat. It might be thought unfair if the owner of a spacious penthouse flat paid exactly the same as the tenant of a small studio flat. Similarly, if you do not have a car-parking space you might be surprised if you had to contribute towards electronic gates, remarking of spaces and provision of keys to the car park. You must read the lease. Some schemes may calculate the contribution according to former rateable values of the flats (the old equivalent of council tax); others might make the calculation according to floor space of an individual flat. Whichever method is used, there will be tenants who feel that they are disadvantaged.

Prospective buyers should be aware that when there is an unscrupulous or inefficient landlord or management company, the apportionments may add up to more than 100 per cent of the expenses or they might be based upon incorrect data (for example, incorrect former rateable values or floor space). In such cases, the tenant must challenge the figures and, as a last resort, the matter may have to go to the Leasehold Valuation Tribunal (LVT).*

Method of payment

The lease will normally describe the service charge as additional rent. This enables the landlord to exercise the remedy of 'distress' and to forfeit the lease (see pages 142–50) without the necessity of serving a formal notice on the tenant. New restrictions have been placed on the landlord's ability to forfeit when the service charge is in dispute (see page 148).

The landlord will wish to have funds available to meet expenditure as it falls due, so the lease will require some form of advance payment. Usually this is achieved by the lease requiring quarterly (or half-yearly) payments from the tenant based upon certified estimates of expenditure. When the accounts are certified at the end of the financial year, adjustments to cover under-payments and over-payments can be made. Any refund to the tenant should be made as soon as is practicable or discounted from the next payment. These matters will often be dealt with in the lease.

Common abuses by landlords

The danger of the existing system is that it is open to abuse by unscrupulous landlords. The most common complaints are of landlords:

- stealing money from maintenance funds
- falsifying tenders so as to make a secret profit
- charging for work not carried out
- failing to carry out works in good time, and waiting until costs of repairs are higher
- omitting to disclose that money is missing from maintenance funds
- creating fictitious management companies which levy high fees for services provided
- charging high fees for answering tenants' queries.

Tenants' rights

Your right to a management audit

The standards of management and maintenance (and, of course, the costs involved) provided by the landlord can be major causes of concern for tenants.

The Leasehold Reform, Housing and Urban Development Act 1993 allows for a quality-control check on the services actually provided by the landlord. The purpose of the audit is to find out whether the landlord is properly carrying out his or her management obligations under the lease. This will help to quell fears that the tenants are not getting value for money and will provide proof of poor management in any court action which arises from an alleged breach of service covenant.

Your rights at a glance

Parliament has come to the assistance of the tenant in some important ways. As a tenant, you have:

- the right to a management audit. This has been extended under the Commonhold and Leasehold Reform Act 2002
- the right to certain information about service charges and accounts. This involves obtaining, on request, a summary of costs on which the charge is based and looking at related documents. This right has been widened by the 2002 Act
- the right for service charges to be reasonable. For the purpose of challenge before an LVT, the definition of 'service charge' has been extended, again by the 2002 Act, to include costs of improvements and administrative charges. Previously, the tenant could not challenge the reasonableness of works that were regarded as improvements
- the right to challenge demands for unreasonable service charges and/or the standard of the works whether intended or completed
- the right to seek the landlord's recognition of a tenants' association
- the right to be consulted about major works. This has been simplified and extended under the 2002 Act.

Residents of flats can serve a notice requiring an audit of the landlord's management of the premises. The entitlement extends only to tenants who hold under a long lease and pay a service charge to the landlord. Such a tenant is known as a 'qualifying tenant' and, although a tenant can own and qualify in relation to more than one flat, there can only be one qualifying tenant for each flat. If the flat is co-owned, only one of the co-owners can serve the notice. Further conditions are attached according to the number of dwellings included in the premises:

- If there is only one dwelling let to a qualifying tenant, the right can be exercised by that tenant alone.
- Where there are two dwellings in the premises let to qualifying tenants, either or both may exercise the right.
- As regards three or more dwellings, it is necessary that at least two-thirds of the qualifying tenants jointly seek the audit.

As well as checking that the landlord is fulfilling his or her management obligations, the audit checks that the sums paid by the tenants are applied in an efficient and effective fashion. The measure of quality control is in a code of practice, intended to promote desirable practices in the management of premises, published by the government.

The audit will be carried out by a professional surveyor or accountant, appointed and paid for by the tenant(s); the auditor is given rights to inspect the premises and accounts. The notice served by the tenant(s) on the landlord must:

- identify the tenant(s)
- identify the auditor
- specify any documents which are to be inspected
- specify a date, between one and two months from the date of the notice, when the premises will be inspected.

The landlord then has one month from the notice to make available any requested documentation. If he or she fails to comply, the auditor can (within two months of the notice) apply to court for an order compelling his or her co-operation.

Your right to challenge
Many leaseholders suffer stress and financial loss because of bad landlords and inefficient management agents. There is, however,

---

Following the audit

The audit should give tenants:

- an awareness of current management standards and practices. This will show whether the landlord is meeting the obligations imposed by the lease and the general law
- valuable information as to, for example, service charge accounts, contracts entered by the landlord and the general state and condition of the common parts of the block
- if appropriate, evidence in order to challenge service charges before the LVT
- some support for an application for the appointment of a manager.

---

some limitation on the amounts that can be legitimately charged. This is laid down by the Landlord and Tenant Act 1985 (as amended by the Housing Act 1996), which imposes duties upon landlords with respect to service charge costs and estimates. As a general yardstick, service charges should be limited to costs reasonably incurred during the past year. In addition, the works and services concerned have to be provided to a reasonable standard. What constitutes 'reasonable' is a matter for the Leasehold Valuation Tribunal (LVT) to determine. These controls have been extended by the new Commonhold and Leasehold Reform Act 2002.

Your right to information
The tenant is free to request written details of the costs and how they have been calculated, and the landlord must respond. Such information must also disclose what bills have been paid and those that remain outstanding. The Commonhold and Leasehold Reform Act has made it a requirement that landlords provide annual accounting statements that give information about money paid into a service charge fund (as well as any standing credit in that fund) and the costs incurred by the landlord. If this requirement is not met, the tenants are able lawfully to withhold payment of the service charge. In addition, the law obliges landlords to provide tenants with a summary of their rights and obligations in

connection with service charges. The landlord must give the tenant reasonable access to any supporting accounts if he or she wants to inspect or even copy them. Tenants have the right to inspect this documentation relevant to their accounting statements within 21 days of the request. Tenants are also able to take copies of the documentation or have copies provided for them on payment of a reasonable fee. Where a written summary of the costs is provided following a request by a tenant, it must be certified by an accountant who is neither a partner nor an employee of the landlord. The accountant's certificate is no guarantee of reasonableness or arithmetical accuracy.

Challenging reasonableness

If the amount is not agreed or admitted, the tenant can apply to the LVT to make decisions as to whether:

- the costs incurred for services, repairs, maintenance, improvements, insurance or management were reasonably incurred
- services or works for which costs were incurred (or are about to be incurred) are of a reasonable standard. The tenant can challenge the service charge before the LVT, whether or not the charge has been paid
- an amount payable before the costs are incurred is reasonable
- the costs about to be incurred are reasonable.

If either party wishes to appeal against the LVT's decision, leave to appeal to the Lands Tribunal★ must be obtained. Accordingly, in theory, the landlord cannot appeal, drag out proceedings or increase costs without good reason. In reality, it could take 18 months or more for the case to be heard and it might be necessary to incur expensive, but crucial, legal advice.

The problem of tenants being billed for unjustifiably high service charges by unscrupulous landlords is returned to in Chapter 18.

Tenants' associations

A tenants' association is one which is representative of the tenants and recognised as such by the landlord, a tribunal known as the Rent Assessment Committee, and the court. (The Committee is a specialised body dealing with landlord and tenant disputes – consult the telephone directory to find the one nearest you.) The Landlord and Tenant Act 1985 allows an association of residents who pay service charges (as long leaseholders in blocks of flats generally do) to apply to the landlord to be 'recognised'. Such an application should be made in writing and state how many flats are represented by the association. This should be more than 60 per cent of the flats in the block. The letter should be sent by recorded delivery or registered post. If the landlord does not respond by sending a notice of recognition, the association can apply to the Rent Assessment Committee for a certificate of recognition.

The officials of the association act as agents for the members as a whole, and the members are liable personally in respect of any obligation incurred by the association. The association will, usually, have no substantial assets.

The importance of a recognised association lies in the collective bargaining power the members have in relation to the landlord. In addition, under the Landlord and Tenant Act 1985 the association has the right to be heard on the question of major repairs before estimates are asked for. A tenants' association can act as a watchdog to ensure that its members and the landlord abide by the covenants contained in the lease. If legal action against the landlord is appropriate, the association can initiate the action on behalf of all its members (not an individual member). Whether recognised or not, however, the association does not have a legal personality and cannot itself go to court. Instead, one member can take representative action on behalf of all the flat-owners even if some are not members of the association.

The association can negotiate with the landlord over a variety of matters including the quality of the services provided, their cost, the contractors to be used and the consideration of estimates, for example. Even where the landlord takes no notice of a complaint, the fact that the association has made it may be considered a preliminary to taking legal action.

The acts of the association may bind only its members (and not other tenants) and, moreover, individual members can disengage themselves from the acts if not in agreement. Unless such tenants notify the landlord to the contrary, however, the latter can assume that the association has the authority to bind all its members.

The Federation of Private Residents' Associations★ will provide an information pack on how to set up a tenants' association.

The rights of tenants' associations

When the landlord employs a managing agent, the rights of a recognised tenants' association are strengthened by the Landlord and Tenant Act 1987. If, when a tenants' association formally applies to the landlord for recognition, there is no managing agent, the landlord must notify the association in writing before appointing an agent in the future. This notification must inform the tenants of the name of the agent; identify those responsibilities of the landlord which the agent is to take over; and allow one month for the association to make comments.

An outline of the rights of tenants' associations

A recognised tenants' association currently has rights over and above those enjoyed by individual tenants. Only an association has the right:

- to put forward names of contractors to be asked to estimate for major works
- to be sent a copy of estimates for major works
- to be consulted about the appointment of a managing agent and be given the opportunity to make comments
- to appoint a surveyor to advise on service charge matters. The surveyor has the right to inspect and copy documents held by the landlord and to inspect common parts. A surveyor appointed by an individual tenant does not have such rights.

Where a managing agent has been employed at the time the association seeks recognition, the association must be informed of the identity and functions of the agent and be allowed to make comments about the effectiveness of the particular agent.

A landlord who has recognised an association must, every five years, formally notify it of any changes in the duties of the managing agent. If the landlord proposes to change the agent, the above procedures as to notification must be followed.

A recognised tenants' association also has the right to appoint a surveyor to advise on matters relating to the service charge. The Housing Act 1996 gives the surveyor extensive rights of access to documents and premises. The landlord must, however, be given written notification of the appointment.

Right to a surveyor at a glance

The terms of a tenants' association's right to appoint a surveyor are as follows:

- only a recognised tenants' association can exercise the right
- a qualified surveyor must be appointed (suitably qualified tenants are not disqualified)
- the association must provide notice of appointment to the landlord. No form is prescribed for this notification
- the surveyor has a right to inspect any documents reasonably required. The landlord must comply with this request 'as soon as is reasonably practicable'
- the surveyor can inspect all buildings containing flats let to members of the association and the landlord must allow this within a reasonable period
- if the landlord fails to comply, the association must apply to court within one and four months of the service of the notice of appointment
- the surveyor's appointment ceases if the association ceases to exist or gives notice to the landlord.

The right to be consulted

Where the landlord wishes to carry out works on the premises (repairs, construction, improvement or maintenance, for example) further restrictions imposed by the Landlord and Tenant Act 1985 apply. First, where the works will cost an individual tenant more than £250, the landlord must formally consult with the tenants about these major works. Second, where the landlord proposes to enter a contract for the provision of services for a period of more than a year (and the cost for an individual tenant exceeds £100), the landlord must consult the tenants before proceeding. This covers long-term maintenance contracts, for example. Third, where the landlord intends to enter a long-term agreement which will involve works being carried out beyond a period of 12 months, an additional duty to consult is imposed. This is regardless of the costs of those works.

The rules are that when a landlord is obliged to consult, and *no* recognised tenant's association exists, the landlord must take the following steps:

- obtain a minimum of two estimates for the proposed works/ service agreement of which one, at least, must be from a person wholly unconnected with the landlord
- provide for each tenant (or display where it is likely to come to the attention of all tenants) a notice which describes the intended works, contains a copy of the estimates and invites comments
- give, as a general rule, at least 30 days' notice of the proposed works/service agreement
- have regard to any observations received. This does not mean, however, that the landlord must act on the comments provided by the tenants.

If there is a recognised tenants' association, the landlord must:

- give the secretary of the association a detailed specification of the proposed works/agreement and allow 30 days within which the association may suggest to the landlord the names of firms from whom estimates should be obtained
- obtain a minimum of two estimates, at least one from a person wholly independent of the landlord
- provide a copy of the estimates to the secretary of the association
- give each tenant a notice describing the works/agreement, summarising the estimates, offering (free of charge) the right and opportunity to inspect and (at the tenant's expense) to take copies of the detailed specifications of the intended works and estimates, and invite observations
- have regard to the comments made by the tenants
- unless there are urgent safety reasons, not start the works/enter the agreement earlier than the date specified in the notice (at least one month's advance notice).

If the landlord fails to take these steps, the chances are that the excess amount – £250 (major works), £100 (long-term service agreements) or £250 (long-term works) – will not be recoverable.

The LVT does, however, have the power to dispense with these conditions, say, if the works are urgent.

Arrears, assignment and recovery of service charges

A landlord can only recover costs for service charges within a limited period. Currently, the landlord must write to the tenants about the charges within 18 months from the time that the costs were incurred. If the landlord fails to do this, he or she cannot recover the costs of those charges. In addition, the Landlord and Tenant (Covenants) Act 1995 restricts the ability of the landlord to recover unpaid service charges from a previous tenant, following assignment of the lease. The Act requires the landlord to notify the former tenant of the debt within six months of it falling due; this notification fixes the former tenant's liability. This liability can be increased only if the notification forewarns the tenant that the debt may be greater when the landlord sends further notification (within three months of the final calculation) which provides details of the increased amount claimed.

Welfare benefits and service charges

If you are in receipt of income support or job seeker's allowance then financial assistance towards the payment of service charges might be available from the Department of Works and Pensions. To qualify, the service charges must relate to accommodation costs such as insurance, management, porterage services, lift maintenance and cleaning and heating of common parts. This does **not** include contributions and charges towards major repairs, sports facilities, satellite or cable TV facilities or the provision of heating and hot water to the flat.

Certification of the charge

Every service charge provision should allow for certification of the charge, state how this is to happen, and stipulate that the cost involved can be recovered as part of the charge. The most common means adopted is for the lease to require the landlord to produce certified or audited accounts as soon as practicable following the end of each financial year. The certificate should be drawn up by an expert (auditor or surveyor). Until the accounts are fully certified, the tenant will normally not be liable to pay the charge. Any time limits specified will not be strict, unless the lease makes them so.

Trust funds

The Landlord and Tenant Act 1987 imposes a trust on all money paid as service charges and on any income from investments of those payments. The landlord, managing agents or management company are the trustee(s). The purpose of the trust fund is to defray the costs for which the charges were raised and, over and above this, it is for the benefit of the existing tenants: the money belongs to the tenants and cannot be taken by the creditors of, for example, an insolvent landlord.

The Commonhold and Leasehold Reform Act 2002 has made it a requirement to set up a trust even when there is only one tenant who is liable to service charge. In addition, in order to safeguard tenants' money, and to bring the law into line with the government's approved code of practice, the new law will require that service charges paid (including reserve funds) must be kept in a separate client account so as to prevent the money being mixed with other funds. It is a criminal offence for the trustee(s) to fail, without reasonable excuse, to use a separate client account, and they face the prospect of a fine of up to £2,500. Tenants and a tenants' association have the right to ask for proof (to be provided by the landlord in 21 days of the request) that their money is going into a designated account, and they can lawfully withhold service charge payments if they have reasonable grounds for believing that it isn't. Local authorities and registered housing associations are exempt from these requirements.

The lease may contain a clause setting up the trust and this might require that any money paid by way of a service charge shall be:

'... in trust for the tenant until applied towards the tenant's contribution towards the costs expenses outgoings and matters mentioned ... Any interest or income of funds for the time being held by managing agents or if none the landlord pending application as aforesaid shall be added to the funds.'

Unless there are any specific terms in the lease about the distribution of the trust fund, the entitlement of each tenant is proportional to his or her contribution to the service charge. When a lease is assigned, the outgoing tenant will not be entitled to a refund of his or her share of the fund; this will be acquired by the incoming tenant. However, the seller should find out how much his or her credit in the fund is worth and, when the contract is being negotiated, ask the buyer for a payment equivalent to this sum.

Reserve (sinking) funds

It is wise for the lease to provide for reserve funds to cover irregular and major expenditure (for example, the replacement of lifts, roof or heating system, and refurbishment). This should ensure that flat-owners will not be faced with too large a bill at any one time because sums will have been put aside to spread the cost over a number of years. It also means that all occupiers contribute and, because contributions are not usually recoverable, not just those occupiers at the time the work is carried out.

There are various matters that should be clarified in the lease:

- the end to which the funds can be put. The circumstances in which the landlord may have recourse to the funds should be spelled out
- where and how the money is to be kept. The landlord or management company must invest the money and the funds are held on trust for the current tenants. This ensures that the money is preserved for the tenants and accrues interest to be added to the fund
- that the accounts be audited each year and the amount of the contribution to the fund be assessed annually by a qualified third party. The tenant should ensure that the landlord can claim contributions only as are reasonable
- if the landlord sells the freehold, because the money belongs to the tenants, the lease should require the trust fund to be transferred to the new buyer, who then will become the trustee
- the predicted expenditure must be limited to the duration of the lease so as to prevent the landlord from amassing a sum for use after the lease has ended.

The Leasehold Valuation Tribunal

The Leasehold Valuation Tribunal (LVT) deals with a broad range of disputes concerning residential property. These include problems concerning valuation for the purposes of collective enfranchisement (see Chapter 18) and lease renewal, and the appointment of managers; it also determines the reasonableness of service charges already levied for works or services provided, or charges for proposed works. An application can be made by any individual tenant or group of tenants (but not a tenants' association because it does not have legal personality). The landlord can also apply – for example, to gain assurance that proposed works are reasonable. The application will provide details of the parties, names and addresses of all tenants contributing to the service charge (if the tenant is applying, those names and addresses known to the tenant), the amount of the service charge currently payable, and a statement of the issues the LVT is asked to determine.

What the LVT cannot do

The LVT cannot:

- force the landlord to refund money
- generally make an order for costs
- order work to be remedied
- enforce a leasehold covenant.

Fees and costs

The fee for the application varies, but cannot exceed £500. This is payable in two stages: £150 (which is non-refundable) when the application is made, and the remainder prior to the hearing. This is the only payment an applicant will have to make, other than the applicant's own legal and other professional costs. Traditionally, the LVT could not award costs against a losing party but it now has the limited power to award costs in the case of unreasonable applications and according to the conduct of proceedings. In cases where the service charge allows the landlord to add legal fees, the tenant may apply for an order preventing the landlord passing on these costs in this way.

LVT fees vary according to the nature of the application and, in certain disputes (e.g. the appointment of a manager), the number of flats.

- There will be a flat-rate hearing fee of £150.
- The application fee payable when a service charge, insurance premium or administrative charge is disputed varies according to the sums involved. The fees are as follows:

Charge	Fee
£0 – £500	£50
£501 – £1,000	£70
£1,001 – £5,000	£100
£5,001 – £15,000	£200
£15,001 +	£350

- If the application is to dispense with the requirement to consult, to determine suitability of an insurer, to appoint a manager or to vary a lease, the fee payable depends on the number of flats. For up to five flats, the fee is £150; for six to ten flats, £250; and for more than ten, £350.
- If a number of applications are heard together, only one hearing fee will be payable. As regards the application fee, the highest one is payable.
- The fee is waived where the applicant (or the applicant's partner) is in receipt of income support or other specified benefits.

New powers
The powers and operation of the LVT have been extended by the Commonhold and Leasehold Reform Act 2002. The changes are as follows.

- The LVT is allowed to decide the liability of leaseholders to pay the service charge, in addition to determining questions of reasonableness.
- Landlords are able to get the LVT to determine that the cost of specific works falls within the scope of the service charge, before the works are started. This will reassure landlords that the cost of proposed works will be recoverable under the service-charge clause.
- The LVT can decide on the tenant's liability to pay an administration charge (for example, for the landlord giving consents such as consent to alterations, or for the processing of late payments of ground rent).
- The LVT has the power to award costs where one party has brought or conducted proceedings vexatiously or unreasonably.

- Appeals to the Lands Tribunal can be made where either the LVT or Lands Tribunal consent (previously, consent had to be from the Lands Tribunal).
- Where both parties agree, the LVT can dispense with a hearing and allow the matter to be dealt with by written representations.

Will you need help to apply?

Many applicants manage without instructing a lawyer as the LVT is designed for use by people inexperienced in law. Nevertheless, legal representation can increase the chances of success so a balance has to be drawn between cost and possible reward. An application can generate much paperwork and detailed information, which has to be understood, stored and perhaps relied upon at the hearing, and this can involve a lot of hard work. It might also help to watch a few LVT hearings (they are conducted in public) and to contact an advice agency.

How to prepare an application

- Collate the evidence and documentation (application forms, copy of the lease, supporting statement, etc.).
- Make sure the application form is correctly filled in.
- Keep it as simple as possible and rely only on relevant documents and evidence.
- Work out beforehand how you are going to present your case at the hearing.
- Decide whether you will need expert or ordinary witnesses.
- Obtain witness statements/reports.

LVT procedures

Although there are no formal procedural rules in the LVT, all tribunals adopt a similar way of conducting their business. This may be broken down as follows.

- A pre-trial review will occur; this is when the nature of the dispute is worked out and certain factual evidence agreed between the parties. By this time, each side will have seen the other's statement of claim. The review occurs before a tribunal member.

- Evidence will later be exchanged which reveals each side's claims. The parties will, therefore, be aware of the strength of each other's case.
- A bundle of documents (i.e. the written evidence) will be prepared by each side. This will be provided to the tribunal and the other side. If carefully compiled, this will be a useful source of reference during the hearing.
- The LVT may decide to take a trip out and view the property in dispute.
- The hearing is informal, open to the public and often held in nearby council-owned premises.
- The tribunal will usually consist of a lawyer, a valuer and a lay person. One of these will chair the proceedings.
- At the hearing the applicant is heard first and is expected to present his or her case orally, simply and politely. Remember that there are no formal rules of evidence operating here.
- The decision is not declared at the hearing, it will be posted to the parties some weeks later.
- The decision cannot be enforced by the LVT. If the losing party refuses to comply, the winner will have to go to court in order to force compliance with the LVT's decision.

What next?

The government is determined to devise further methods by which tenants can exert control over landlords and their managing agents. The following plans are under discussion:

- to increase the requirements for the landlord to consult with tenants over the employment of contractors, and to ensure regular re-tendering
- to oblige the landlord to provide more cost-effective insurance and disclose any commission paid
- to maintain management standards, possibly by a licensing scheme for management agents
- to ban bad agents from managing buildings. Even the Royal Institution of Chartered Surveyors (RICS)★ has admitted that standards within the sector vary and, 'in the very worst cases, managers can act in a fraudulent manner'.

Chapter 14

Management and management companies

Much responsibility may fall on the landlord in the maintenance and repair of the common parts and the provision of services. A building cannot manage itself and steps have to be taken to provide services, repair, insure, pay bills and enforce tenants' covenants. The expenditure will be recovered from the tenants' service charges. Unless the building consists of no more than two flats, normally there will need to be some system of management of the premises. While everything is going well and the building is maintained, a tenant might not be concerned about who provides the services. But if the landlord, the managing agent or the management company is neglectful and the building is falling into disrepair, it becomes a serious problem and an urgent issue for the tenants. It might, under such circumstances, be better for the tenants either to buy out the landlord's freehold interest and set up their own management company, or to form a Right to Manage company, under the Commonhold and Leasehold Reform Act 2002, and take over management without buying the freehold. There are statutory rights which entitle tenants to purchase and/or take over their landlord's interest in the building (see Chapters 15 and 18).

Management may take various forms, and the more common ones are considered below.

Direct management

In this form of management, the landlord manages the building directly or through agents, carries out the maintenance obligations and is reimbursed by the revenue from ground rents and service charges. The flat-owners have no say in the management of the building. Usually, the landlord employs a managing agent and the fees for such professional assistance are passed on to the tenants. The agent might be a member of the Association of Residential Managing Agents (ARMA)⋆ and have undertaken to abide by the codes of practice issued by ARMA. The benefits of professional management include having:

- an organised approach to funding and costing matters
- more informed estimates of the work needed and duration of work
- an independent judgment of what constitutes good repair
- an impartial resolution of disputes
- professional back-up and office facilities
- professional indemnity insurance against acts of incompetence or negligence.

If the flats are in a block, the landlord may be keen to be free of what is an onerous and unenviable responsibility and may look to one of the other forms of management.

Concurrent lease

Here the landlord grants to managing agents a concurrent lease, interposed between the landlord and the flat-owners, so that the agents acquire the rights and obligations of the landlord for the duration of the lease. The agents should be a reputable business (perhaps of surveyors) with sufficient assets to carry out their obligations. They will be responsible for collecting the ground rents and the service charges (which will include their fee). The flat-owners should, in theory, not have to worry about the shift in responsibility. The landlord remains liable on the covenants to the tenants.

Tenants' management company

In its basic form a tenants' management company draws its membership exclusively from the flat-owners and owns the freehold to the building. The original landlord, having disposed of the freehold (and, if the lease was created after 1 January 1996, having the opportunity to be released from covenants), essentially drops out of the picture.

The tenants can buy an 'off the shelf' company from a firm which specialises in creating companies; they are thereby free of the administrative work involved in compiling the documentation and registering the company. Except in relation to enfranchisement and the right to manage, it is up to the tenants what type of company to operate: a company limited by shares or by guarantee, or one of unlimited liability; however, as the issue of share capital and the concept of unlimited liability are out of place in a management company, it is likely that it will be a company limited by guarantee. At a later stage, if the tenants wish, they can wind up the existing company and create another one which better suits their needs.

Powers and purpose

The company will need to set out its purpose and powers in the documents which create the company: the memorandum and the articles of association.

The **memorandum of association** will disclose the following:

- the name of the company, which will usually be the name of the block or the street where the flats are situated
- the objectives underlying the company's formation. Normally these will be to acquire the freehold, to manage, to borrow money if necessary, and to enhance the value and beneficial features of the building
- the limitation of each member's liability to a nominal sum (for example, £1) in case of debt or legal action being brought against the company
- the restriction of membership to flat-owners.

The **articles of association** will contain further fine-tuning and will usually deal with the following:

- the recognition of the purposes as set out in the memorandum of association
- the cessation of membership on the sale of the flat
- the provision of voting rights for each member
- the procedure for calling annual general meetings and extraordinary general meetings and the regulation of proceedings at such meetings
- the election procedure for directors and the power to appoint a secretary

- the necessity to produce annual audited accounts and the place where those accounts are to be kept.

By virtue of forming a management company, the tenants can in theory do as they please with the building. In practice, however, to avoid disputes and to achieve unanimity, much turns on strong and effective leadership within the company.

Who runs the shop?

The company must be run by someone and have a board of directors and a secretary. Often the board of directors is elected by and from the flat-owners, the secretary (often a solicitor) being appointed by the board. An auditor will also have to be employed. The fees for such professionals will be taken from the ground rents and service charges.

Normally it is desirable for the actual management of the building to be placed in the hands of a professional (such as an estate agent or surveyor). The manager is appointed by the board to see to repairs, maintenance and provision of services, and the collection of ground rents and service charges. The manager remains accountable to the company. If there were no manager, obviously there would be some financial savings, but the burden would be likely to fall on a few conscientious flat-owners and the risk is that the building might fall into neglect.

Once the freehold is vested in the company, the position of a flat-owner is not really affected. The value of any individual lease is untouched. The management company becomes the new landlord and the covenants continue between it and the flat-owners.

It is better for all flat-owners to become members: indeed, pressure may be brought to bear on a buyer when an existing lease is assigned, in the form of a covenant in the assignment which compels him or her to become a member of the company. The disadvantage of non-membership is that the tenant has no say in the running of the company and the management of the building.

Tenants who set up such a freehold-owning management company should ensure that there is only one share/vote per flat and that, where there remain some tenants who do not wish to participate in the purchase of the freehold, their votes are left unused.

The financial liabilities of the individual flat-owner will, in practice, be the same whether a member or not because all tenants will still have to pay the appropriate service charge.

Interposed management company

It is possible for a tenants' management company to exist while the landlord retains the freehold title: the company can take a lease of the whole building, covenant to carry out the landlord's obligations and collect the service charges and ground rents. A covenant will be given which allows the landlord to terminate the company's lease if the management is not good enough. This is the same as a concurrent lease (see page 202), except that it is the tenants' management company which becomes the managing agent. This does not affect the individual flat-owners' leases. The landlord remains liable on the covenants in the original leases.

The flat-owners, as members of the company, have to ensure that the company can finance the day-to-day running of the block. A deposit may be required from each tenant to establish a float to finance initial repairs if the service charges previously received by the landlord are insufficient. It is usually desirable that a 'profit rental' be agreed with the landlord. This simply means that the company receives more in ground rents from the tenants than it pays out to the landlord (who would normally agree to this because the work and responsibility of managing the building have been passed on to the company). This helps to top up the company's sinking or reserve fund.

Right to Manage company

Right to Manage (RTM) companies are a central part of the new reforms allowing tenants to take over the management of their block without having to prove fault on the part of the landlord – reforms introduced under the Commonhold and Leasehold Reform Act 2002 and covered in Chapter 15. Any managing body must, of course, have the ability to enter into contracts and to bring legal action against individual tenants or third parties. The government has therefore thought it best to control the setting up and character of RTM companies, and the advantage of this is that it ensures that the company will be properly formed and have enough powers to manage the block effectively – it will be democratic and have clearly spelled-out rights and responsibilities. As it is the RTM company that will formally notify the landlord that it is claiming the right to manage, until the company is formed the tenants cannot exercise the new right to manage.

Forming an RTM company should be a straightforward matter. It can be done by the tenants themselves or with the help of a solicitor or a company agent. A company agent can provide ongoing services and offer a company secretary and registered address.

The requirements imposed on a Right to Manage company are that:

- it must be a private company limited by guarantee
- its founding documents (the company's memorandum and articles of association) must define the company's purposes as including the right to manage the property
- it must not be a commonhold association (see Chapter 2) – the two are, therefore, mutually exclusive
- there can only be one Right to Manage company managing a block of flats at any one time. This is designed to prevent competing bids for the management of the block
- it cannot hold the freehold. If the RTM company does later acquire the freehold of the block, it ceases to be an RTM company. It then becomes a Right to Enfranchise company with management powers and duties (see Chapter 18).

Membership and regulations

The people entitled to be members of the RTM company are qualifying tenants in the block and the landlord. A buyer of a member's flat will automatically become a new member. Voting rights will be weighted to ensure that the landlord remains in a minority. The government has made regulations about the precise content and form of the company's founding documents and these regulations should be adopted by the company. Some regulations will bind the company even if not specified in its memorandum or articles of association. Indeed, some regulations will override any contrary provisions in the founding documents.

Functions

The Right to Manage company benefits from several rights, but has some limits on its powers. For example:

- The company will take over the management functions of the landlord relating to services, repairs, maintenance, improvements, insurance and general management.
- The landlord will be obliged to pay over any accrued and unused service charges held at the acquisition date. The idea is that the RTM company will then receive service charge payments directly from the tenants.
- Any obligation owed by the RTM company will be owed to each tenant and landlord.
- The company must keep under review whether tenant covenants are being complied with and report any breach to the landlord within three months.
- With the exception of forfeiture, the company is able to exercise any enforcement rights, that were previously the landlord's, against any tenant.
- The company can grant a tenant permission either to assign or sub-let his or her flat, or to carry out alterations and improvements, but only if it gives the landlord at least 30 days' advance notice. In any other case of giving approval, the landlord must be notified at least 14 days in advance. If the landlord objects, the approval can only be given with the subsequent written agreement of the landlord or the permission of the Leasehold Valuation Tribunal (LVT)*.
- If the landlord becomes unhappy at the way the RTM company carries out its management functions, he or she can apply to the LVT for the appointment of an independent manager.

Local authority landlords

Under the Housing Act 1985, local authorities are allowed to enter into management agreements with third parties, including, in the case of housing estates, a tenant management organisation (TMO). The local authority proposing to make arrangements must inform tenants of the terms of the agreement and the identities of the managers. The tenants are entitled to make their views known before the decision is taken, but there is no right under the Act to block the authority's plans. The authority must also make provision for tenants to make their views known as to the standards of service provided by the managers.

When it is a TMO that seeks to manage, the local authority is obliged to provide financial and other forms of direct support. The process for a TMO is as follows:

- It must be open to any tenant of a relevant flat to join the TMO.
- The majority of the TMO's members must back the proposal to manage.
- The TMO must serve a right-to-manage notice on the authority landlord and give a copy to each tenant affected.
- If reasonable, the local authority will ballot all affected tenants.
- If a notice is accepted, the TMO will select an approved training agency and the nominated agency will decide whether it is reasonable to proceed.
- If the majority of tenants support a management agreement, the TMO will be trained in management skills according to a programme developed by the government.
- If the programme is successful, the TMO will be certified to proceed and will need to be registered as a company in order to do so.
- A further ballot will then be taken of the tenants and, if a majority agree, the agreement will finally go ahead.

Chapter 15

Repair covenants and management rights

The state of repair of houses and flats is a crucial issue. First, it affects the comfort and enjoyment of people living in the property (and, in some cases, their safety: see Chapter 16). Second, it dictates the value and marketability of the house or flat. Third, it affects whether a mortgage will be granted to a prospective buyer. For leaseholders of flats, disrepair brings with it other concerns. The lease will place obligations on the leaseholder or the landlord to put and keep the property in repair. If these obligations are not met, the defaulting party can be sued for compensation by the other or be ordered by a court to carry out the repairs. The leaseholder, moreover, could be faced with an attempt by the landlord to put an end to (that is, to forfeit) the lease. The landlord's costs of repairing the property will also be passed on, via the service charge, to the leaseholders, and a prospective buyer of a flat in a rundown building might well be dissuaded from buying the lease if the service charge is likely to be high over the next few years.

The covenants to repair are, therefore, central to any lease of a flat. It is crucial that flat-owners read their leases to discover who is responsible for repairs. As mentioned in Chapter 14, where it is the landlord's responsibility but the landlord fails to carry out the necessary works, leaseholders have increased rights to take over management of the block from the landlord under the new right-to-manage scheme.

Express covenants

The covenants to repair will often be explicitly stated within the lease. In certain situations, and where the lease is silent, covenants can be read into it (that is, they are implied); for those that are implied, see Chapter 16.

The clauses relating to repair must be carefully drafted and a variety of important matters should be addressed, such as whether the burden is to be carried by the landlord or tenant, the type of disrepair to be covered, and the standard of repair work required.

Burden

Not surprisingly, landlords will seek to place the responsibility of repair, as far as is possible, upon the tenant. However, when the lease is of only part of a building – as is the case with a flat – it is often unrealistic to place major repair obligations on each tenant. The landlord will need to assume repair responsibilities in relation to those parts of the structure which it would be impractical for any (or all) of the tenants to maintain (for example, the roof or the lift). Otherwise, difficulties and potential unfairness would arise when working out the obligations of each tenant and whether contributions are to be made by other tenants. It is likely, therefore, with multi-occupancies that the landlord will take on board major repairs and recoup the costs through a service charge. In such cases, the tenant will normally remain liable for repairs in the flat.

Types of covenant

Although the wording and detail of repair covenants can vary greatly, under a typical long lease the tenant's repair covenants are:

- to keep the premises in good repair. This will normally refer only to internal repairs, with the landlord usually liable for structural and external matters. In a small block, however, the covenant may stipulate good repair both internally and externally
- to do specified works of repair or maintenance at stated intervals: for example, to paint the outside once every three years and the inside once every five years
- to deliver up the premises in good repair at the end of the lease or to pay a required sum if they are not.

If the premises are in disrepair at the start of the lease, a covenant by the tenant either 'to put' or 'to keep' them in repair imposes the obligation on the tenant to remedy existing defects.

The landlord may enter into a covenant to repair (for example, when the building is let to various tenants in separate flats). Again there are many ways in which this covenant could be drafted. Commonly found examples mention 'the structure and exterior' of the building, but it is necessary to appreciate that the exact wording used determines the extent of the landlord's responsibility. A straightforward example of a landlord's covenant would be:

> 'To maintain and repair and keep in good order and condition the roof foundations gutters and main structure of the building.'

Where the landlord enters into a covenant to repair and a defect arises on the premises leased to the tenant, the covenant is breached when, having been notified of the disrepair, the landlord fails to repair within a reasonable time. When defects arise in other parts of the building, the landlord's breach arises as soon as the defect appears. These rules are implied and may be altered, if both parties agree, by express wording in the covenant.

Limiting responsibility

The landlord's responsibility can be limited within the lease. This can be resisted by the prospective tenant during the initial negotiations before a lease is granted. Once the lease is granted, however, the covenants will automatically bind the next buyer of the lease and there will be little or no scope for renegotiation with the landlord. This limitation of the landlord's responsibility can be done in several ways:

- damage caused by the tenant or by unauthorised alterations may be excluded
- the covenant may not cover all areas of the building and deliberately be insufficiently comprehensive
- the repair obligations may be reduced by expressions such as, for example, 'the landlord's best endeavours' to keep the property in repair.

Meaning of 'repair'

The meaning of 'repair' itself is not clear-cut. Repair may be defined as restoration by renewal or replacement of a part of the building, but does not include a reconstruction or renewal of the whole (or a substantial part) of the building or what can be described as an 'improvement'. Accordingly, disrepair relates to the physical state of the property and not merely a lack of amenities or inefficiency. Whether work is classified as 'repair' is, therefore, a matter of common-sense and degree. The approach adopted by the courts to this question is to examine the terms of the lease in the context of the particular building, its state of repair at the start of the lease and the work required as a whole. Generally speaking, it makes little difference whether the tenant's covenant is expressed as keeping the premises 'in repair', 'good repair', 'tenantable repair' or any other similar phrase. All that is necessary is that the covenant states the premises to be repaired, that they are to be maintained in that condition and, as regards tenant's covenants, are to be left in a state of repair at the end of the lease.

What repair covenants cover

Subject to contrary provision in the lease, a covenant to repair obliges the person making the promise to:

- put the premises into repair, even if the building is old and dilapidated. This is another reason why the tenant should commission a detailed survey before taking the lease
- repair each part as and when it needs repair. This carries with it the making good of the decorative state of the premises
- carry the risk of accidental damage or destruction. Hence the need for a comprehensive policy of insurance
- within limits, correct defects in the building arising from design or construction faults. This will often form an express part of the covenant. If it does, and in order to protect the tenant, a compulsory litigation clause might be included within the lease requiring the landlord first to sue the builder and architect, as appropriate.

Subject to the wording of the covenant, the person making the promise will not normally be required to rebuild premises which are beyond repair; to replace a badly designed or constructed part of the building, unless it has fallen into disrepair; to put the property into perfect repair; or to clean drains and pipes, etc. It may also be the case that a tenant's covenant will expressly exclude liability for 'fair wear and tear' (that is, disrepair caused by ordinary, natural causes). This does not mean, however, that the tenant can idly stand by and watch the ravages of time take their course. He or she would still be required to take reasonable action to preserve the building (for example, by treating external woodwork) and to repair consequential damage to the property following 'fair wear and tear'.

Potential problems

Both parties should pay close attention to which parts of the building are covered by the covenants to repair. There should be a clear demarcation between the responsibilities of the landlord and those of the tenant(s). The landlord might be obliged to repair the exterior, the structure or the foundations, timbers, load-bearing walls and roof, for example. Despite the common use of these expressions, some uncertainty can still arise.

First, the term 'exterior' is somewhat unclear and the covenant must make clear what it refers to. For example, is it the exterior of the whole building or the exterior of the tenant's part of the building? Does it include access ways or staircases? Does it refer only to the finish of the building or extend to what lies beneath the finish?

Second, the lease should expressly state whether 'structure' includes internal walls, partitions and windows in addition to the roofs, external walls and foundations.

Third, the listing of different parts of the building may add precision, but there is a danger that an important part may be accidentally omitted and the conclusion might then be that the omitted part has been deliberately excluded from the scope of the covenant.

A modern drafting technique is to define clearly the tenant's property within the premises section of the lease and to tie in the repairing obligations with that description. Accordingly, the lease may define the tenant's premises as being the space within the surrounding walls, floors and ceilings. It may also make specific reference to internal walls, wall finishes, windows and landlord's fixtures (for example, sanitary fittings). If so, what is not mentioned is considered to be within the ambit of the landlord's repair covenant.

Standard of repair

Regardless of the wording of the covenant, the standard of repair is in all cases geared to the age, character and locality of the premises.

The aim is to achieve a level which would make the premises reasonably fit for the occupation of a reasonably minded tenant likely to take the lease. The landlord can, however, exert a tighter control over the quality of repair; a simple method would be to insert into the covenant a clause which requires the tenant to repair 'to the satisfaction' of the landlord or the landlord's surveyor, or to repair under the 'supervision' of the latter.

Decoration

As part of the repair obligations, the tenant will usually be obliged to decorate and redecorate. Sometimes the work required is set out in detail, but often the tenant's obligation is general. The timing of the work is also normally spelled out. Where the tenant is made responsible for external decoration, it will normally be required every three years; internal decoration usually at five-yearly intervals. Often there is the extra requirement that decoration will take place in the last year of the lease. The timing, however, can be left more open-ended. The covenant may require decoration 'as often as is reasonably necessary' or 'as often as in the opinion of the landlord is reasonably necessary but not more than once every three years'.

The landlord may give a covenant to decorate, but will then recover the cost from the tenants via the service charge. The landlord will often avoid specifying times and will reserve flexibility. A landlord's covenant could read:

> 'To decorate in good and workmanlike manner and with appropriate materials the exterior and common parts of the building as often as in the opinion of the landlord is reasonably necessary.'

Alterations and improvements

It is not uncommon for a tenant to seek to alter and improve the premises leased. If the lease is silent on the matter, the tenant is restricted only by planning controls, any express covenant to leave the property in repair at the end of the lease, and the general law which prevents the tenant damaging the value of the landlord's freehold interest. The landlord can, generally speaking, prevent the carrying out of such works only if they seem likely to damage the property, reduce its value or adversely affect its character. It is not unusual, therefore, for the landlord to impose restrictions expressly in the lease. The tenant needs to be aware of any hidden obligations to improve, and the statutory provisions by which any restrictions imposed by the landlord can be modified.

Landlord's restrictions

It is the usual practice for the lease to include express tenant's covenants designed to ensure that the soundness, nature and value of the property are maintained. These covenants can vary in wording and detail, but most tend to be comprehensive in coverage. An example of this type of covenant would be:

'Not without the landlord's previous written consent at any time during the said term to cut maim or remove any of the main walls beams columns timbers floors or any structural parts of the demised premises or commit or permit any waste or damage to the demised premises or to the floors or timbers thereof or to make or permit to be made any alteration in or addition to the main structure or in any external decoration thereof (except as aforesaid).'

Although the reference to 'cutting and maiming' in the above covenant is somewhat old-fashioned, it is still commonly used in leases. When used, the phrase can prohibit even minor jobs such as the drilling of holes and the fixing of wall lights without the landlord's consent.

The term 'alteration' embraces also 'improvement' and is directed at works which will affect the construction or the appearance of the building. This would not, however, cover small jobs such as attaching shelves, mirrors and mantelpieces, for example. The use in the covenant of the word 'addition' gives the landlord further protection because it extends to works that would normally fall outside the meaning of 'alteration'. The prevention of alterations to the external appearance would not prohibit major preservation work on the premises.

The covenant might also oblige the tenant, at the end of the lease, to restore the premises to the same condition as they were in prior to the alteration or improvement. Other restrictions could be attached: for example, to obtain the landlord's consent before applying for planning permission; to submit for approval by the landlord all plans and specifications; and to pay the landlord an indemnity for any damage and liability incurred.

Absolute or qualified?

A covenant against alterations may be absolute (that is, all alterations are prohibited) or qualified (that is, prohibited except with the consent of the landlord). An absolute covenant does not require that the landlord refuse consent to the proposed works only on reasonable grounds; therefore his or her reasons for refusal cannot be challenged.

A qualified covenant will expressly refer to the need for the landlord's consent and this consent cannot (despite whatever may be said in the lease) unreasonably be withheld. However, there is nothing to stop the landlord from attaching reasonable conditions to the consent. These may, for example, require the tenant to pay compensation to the landlord for any loss and the reinstatement of the premises at the end of the lease.

Hidden obligations

Although there is no implied obligation to improve the premises, it is possible that such an obligation might be concealed within a tenant's covenant. This could occur in the following situations.

- A covenant to comply with statute law might carry with it the obligation to carry out improvements required under a particular Act of Parliament or Regulation (for example, to put the property into a habitable condition or to have a gas vent installed).
- The performance of a covenant to repair could involve the tenant in carrying out improvements as dictated by modern building techniques and prevailing building regulations.

A buyer will have to trust in the skills of the conveyancer in order to discover such hidden pitfalls.

Ensuring good management: statutory help

During the tenant's ownership of the flat, the covenants and their enforcement are only as effective as their wording in the lease is accurate and certain. There may be disagreement between the tenants and the landlord as to the need to repair, and the repair covenant itself may be unclear. There may also be complications as to who is to pay for any works and to what extent. If the situation cannot be resolved, Parliament has stepped in to help tenants, reforming the situation by way of the Commonhold and Leasehold Reform Act 2002. The basic idea is that it is unfair for landlords to have complete control over management when they hold such a comparatively small stake in the building. The new legislation introduces a new right for tenants: the **right to manage**. The attraction of this right is that it does not require proof of any fault on the landlord's part and allows tenants to manage the building collectively without having to buy the freehold. Simply put, it offers an alternative option for tenants who are unhappy with the management of the building.

This section covers the rights held by tenants with long leases.

Long leaseholders' rights at a glance

A long lease is one that was originally granted for over 21 years. Long leaseholders have the following rights given to them by legislation:

- the right to information about the current landlord's name and address
- the right to seek appointment of a manager
- the new right to manage
- the right to acquire compulsorily the landlord's interest in the building
- the right to vary the lease.

Right to information about the landlord

The landlord must comply with the following obligations:

- The landlord must provide the tenant(s) with an address in England or Wales where notification can be sent. This might be the address of the landlord's agent, such as a solicitor. If the landlord's address is outside England or Wales, an address in

England or Wales must also be provided. Until this information is provided, service charges and ground rent are treated as not being payable.

- The name and address of the landlord must be put on any written demand for service charges. The service charge is not payable until the landlord complies.
- If a new landlord takes over, the name and address of the new landlord must be given before the next ground rent is due or within two months of the new landlord acquiring the freehold, whichever is the later. Failure to do so is a criminal offence.

Right to appoint a manager

Where the whole or part of a building consists of two or more flats, any tenant of the block has the right, individually or with other tenants, to ask the Leasehold Valuation Tribunal* to appoint a manager to run the block or to carry out certain management functions. This right is given by the Landlord and Tenant Act 1987 and arises where the landlord's management of the building has been unsatisfactory. The Commonhold and Leasehold Reform Act 2002 extends the right to where the management is carried out by a third-party manager. The grounds for obtaining the appointment of a manager are:

- the landlord is in breach of a leasehold covenant relating to management of the premises
- the landlord has demanded, or is likely to demand, unreasonable service charges
- the landlord has failed to hold service charges in trust or in a separate client account (this is a newly introduced ground)
- the landlord has failed to comply with any relevant provision of a government-approved code of management practice (as produced by the Royal Institution of Chartered Surveyors*)
- in all cases, it must be convenient and just to make the order.

Exclusions

There is no right to appoint a manager when:

- the flats are in a converted building (not a purpose-built block of flats) where the landlord is also a resident. The Commonhold and Leasehold Reform Act restricts this exclusion so that it does

not apply if at least half the flats in the building are held under
long residential leases

- the landlord is a public body, for example, the Crown, a local
authority, a housing action trust or registered social landlord

- the premises are included within the functional land of any charity.

Procedure

In order to exercise the right, the tenant(s) must serve a preliminary
notice on the landlord. (This obligation can, however, be dispensed
with by the Leasehold Valuation Tribunal if it is not reasonably practicable to notify the landlord: for example, if the landlord cannot be
traced.) This notice must tell the landlord that the intention is to
seek the appointment of a manager, specify the ground(s) on which
the order will be sought and invite the landlord to remedy the specified problems within a stated, reasonable period. If the landlord
does not put the problems right within the period specified in the
notice, the tenant(s) may then apply to the LVT for the appointment
of a manager. (An application must be made by one or more tenants,
and cannot be made by a tenants' association.) The application must:

- provide details of the applicant(s), the landlord and all tenants
in the building

- provide details of any mortgage lender of the landlord

- include a copy of the lease and the preliminary notice served on
the landlord

- state the ground(s) on which the LVT will be asked to make the
order.

Once the order is made, the LVT has a wide discretion as to what is
included and the conditions to be imposed as part of the manager's
appointment, including time limits. The order can be permanent,
of limited duration or suspended in effect (to give the landlord an
opportunity to manage properly); it can also be revoked or varied
subsequently at the request of either the tenant(s) or the landlord. If
it is an immediate order, the manager will then assume responsibility for the building and rectify the default. The order will include
the name of the manager, his or her functions, and the remuneration. The functions will include repair, maintenance and
insurance. Payment to the manager might be shared between the
landlord and tenant(s). In order to make the order binding on any

future buyer of the landlord's freehold, the order can be registered at the Land Charges Registry (for unregistered land) or Land Registry (for registered land).

The cost of obtaining a management order is not as prohibitive as it once was, but it offers little assistance where the landlord has insufficient funds to finance whatever is lacking (repairs, maintenance, insurance). However, an order still has value because it can be followed by an acquisition order allowing the tenants to make a compulsory purchase of the freehold (see page 225).

Right to manage

Taking over the management of the building from the landlord has obvious attractions to tenants. It gives them control over the level of service charge set, and allows them to appoint their own management agents and select their own insurers. Taking over control from the landlord is a major motivation for tenants to group together to force the landlord to sell the freehold under collective enfranchisement (see Chapter 18). However, under this new right-to-manage scheme, tenants do not have to buy the freehold in order to gain control, are not required to pay compensation to the landlord, and do not have to show that the landlord has a poor management record. This new right allows a group of qualifying tenants to take over management responsibilities through a nominee managing body called a Right to Manage (RTM) company: see Chapter 14. The landlord's consent is not required and there is no need for any court order. The company will step into the shoes of the landlord and will take over maintenance and repair of the building, insurance (if it was the landlord's responsibility), and the collection of service charges. In return, the RTM company must ensure that the landlord's interest in the building is not adversely affected by the company's actions or failures. The landlord continues to collect ground rents. Remember that only management passes to the RTM company. The process does not affect the leases or ownership of the freehold.

Qualifying for the right

In order for leaseholders to qualify for the right to manage, certain eligibility requirements are imposed, to prevent a minority of residents from taking control of the block. These are:

- leaseholders must own a long lease (one originally granted for more than 21 years)
- they must become members of a Right to Manage company which is properly constituted for the purposes of collective management
- the block must include two or more flats held by qualifying tenants
- the participating leaseholders must occupy at least half the flats in the block
- the right extends to associated premises such as garages and gardens, but only if they are for the sole use of residents in the block.

Are the premises excluded?

The right to manage does not extend to all types of premises. The following fall outside its scope:

- properties where the number of flats held by qualifying lease-holders is less than two-thirds of the total number of flats in the building
- properties where more than 25 per cent of the total internal floor space is used for non-residential purposes (for example, where there are flats above a shop and the shop forms more than a quarter of the building)
- properties where there is a resident landlord. This applies to conversions (not a purpose-built block) where there are no more than four living units (flats, bedsits, etc.) and the landlord (or an adult member of his or her family) lives in one unit and has done so for the previous 12 months
- where the landlord is a local authority. Such landlords are subject to other right-to-manage provisions (see below)
- where the RTM company has lost management of the premises within the preceding four years, unless permission to exercise the right again is given by the LVT
- any property which is already subject to the right to manage.

Exercising the right

A Right to Manage company can serve a 'discovery notice' on the landlord to find out relevant information about the identity of the other tenants in the block and whether the building qualifies under the scheme. The landlord has 28 days in which to respond. All qualifying leaseholders must be given an opportunity to participate in the right to manage and become members of the RTM company. They will be given a 'notice of invitation to participate'. At least 14 days must then lapse before the RTM company can notify the landlord that it is claiming the right to take over management, which it does by serving a 'claim notice' on the landlord. In normal cases, a copy of the claim notice must be provided to all the leaseholders (including those who did not wish to participate).

If the landlord cannot be traced, the RTM company can dispense with serving a claim notice and apply directly to the Leasehold Valuation Tribunal. The company must, however, advertise in order to try to find the landlord.

The usual procedure starts when the claim notice is served on the landlord. The landlord may serve a counter-notice either admitting the right to manage or challenging the validity of the tenants' claim. The RTM company then has two months within which to apply to the Leasehold Valuation Tribunal. The company can withdraw the application or decide to proceed. Once the LVT's order is made, the company will be liable for the landlord's reasonable costs.

If it later turns out that the company is not running the block satisfactorily, any tenant can apply to the LVT to argue for the appointment of an independent manager. If the tenants later decide to buy the freehold from the landlord under the enfranchisement provisions, the RTM company will have to be converted into a Right to Enfranchise (RTE) company (see Chapter 18).

Contents of the participation notice

The invitation to participate must:

- state that the RTM company intends to acquire the right to manage
- state the names of members of the RTM company
- invite recipients to become members
- contain prescribed information
- be accompanied by a copy of the RTM company's founding documents (i.e. memorandum and articles of association) or offer the opportunity to inspect such documents.

The disadvantages of exercising the right to manage

Although the process is reasonably straightforward, tenants must remember that they will incur duties and responsibilities.

- Much work has to be done before the service of the claim notice (e.g. setting up the company, arranging bank accounts and dealing with existing contracts).
- The tenants (via the RTM company) are assuming total responsibility for budgets, management, services, repairs, etc. A programme of maintenance for, say, a 25-year period will have to be devised.
- The tenants will normally have to select (and deal with) a professional managing agent to run the block.
- The RTM company is required to comply with government-approved codes of practice.
- The tenants will need to learn about company law and procedures; participate in regular meetings; be prepared for ongoing commitment to the RTM company; deal with problem tenants who do not pay service charges; and take on potential liabilities as officers of the company.
- The RTM company will be accountable to the landlord if there is neglect or mismanagement.
- The landlord is entitled to be a member of the RTM company and this can lead to trouble. Any intermediate landlords (e.g. head lessee) are also entitled to be members. All members have voting rights.

Contents of the claim notice

The claim notice served by the RTM company must:

- be served at least 14 days after each tenant has been given a notice of participation
- be in a prescribed form; but the notice will not be invalidated by inaccuracy of any of the particulars required
- specify the premises and contain a statement showing that the premises are within the right-to-manage provisions
- state the full names and flat number of each tenant who is a member of the company

- provide particulars of each member's lease (for example, its duration and when it was created)
- state the registered office of the RTM company
- specify a date, not earlier than one month after service of the claim notice, within which the landlord may respond by a counter-notice
- stipulate a date, at least one month later than that previously specified, on which the RTM company intends to acquire the right to manage.

Right to compulsorily purchase the freehold

The right to buy the freehold against the landlord's wishes (usually when the landlord has badly managed the block) is offered by the Landlord and Tenant Act 1987. Due to the likely disrepair of the block, this is not always an attractive bargain to enter. This right applies to long leaseholders of two or more flats in the same building, who have the same landlord. Following service of notice on the landlord, a majority of such tenants may apply to the court (not the LVT) to require the landlord to transfer the freehold to the tenants. The court can dispense with the notice if it is not reasonably practicable to serve it, so an order can be made even if the landlord cannot be found. The court order may be obtained if *either* of the following grounds is established:

- the landlord is in breach of any leasehold covenant relating to repair, maintenance, insurance or management and the breach is likely to continue; *or*
- an order for the appointment of a manager has been in force for at least two years before the date of the current application.

On the granting of the order, the freehold will be conveyed into the name of a nominated person or a management company set up by the tenants. If the parties cannot agree the terms of the purchase, the court will work out the terms for them, and the basis for this must be what is fair and reasonable according to the market value of the premises in their present condition (reduced to take account of there being no vacant possession because the flats are occupied). Once granted, the order terminates any interest the landlord held in the premises.

Exclusions

This right to acquire the landlord's freehold does not apply if:

- the block is a converted building (that is, it is not a purpose-built block) and the landlord resides there
- the landlord is a public body or a registered social landlord
- the premises are included within the functional land of a charity
- more than 50 per cent of the internal floor area of the premises is used for non-residential purposes
- the total number of flats held by qualifying tenants is less than two-thirds of the total number of flats contained in the premises.

The right to vary the lease

It is possible that the lease as drafted is defective in some way (for example, it does not adequately cover repair). Unless the tenant and landlord agree to change the lease, it is necessary to go to court for the defect to be corrected. Before the Landlord and Tenant Act 1987, any variation of a lease proved to be a costly venture because, unless the landlord consented, it had to be done via the High Court. Moreover, there was no method which readily catered for the variation of more than one lease at a time.

The 1987 Act introduced a fundamental change by allowing the County Court to amend a defective lease on the request of either the tenant(s) or the landlord without the consent of the other party. This jurisdiction has now been transferred to the Leasehold Valuation Tribunal★ by the Commonhold and Leasehold Reform Act 2002. The grounds on which an application may be based are that the defective lease fails to make satisfactory provision on one or more of the following matters:

- the repair and maintenance of the flat or the building
- the insurance of the premises
- the repair and maintenance of any installations and/or the provision of any services reasonably necessary to ensure that the occupiers have a reasonable standard of accommodation
- the recovery of expenditure incurred for the benefit of the other party (for example, insurance, service charges and legal expenses)

- the computation of the service charge payable under the lease
- a fixed administrative charge specified in the lease or a specified formula for determining such a charge (this was introduced by the Commonhold and Leasehold Reform Act 2002).

Tenants should be aware that any variation which increases the obligation of the landlord is likely to result in a higher service charge levied on them.

Multiple variations are available to cover the situation where the tenants share the same landlord (even if the flats are in different buildings). This is so even if the leases are not identical.

Although a single tenant may apply in relation to a single lease, before the LVT can make a single order varying two or more leases (whether or not in the same building), the application must be supported by at least 75 per cent of the parties concerned and not opposed by more than 10 per cent. If there are fewer than nine leases involved, all or all but one of those tenants must consent.

The LVT can vary the lease(s) as it sees fit. There are, however, no guidelines to help it in its decision to vary. The general rule is that a variation order will be made unless it would be unreasonable to grant the order or would substantially prejudice the landlord or the tenant.

Any variation order binds the parties to the lease(s). A memorandum of any variation made will, usually, be endorsed on the lease(s).

Chapter 16

Fitness, repair and safety

In a block of flats, the landlord usually retains possession and control of the common parts and will covenant for their repair and maintenance. The tenant will then be responsible for the maintenance and repair of the individual flat concerned. As regards those flats not in a block, the liability to maintain and repair both the building and the flat traditionally rests on the shoulders of the tenant.

In addition to those covenants which are explicitly stated in the lease, there are a variety of obligations imposed by the general law which are not. Many of these obligations will be imposed on the landlord. This chapter looks at the issues of repair and safety, and describes briefly what safeguards the law provides to a tenant.

Fitness and disrepair

The problem of unfit housing is acute in the UK. Although the problem seems to be worst in London, in most big cities properties appear to be falling into disrepair faster than existing disrepair can be remedied. The preservation of housing stock is clearly of social importance. The public interest suffers if repairs are not carried out because buildings then decay and become dilapidated. The courts and Parliament have, therefore, gradually introduced laws which place some obligations on the landlord to maintain and repair.

Although the general rule of *caveat emptor* ('let the buyer beware') applies to flats – that is, a person buying a flat is offered no guarantee about its state, and has to carry out his or her own tests to check that it is satisfactory – it does give way in certain and limited circumstances recognised by the courts and Parliament. Irrespective of what is said in the lease, certain obligations are imposed on the landlord by law. The only obligation imposed by law upon the tenant is to use the premises in 'a tenant-like manner' and not to commit 'waste'. This could make the tenant liable for causing wilful or negligent damage and, moreover, places the responsibility for minor flat maintenance upon the tenant.

The somewhat hesitant progress made by the courts towards establishing a basic standard of habitation under a residential lease has been achieved by applying the laws of negligence and nuisance, and also by reading into residential leases certain contractual obligations on the part of the landlord. The government intends to place new duties on landlords and to give local authorities extended powers to enforce them.

The Landlord and Tenant Act 1985

The 1985 Act imposes obligations on the landlord as regards leases (of both houses and flats) for fewer than seven years. Provided that the landlord has been notified of the disrepair, he or she is then subject to an implied covenant:

- to keep in repair the structure and exterior (including drains, gutters and external pipes) of the whole building
- to keep in repair and proper working order the installations for the supply of water, gas, electricity, sanitation and heating.

The obligation of the landlord extends not only to the flats let but also to the common parts. The landlord cannot contract out of or otherwise sidestep this duty. However, the duty does not extend to repairs attributable to the tenant's fault or which arise because of fire, flood or inevitable accident. The standard of repair required varies according to the age, locality and character of a particular property. The landlord has the right to inspect the premises on giving 24 hours' written notice. Local authorities have wide powers under the Housing Act 1985 to require a landlord to carry out repairs (see pages 236–41).

Defective Premises Act 1972

This Act imposes on a builder, architect and others involved a duty to build or extend premises properly. The requirement is that the work is done in a workmanlike or professional manner with proper materials. If the property is not fit for habitation when completed, the tenant may recover damages. This duty does not apply (and is not necessary) if the premises are covered by a National House Building Council (NHBC)* guarantee (see Chapter 8).

Quiet enjoyment

The covenant of quiet enjoyment, which is implied into every lease, may also help in maintaining the quality of the premises. A landlord who, for example, undertakes to maintain the roof of a building, but fails to keep it watertight, will be in breach of the covenant for repair and also that for quiet enjoyment if the tenant's flat is affected. It would be similar if, in winter, the landlord failed to lag a water-pipe which was within his or her control, and the pipe burst causing damage to the tenant's premises.

There would be a clear breach of the covenant (and possibly it would constitute the criminal offence of harassment of tenants) if the landlord intentionally disconnected the tenant from mains services. The tenant could initiate civil proceedings in the County Court and seek compensation or an injunction.

Safety in the home

The home is a potentially hazardous place. Countless domestic accidents occur each year and most accidents involving children arise in the confines of the family home. As a general rule, it is the tenant (and not the landlord) who is liable for any injury happening on the leased premises. There are, however, some circumstances in which the landlord, or someone else, will be liable. Some of the exceptions to the general rule have been created by the courts, while others arise from Acts of Parliament.

Contractual duty of care

A duty of care is imposed on the landlord of a block of flats to preserve the amenities and the common parts of the building enjoyed by the tenant. The landlord is, therefore, under a duty to take reasonable care to keep such things as lifts, rubbish chutes and stairways safe and efficient. An aggrieved tenant can apply to the court for an order compelling the landlord to carry out whatever repairs are appropriate; if loss is suffered, the tenant can seek financial compensation.

This duty can offer redress for the tenant who suffers physical injury due to the unsafe condition of the landlord's part of the building. A tenant who is hurt, for example, by a fall on a dilapidated staircase or by tripping over a loose carpet in an unlit entrance hall is likely to recover compensation for breach of this contractual duty. The duty extends not only to hidden defects, but also to those which are obvious. A landlord could be liable, therefore, for the failure to clean a snow-covered step or an icy path. Persons other than the tenant (for example, family – even if living in the flat – and visitors) will not have a contract with the landlord and must rely instead on the law of negligence. This is, however, subject to the Contracts (Rights of Third Parties) Act 1999 which, in limited circumstances, allows third parties to sue on a contract which is intended to benefit them (see Chapter 10).

Liability in negligence

Irrespective of any contractual obligation, the law of negligence places on the landlord a duty to take care and expects him or her to act as a 'reasonable' landlord. If there is a breach of this duty, the landlord's liability will extend to all those who are reasonably foreseeable as being affected by the negligence (the tenant, the tenant's family and visitors, for example), so any of them can sue.

The law of negligence has an important function when damage arises from disrepair of parts of the building retained by the landlord. If the landlord, for example, retains responsibility for service ducts and the roof, but fails to prevent an infestation of vermin in the ducts, to clear a gutter or to repair a down-spout, the tenant could recover compensation from the landlord for any damage to property arising from such failure. In limited circumstances, the landlord might, moreover, be held liable for damage caused by a third party. An example of this is where the landlord controls a security system within the building which fails (alarms have been ineffectively installed or the porter falls asleep) and, as a result, vandals enter a flat and cause damage. In this situation the landlord might be found liable in negligence.

If the landlord is the builder, he or she might be liable under the general law of negligence for dangerous defects in the design or construction of the flat which cause injury to a tenant. This duty is designed to ensure that occupiers and visitors are reasonably safe. If the landlord is not the builder, there might still be liability under the Defective Premises Act 1972 (see page 234).

Where the landlord retains control over any part of the building (lifts, entrance hall, forecourt and other common parts), he or she will be regarded as an occupier of those parts. The tenant will be regarded as the occupier of the flat. Under the Occupiers Liability Act 1957, an occupier owes all visitors a 'common duty of care', that is, a duty to make anyone who is lawfully there safe in using the premises. The degree of safety that an occupier has to ensure is higher for children than for adults: the landlord must be prepared for children to be less careful. If the landlord has ceased to be an occupier (that is, the whole building has been leased), the burden will fall on each individual tenant or the tenants' management company. A more limited duty is owed by an occupier to a trespasser under the Occupiers Liability Act 1984.

The landlord may attempt to avoid liability in negligence by displaying an exclusion notice (that is, a statement that he or she accepts no responsibility for loss or injury incurred on the premises howsoever caused). Such notices are ineffective as regards death and personal injury. With respect to damage to property, they are effective only provided that they can be shown to be reasonable.

Liability in nuisance

The law of nuisance covers a multitude of sins and may enable the tenant to sue the landlord where the latter unreasonably interferes with the former's use or enjoyment of the premises.

When a landlord leases property in a state which constitutes a nuisance (for example, it has a leaking pipe or a defective roof), and this results in loss or injury to the tenant or his or her property, the landlord will be liable. Where the nuisance is caused by an act of the tenant, the landlord will not usually be liable. This means that if the landlord remains liable under the lease for repair and maintenance of the part of the building which contains the source of the nuisance, he or she will be liable for that nuisance. If the obligation to repair or maintain falls on the tenant and extends to the source of the nuisance, the landlord will not normally be liable. Similarly, the landlord will not usually be liable to a tenant for a nuisance caused by another tenant.

As with negligence, the tenant would need to establish fault on the part of the landlord and demonstrate loss (that is, interference with comfort and/or physical damage or injury). Unlike negligence, only the tenant can commence legal proceedings; the tenant would, therefore, have to sue on behalf of family members or visitors.

Rylands v Fletcher

A further remedy, akin to nuisance, exists under what lawyers call the rule in *Rylands v Fletcher*, which makes a landlord liable for things brought on to the land (for example, stored water, oil and even electricity) which then escape and cause damage. A tenant could seek a remedy under this rule even though there is no fault on the landlord's part. It is strict liability and probably (there are conflicting views) extends not only to damage to property, but also to personal injury.

Health and Safety at Work Act 1974

Although those who drafted this Act may not have intended it, aspects of this legislation have been applied to residential leases. A duty is imposed on the person who has control of the premises 'in connection with the carrying on by him of a trade, business or other undertaking'. This embraces an individual landlord (or a management company) of a block of flats. The duty is to take reasonable care to ensure that all means of access and exit on the premises, together with plant and machinery provided for use on the premises, are safe and without risk to health. Liability could arise as regards unsafe lifts and the dangerous state of common parts, for example.

If the landlord ignores the repair and maintenance of such amenities as lifts, stairways and electrical installations in the common areas, the tenant may request the local authority to serve an 'improvement notice' on the landlord which will compel the latter to fulfil the obligations. Failure to comply with the notice constitutes a criminal offence.

New Health and Safety Regulations are introduced from time to time. The Management Health and Safety at Work Regulations 1992, for example, impose stringent rules (and harsh penalties) on the managers of property concerning the safety of employees (for example, porters, cleaners and maintenance workers) and others on the premises. This could render a landlord liable to anyone injured on the premises. Similarly, the Gas Safety (Installation and Use) Regulations 1994 are designed to protect tenants from carbon monoxide poisoning from the faulty installation and use of gas appliances. This makes landlords responsible for making sure that gas appliances are maintained in good order and checked for safety (by a registered CORGI fitter) at least every 12 months. This responsibility extends only to appliances and pipework 'owned' by the landlord. This means that if the landlord provides gas heating as part of the services of the flat or common parts, the Regulations will apply. The legal position is more uncertain where there is no block of flats and each tenant is responsible for his or her own gas appliances. It would be necessary to show that the landlord owned the appliance. Although it could be argued that a gas fire and boiler (but not a gas cooker and refrigerator) were landlord's fixtures, it is doubtful whether the courts would extend the landlord's liability to tenants with long leases.

The Defective Premises Act 1972

The Act places an obligation on the landlord to take reasonable care to prevent personal injury or damage to property which might be caused by defects (which exist at the commencement of the lease or which emerge subsequently) in the premises leased. This obligation, however, is limited to where the landlord:

- has entered into a repairing covenant or has reserved the right to enter and carry out repairs
- knew or ought to have known (for example, by inspection) of the disrepair
- has failed to take reasonable care in respect of repair and maintenance.

Where a tenant is injured by tripping over an uneven paving stone or when a communal garden wall collapses, for example, the landlord will be liable under the Act. This is so even if the danger has been caused by the faulty repair work of a previous landlord or tenant. The duty concerns hazards on the land which make it unsafe. The liability of the landlord, moreover, cannot be excluded by any 'exclusion' notice or term in the contract.

The Environmental Protection Act 1990

This Act, under which a local authority may intervene in cases of alleged housing disrepair, offers a further avenue of redress to the tenant. Any premises that are in such a condition as to be dangerous to health (for example, defective wiring, ill-fitting windows, blocked drains, extensive damp and mould) or to constitute a nuisance (an unreasonable interference with the tenant's enjoyment and use of the flat) fall within the definition of a statutory nuisance within the Act. (Inadequate soundproofing is not covered, nor is traffic noise, but the tenant could gain some redress against a neighbour who played amplified music.)

The Act deals with the consequences of the defect rather than with the defect itself: there has to be a health hazard arising from the defect complained of. Take, for example, a defective roof. The disrepair is not itself the statutory nuisance, but if the roof leaks, and the water damages the tenant's flat, this would become the nuisance. The Act, therefore, becomes important where the landlord retains control or possession of some part of the building and the damage emanates from that part.

The tenant has two possible ways of getting redress. First, he or she can go direct to the Magistrates' Court for a 'nuisance order' (that is, a summons) against the landlord. A hearing will then be conducted and, if the court finds in favour of the tenant, an abatement order will be issued. Funding from the Community Legal Service is not available for this private court action, but costs can be awarded against the landlord and a compensation order can be made by the court.

Alternatively, the tenant may complain to the Environmental Health Department of the local authority and is entitled to have the complaint investigated. If it is found that the defects amount to a statutory nuisance, the local authority will serve an abatement notice on the landlord. This notice will specify the nuisance and may require the landlord to carry out specified repairs. Subject to a landlord's appeal, a failure to comply by the date set in the notice will constitute a criminal offence. The local authority has the alternative option to do the work itself and invoice the landlord for the work.

Local authority action

Originally the Housing Act 1985 set out to ensure that buildings (including flats) used for residential purposes met certain basic standards. Houses and flats which were unfit should have been repaired or withdrawn from domestic use. The Act gave local authorities wide-ranging powers to deal with disrepair and poor-quality housing. These powers are increased by the Housing Act 2003 which introduces a radically new scheme of enforcement.

The local authority is obliged to inspect its area from time to time in order to decide whether any action under the 1985 Act is necessary. The government can compel a local authority to carry out this inspection if necessary. The authority does not have to act on the request of local residents.

When faced with unfit accommodation, the authority has a number of courses of action available. It is also given broad powers to enter premises to carry out its inspection or, where relevant, repairs.

New standards

The 2003 Act gets rid of the old 'fitness for human habitation' test and replaces it with entirely new standards for condition of residential accommodation. The Act recognises two classes of hazard: category 1 hazard and category 2 hazard. For these purposes a hazard is any risk of harm (even temporary) to the health and safety of an occupier that arises from a deficiency in the flat or common parts. The deficiency might arise from, say, construction work or from an absence of repair and maintenance. The exact category in which a property falls depends upon a numerical scoring system specifically prescribed by the government for calculating the seriousness of hazards. The local housing authority may, as a general rule, charge for taking enforcement action against an owner. Further guidance to local housing authorities is provided by Parliament.

If there is a category 1 or category 2 hazard, the local housing authority will be under a duty or have the power to take one of the following steps:

- serve an improvement notice
- make a prohibition order

- make a demolition order
- declare a clearance area (only in relation to category 1 hazards).

An improvement notice

An improvement notice may be served in relation to both category 1 and category 2 hazards. The same notice may relate to more than one category 1 or category 2 hazard on the same premises. The notice will identify the category of hazard to which it relates, specify the hazard, describe the remedial action to be undertaken, state a time for compliance at least 28 days hence and provide details of the recipient's rights. The general rule is that the notice will be served on the landlord as regards common parts and the tenant as regards the flat. Once served, the improvement notice becomes operative at the end of 21 days. It can, however, be varied or revoked by the local housing authority. Revocation would, for example, be relevant where the hazard ceases to exist.

The recipient of the notice can enter an appeal within 21 days following its service. It is a criminal offence not to comply (without reasonable excuse) with an improvement notice. The duty can be enforced by the local housing authority which has a power to enter the premises on giving seven days' notice and, with authorisation of the Magistrates' Court, to remove any obstructions to entry. The court can also order that the hazard be remedied by the local housing authority at the owner's expense.

A prohibition order

The local housing authority can issue a prohibition order in relation to category 1 and category 2 hazards. An order can be made concerning a block of flats if the hazard exists in one or more of the flats. The same order may relate to more than one category 1 or category 2 hazard. The prohibition order will prevent the use of the premises (or any part thereof) except for a purpose authorised by the local housing authority. In particular, the prohibition may restrict occupation of the premises. The order must be served on every owner and occupier of the premises to which it relates. An appeal may be made to the County Court within 21 days of the order being served, but no appeal can be brought by a tenant unless the tenant has more than three years remaining unexpired on the lease. If no appeal is brought, the order becomes effective at the end of 21 days from the date of service. Procedures exist which allow the local housing authority to vary or revoke a prohibition order.

It is a criminal offence to fail to comply with a prohibition order or to obstruct the local housing authority from carrying out its functions. The local housing authority is given a power to enter the premises after giving seven days' notice. It can also apply to the Magistrates' Court for a court order allowing it to take action to remove obstructions and to carry out its duties (i.e. preventing occupation of the premises). In addition, either the landlord or the tenant of premises affected by the prohibition order can apply to the court to terminate the lease or to vary its terms.

A warning notice

Warning notices can be mandatory or voluntary. Mandatory warnings concern category 1 hazards whereas voluntary warnings relate to category 2 hazards. The warning notice can relate to more than one hazard and must specify the hazard, the remedial action to be taken and other courses which are open to the local authority (e.g. to serve an improvement notice). The serving of a warning notice does not prevent the local housing authority from taking further action in relation to the hazard.

A demolition order

The local housing authority can make a demolition order where one or more category 1 or category 2 hazards exist on the premises or, in relation to a block of flats, exist in one or more flats.

A clearance area

The local housing authority may declare an area to be a clearance area if each of the residential buildings in the area contains at least one category 1 hazard or the residential buildings in the area are dangerous or harmful to the health and safety of the inhabitants.

Compulsory improvement

There are two other situations in which a local authority may require the improvement of a dwelling by a leaseholder, even if it is not in a state of disrepair and unfitness. These are where the premises are in a local authority 'action' or 'improvement' area and the property is lacking in standard amenities (for example, a fixed bath or shower, a wash-basin and a sink supplied with hot and cold water, and a toilet). The flat must have been built or converted since 3 October 1961 and the dwelling must be capable of being brought up to standard at reasonable cost. A local authority grant might be available to assist a leaseholder.

Grant aid: a snapshot

It is difficult to state accurately the type, extent and amount of financial assistance which is available from a local authority, because the schemes are constantly being revised and are governed by complex regulations. It is essential to check the schemes and regulations that are current at the time of the application. Some may depend on your being over 60 years of age; some require you to have owned and occupied the flat for a set period (e.g three years); and others depend upon your being in receipt of welfare benefits. No work should be carried out prior to a grant application being considered. In order to claim a grant, the applicant must be either the landlord or a leaseholder with a fixed term which has at least another five years to run.

The grant system was overhauled by the Housing Grants, Construction and Regeneration Act 1996, and the following is merely a brief introduction to the types of grant available:

- **renovation grants** to improve or repair a house or a flat. The property must be at least ten years old. The grant is discretionary and means-tested (that is, it is geared to the financial status of the applicant); the test varies according to whether the claimant is the landlord or the leaseholder. The grant can be awarded to help towards complying with a local authority repair notice, providing insulation and space heating and/or improving internal amenities and services
- **common parts grants** to finance the improvement or repair of common parts in a building which contains flats. The claimant can be either the landlord or the leaseholder in the building and the grant is dependent upon three-quarters of the flats in the building being occupied. The works that are eligible for grant aid are listed and the list is available from your local authority
- **disabled facilities grants** to provide assistance with the costs of making the flat and common parts suitable for a disabled

leaseholder. Some of these grants are mandatory, most are discretionary. The maximum payable here is £25,000

- **homes in multiple occupation grants** (HMO grants) to help those living in a block of flats, for example, to pay for the installation of basic amenities, fire escapes and related repairs
- **home repair assistance** payable to a leaseholder who is on certain welfare benefits. The maximum amount payable here is £5,000
- **burglar alarm grants**
- **energy-efficiency grants.**

Other assistance

A wide range of schemes exists to encourage and help home-owners to repair and maintain their homes. These include:

- **handy person schemes** which are provided by local author-ities, housing associations and voluntary sector bodies. A person is employed to carry out minor jobs for elderly or disabled home-owners. The service is usually free of charge or, at most, is charged at cost. Handy person schemes are likely to remain a specialised service aimed to assist vulnerable tenants
- **subscription-based repair schemes** which are operated by private companies on a national scale. The home-owner pays an annual fee to become a member of the service in return for a range of specified benefits. These schemes are popular with middle-aged and/or retired leaseholders who, of course, have the money to pay the annual premium. Some schemes are limited to emergency repairs only
- **subscription-based maintenance services** which are likely to be locally based. Although uncommon, this type of scheme will offer limited repair and maintenance cover in return for an annual fee. The average subscribed person is the well-to-do pensioner
- **advisory and information services** are provided by many local authorities and housing associations. The aim is to provide oral advice and to produce helpful booklets on DIY projects. In some areas, tool loan schemes have been estab-lished and surgeries held to discuss repair problems and how to sort them out. Some surgeries and classes are specifically aimed at women or minority ethnic groups

- **home maintenance surveys** are sometimes provided without charge by local authorities and housing associations. These involve property inspections and the supply of a report identifying any problems discovered by the surveyor. The scheme might recommend builders and cater for an inspection of the work when completed. Those who benefit from this scheme are mainly over 60 years of age and on low incomes.

Coal-mining subsidence

The Coal Mining Subsidence Act 1991 requires the 'responsible person' (for example, the Coal Authority) to notify owners and occupiers (that is, landlords and tenants) of any land which may be affected by mining proposals. This notice will highlight the possibility that the property might be affected by coal-mining subsidence and alert the landlord and tenant to keep a watch for tell-tale signs (cracked plaster and sticking doors).

If damage owing to coal-mining subsidence occurs, property owners (including holders of long leases) can apply to have the premises repaired or may be entitled to compensation.

The claim

A claim for subsidence damage should be made as soon as any damage occurs. The latest time for making a claim is six years from when it was reasonable for the damage to have been discovered. The claim should be against the mine owner, who will then inspect the property. Generally, the mine owner will carry out or authorise any necessary repairs according to a previously agreed itemised schedule of repairs. The repairs will, however, be carried out only once the land is stable, and what is termed a 'stop notice' can be issued to delay permanent repairs. Emergency works can be carried out prior to the claim, but the mine owner must be informed as soon as possible what works have been carried out and the reasons for such works.

Compensation

In exceptional circumstances, the mine owner will, instead of making repairs, pay compensation. These circumstances include:

- where repairs are not physically possible because the building is too badly damaged

- where the cost of repairs is significantly greater than the reduction in the value of the property
- where the condition of the property is such that it is impossible to repair in isolation the damage attributable to subsidence.

Other liabilities

Apart from repair and compensation, the mine owner will have to pay for the claimant's legal and surveying expenses as well as costs (postage, phone calls, etc.) associated with the claim. If the property becomes unsafe or uninhabitable because of the subsidence damage, the claimant will also be entitled to receive payment for equivalent alternative accommodation. The responsibility of looking after the house while the owner is in alternative accommodation rests with the mine owner, so the latter will be obliged to keep the property secure and weatherproof. The mine owner will also pay reasonable moving and storage expenses, and excess living costs (for example, light, heat and travel costs).

If the property cannot be sold because of subsidence damage, the mine owner might be required to purchase it at its undamaged value. The claimant must, however, demonstrate a good reason for selling the property (for example, a new job in a different area). When the property has to be demolished, the mine owner must either rebuild it or pay compensation based on the full market value of the property. An extra 'home loss' payment may also be provided.

Dispute resolution

While many disputes will be settled without major problems, the claimant has the potential to take the case before the Lands Tribunal.★ Arbitration is, however, a quicker, cheaper and less formal way of settling disputes. Two independent arbitration schemes have been set up by the Chartered Institute of Arbitrators★ to deal specifically with subsidence claims:

- the Householder's Arbitration Scheme, which, on the payment of £80 (plus VAT), will deal with uncomplicated disputes
- the General Arbitration Scheme, which, on the payment of £120 (plus VAT), deals with more complex disputes.

Chapter 17

Ending the lease

While the lease is in existence the tenant is, for all intents and purposes, the owner of the flat. The landlord has no right to enter the premises, unless it is to follow up a right given by the lease (for example, to view the state of repair) and cannot sell to anyone else the right to occupy the flat. Moreover, for leases created before 1 January 1996, the original parties remain liable to observe the covenants throughout the duration of the lease (see Chapter 10); for leases granted after that date, the Landlord and Tenant (Covenants) Act 1995 allows the tenant to be automatically discharged from covenants following assignment of the lease, and the landlord to apply for such release on the sale of the freehold. Clearly, in all cases, the leasehold covenants end when the lease ends. It is, therefore, important to know how and when a lease is terminated.

A lease can be brought to an end in a variety of ways. A fixed-term lease (the type of lease with which this book is concerned) will normally continue until the term of years expires. It is, however, possible for the lease to be terminated prematurely either by the landlord forfeiting the lease for breach of covenant by the tenant, or by one party buying out the other's interest. When the tenant sells or gives up the lease to the landlord this is known as **surrender**; when the tenant buys the landlord's freehold, this is called **merger**. Each of these methods is described in this chapter, along with safeguards provided for the tenant by Parliament.

Expiry of time

A fixed-term lease (that is, one that runs for a specified number of years) must, at some stage, expire. The lease comes to an automatic end on the expiry of the period agreed; this is known as effluxion.

There is no need for any notice to be served and, at common law, the landlord will be entitled to possession (that is, to evict the tenant) without further ado. The exercise of this right by the landlord has, however, been modified by Parliament.

When drafted, the lease will specify the number of years it is to run for and stipulate the commencement date of the term. The exact date of expiry, if not expressly stated, can easily be calculated. So, for example, a lease granted for 38 years from 4 January 1967 will not automatically expire until the first moments of 5 January 2005. Although the landlord may wish the tenant to vacate the property after midnight on 4–5 January, the tenant will, thanks to the provisions of the Local Government and Housing Act 1989 (see below), normally be allowed to remain in lawful occupation. This is known as security of tenure.

Parliamentary safeguards for the tenant

There are two main measures that Parliament has taken to protect the tenant from eviction at the end of the term of the lease.

The Local Government and Housing Act 1989

This Act protects long leaseholders after their lease has expired, providing their situation falls within its scope. Most long leases will fall within the protection of the Act. Since 15 January 1999 this legislation has replaced entirely Part I of the Landlord and Tenant Act 1954.

Scope

A lease will fall within the protection of this Act provided that it is a long lease (that is, granted originally for over 21 years) and is at a low ground rent. This means either no ground rent or (if the lease was originally granted before April 1990) a rent which did not in April 1990 exceed two-thirds of its rateable value or (if granted on or after 1 April 1990) does not exceed £1,000 a year in Greater London or £250 a year elsewhere. For these purposes rent does not include service charges and insurance premiums, which are some-times described as 'rent' in the lease.

A flat may be excluded because of its high value. The test for high value also differs according to when the lease was granted. If granted before April 1990, the test is simple: the former rateable value of the flat must not exceed £1,500 (in Greater London) or £750 (elsewhere). Due to the abolition of domestic rates in 1990, a different test applies to those leases granted on or after 1 April of that year: the new calculation is to divide the price the first lease-holder paid for the flat (which will be stated in the original lease) by the number of years of the lease. If the result exceeds £25,000, then the flat falls outside the scope of the Act.

Some other exclusions apply: for example, the Act does not extend to those who hold leases from local authorities and housing associations or those who have already claimed a new lease under the Leasehold Reform, Housing and Urban Development Act 1993 (see Chapter 18).

In addition, the leaseholder must occupy the flat as a sole or main residence.

The protection

The importance of the 1989 Act is that it allows a tenant to stay in possession of the flat after the lease has expired. The landlord must serve a notice on the tenant if possession is sought and state a statutory ground of possession on which he or she intends to rely. The tenant then has to serve a counter-notice within two months stating whether he or she will or will not give up possession. If the tenant chooses to stay in the flat, the landlord must apply to the County Court for a possession order. This application must be made within two months of the tenant's counter-notice. Outside these time limits, the landlord's notice/application is invalid. The landlord can, however, then notify the tenant that an assured tenancy of the flat is on offer and specify the proposed terms. The landlord can also apply for an increased interim rent to cover the period until the assured tenancy is granted. If dispute arises, the matter can be referred to the Rent Assessment Committee.★

The landlord can obtain a possession order only on one (or more) of a limited number of statutory grounds as specified in the landlord's notice. These include where:

- the landlord has offered an assured tenancy under the Housing Act 1988
- the tenant has failed to pay rent or observe the terms of the lease concerning insurance

- the tenant has caused a nuisance or an annoyance, or has been convicted of using the premises (or allowing them to be used) for an illegal or immoral purpose (for example, as a brothel)
- the landlord, the landlord's adult children, parents or parents-in-law reasonably require the flat for their own occupation
- there is suitable alternative accommodation available for the tenant
- the landlord proposes, for the purpose of redevelopment after the expiry of the lease, to demolish or reconstruct the whole or a substantial part of the premises.

For the tenant, an assured tenancy is not as good as having a fixed-term lease, but it is better than being made homeless. A shrewd tenant may be able to negotiate a capital sum in return for leaving the premises. This might be the only way the landlord can regain possession. Alternatively, the tenant might be able to negotiate a new lease from this vantage point. An assured tenancy can be ended only in accordance with the Housing Act 1988.

The Local Government and Housing Act 1989

At the end of your lease, you will have the right to continue to occupy your flat, essentially on the same terms, provided that:

- you hold under a long lease (a lease originally granted for over 21 years)
- you live in the flat as your only or main home
- you pay no rent or a low rent
- your flat is not of high value
- your property is not otherwise excluded from the Act
- your landlord has not served a notice offering a periodic tenancy (for example, an assured tenancy) or seeking possession on the permitted grounds. If a notice has been served, consult a solicitor or the Citizens Advice Bureau and make sure that you serve a counter-notice on the landlord within two months
- you do not serve at least one month's notice terminating your long lease. If you do serve a termination notice, you must leave on the date that it expires.

The tenant may counter the landlord's notice by claiming a new lease or (in conjunction with other tenants) the right to buy the landlord's freehold. The tenant(s) will have to serve the appropriate notices within the time limits set out in the Leasehold Reform, Housing and Urban Development Act 1993 (see Chapter 18).

The Protection from Eviction Act 1977

This Act protects all tenants of residential premises by making the unlawful eviction or harassment of the tenant a criminal offence and a civil wrong. To prove harassment, the tenant must satisfy the court (usually the Magistrates' Court for criminal cases and the County Court for civil proceedings) that the landlord or any other person committed acts which were likely to interfere with the peace or comfort of the occupier or withheld services reasonably required for occupation, and that these acts were intended to cause or be likely to cause the occupier to leave the premises. Examples of harassment would include threats, nuisance, intimidation, deliberate failure to do necessary repairs and changing the locks.

To evict a residential occupier lawfully the landlord must obtain an order from the court authorising his or her re-taking possession of the flat. This is unless the landlord reasonably believes that the tenant no longer lives in the flat.

The police have the powers to prosecute for either offence (eviction or harassment), but often the task falls on the shoulders of the local authority. Many local authorities have Tenancy Relations Officers, whose function includes dealing with harassment and eviction matters. A private prosecution is also a possibility. Nevertheless, few offenders are ever prosecuted. This is because very few eviction and harassment incidents are reported, and because local authorities tend to deal with the matter without recourse to the criminal court. In addition, although the penalties potentially include imprisonment and a hefty fine, the court has a habit of imposing a low penalty on a convicted offender.

Premature ending of the lease

Forfeiture

Forfeiture, a means by which the landlord can bring the lease to a premature end when the tenant is in breach of a leasehold covenant, is considered in detail in relation to remedies for breach of covenant (see Chapter 10). Tenants cannot forfeit if the landlord is in breach. Most leases contain a forfeiture or re-entry clause which allows the landlord to put an end to the lease. Forfeiture, however, is hedged with complex and technical rules and, moreover, is not often granted by the courts. The tendency of the courts is, as far as is possible, to assist the tenant and not to allow forfeiture. Although it is a means of early termination, forfeiture is an unpopular, unpredictable and often unsuccessful avenue for the landlord to pursue. As shown in Chapter 10, the landlord's ability to forfeit for non-payment of service charges and ground rent is severely restricted.

Surrender

Surrender involves the tenant giving up or selling the lease to the immediate landlord. The lease then becomes part of the landlord's reversion and is at an end. At first glance, it might be difficult to envisage why a tenant would willingly give up the lease to the landlord. It might, however, benefit the tenant in the following situations:

- where the landlord offers the tenant money
- when the surrender of the old lease is conditional upon the landlord granting to the tenant a new and longer tenancy
- towards the end of a long lease and when the property is in disrepair – the tenant might prefer to give up the flat voluntarily rather than defend forfeiture proceedings for breach of repair covenant.

Surrender usually occurs by negotiation. It can be express or implied.

- An express surrender must be contained in a formal deed, but no special wording is required, provided that the intention to give up the lease is made clear. There must be agreement of both parties and there must be delivery up of the premises to the landlord.
- An implied surrender can arise without a deed. There must be an act by the tenant which shows the intention to give up the lease (for example, the moving out of possessions or returning keys) and the act must be accepted by the landlord.

Subject to contrary agreement, on surrender the landlord is entitled to sue the former tenant for breaches of covenant which occurred before the date of surrender. However, the tenant is not obliged to carry out any covenants (for example, to repair or to redecorate) that would have arisen at the expiry of the lease. The landlord might seek self-protection by inserting a condition into the deed of surrender that such obligations are performed prior to surrender.

As regards sub-leases, the surrender of the head-lease does not affect their validity and the landlord will remain bound by the rights of sub-tenants. Therefore, the landlord should ensure that he or she knows of all sub-tenants and that the tenant ends any sub-leases, before accepting the surrender.

Merger

Merger is the mirror image of surrender and occurs when the tenant buys out the landlord's freehold (for example, by exercising an option to purchase: see Chapter 19). This is not the same as collective enfranchisement (see Chapter 18) because here it is an individual and not a group of tenants buying the freehold. The general rule is that when the respective estates of landlord and tenant merge, the lease comes to an end and the landlord's reversion is said to 'drop down' and 'drown' the tenant's lease. Merger can arise only at the tenant's instigation because the landlord can never force the tenant to purchase the freehold. As with surrender, merger does not affect any existing sub-leases. A merger clause will usually be incorporated into the conveyance of the freehold (for a specimen merger clause see pages 131–2). If a merger occurs, other tenants in the building will have a new landlord (that is, the former tenant who buys the freehold).

Acquiring the freehold by private negotiation and sale is a less daunting and complicated procedure then collective enfranchisement.

Disclaimer

Under the Insolvency Act 1986, if a tenant becomes bankrupt, his or her trustee in bankruptcy (that is, the person appointed by the court to represent his or her interests) may 'disclaim' the lease if it constitutes property that is not readily saleable or gives rise to a liability to pay money or perform some other onerous act. All leases will, therefore, be within the power of the trustee to disclaim. On disclaimer, the lease is ended and the bankrupt is discharged from all further liability in respect of it.

With leases granted before 1 January 1996, if the bankrupt is someone who had bought an existing lease of the flat from a previous owner, disclaimer will not absolve the original tenant (that is, the first leaseholder of the flat) from liability under the covenants. Of course, if the bankrupt is the original tenant, then he or she will be freed from the covenants. All outstanding claims will be made against the bankrupt's assets.

With leases created after 1 January 1996, the original tenant will be liable for a subsequent tenant's breaches only if the original tenant has agreed to become a guarantor for the later one. In such a situation, on the bankruptcy of the latter and the disclaimer of the lease, the former will be discharged from further liability.

Chapter 18

Collective enfranchisement and lease renewal

The Leasehold Reform, Housing and Urban Development Act 1993 contained reforms which struck at the heart of the relationship between landlord and tenant. Aimed at overcoming the difficulties associated with the ownership of a wasting asset – primarily the depreciation in the value of the flat and the inability to sell towards

---

Other ways of buying the freehold

Collective enfranchisement is not the only way of buying the freehold to a flat. Other methods, some of which have been discussed in earlier chapters, are listed below.

- The Landlord and Tenant Act 1987 grants statutory rights to tenants to buy the freehold where the landlord allows the premises to fall into severe disrepair (see Chapter 15).
- Tenants can form a management company and buy the freehold from the landlord (see Chapter 14), but only if the landlord consents. This type of management scheme will be used by groups of tenants when they participate in collective enfranchisement.
- A tenant can buy out the landlord's freehold by merger, that is, by exercising an option to purchase (see pages 279–80 and Chapter 17) or by otherwise negotiating a purchase outside the statutory schemes.
- Tenants can buy out the landlord's freehold if the landlord intends to sell it on the open market. This statutory right of first refusal is considered in Chapter 19.

---

the end of the lease – these reforms allowed certain tenants of flats to join together and buy the freehold of the whole building (**collective enfranchisement**), and the individual tenant to obtain, on payment of a capital sum and a nominal (peppercorn) rent, a new 90-year lease of an individual flat (**lease renewal**). Further reforms have been introduced by the Commonhold and Leasehold Reform Act 2002 and these focus primarily on the criteria for qualification and valuation. The idea that tenants can purchase the freehold to their premises is not new (see box on page 251). Nevertheless, it is only since 1 November 1993 that tenants of flats have had a general entitlement to buy out their landlord's interest collectively if they and their building qualify. In addition, the right of a tenant of a private-sector flat to renew the lease represents another major development, although it has been a right enjoyed by business tenants for well over 40 years and available to tenants of houses since 1967. This chapter deals with the measures available to tenants since 1993. Under the Commonhold and Leasehold Reform Act 2002, collective enfranchisement can only be carried out by tenants who have formed a Right to Enfranchise company, while a single tenant may still act individually to renew his or her lease.

Words of warning

The 1993 Act is complex and highly technical in language and procedure, and even solicitors find it difficult. The bulk and detail of the legislation are intimidating, and the process involved may prove both time-consuming and expensive. Successful contested enfranchisements are rare. The eligibility criteria for enfranchisement are extremely tight, and many tenants will find that they do not qualify. Nevertheless, once all the hoops have been jumped through – and a lot of determination and perseverance are needed for that to happen – the freeholder cannot prevent enfranchisement or the grant of a new lease. The set procedures must be followed within the specified time limits; if they are not, the tenants can be landed with increased costs and long delays or even suffer from the application being deemed withdrawn in certain circumstances. For those who persevere, however, the rewards are often worth the effort. The Leasehold Advisory Service,★ a government-funded organisation, advises tenants interested in either buying the freehold or renewing their lease.

The potential expense, aggravation and long-term responsibilities associated with enfranchisement can be off-putting (especially with large blocks of flats) and it is anticipated that many tenants will instead be content with the renewal of their leases. This is attractive in the long term, particularly if the tenant is happy with the landlord's management of the premises; moreover, further renewals may later be obtained.

Since the processes for both collective enfranchisement and lease renewal involve a daunting chain of notices and counter-notices, it is advisable to engage the services of a legal adviser. By virtue of the Housing Act 1996, the government may give financial assistance to enable such advice to be sought. Any money advanced will, however, have to be paid back. For enfranchisement a qualified valuer must also be used.

How well is the scheme working?

Research undertaken by the government, and based upon leaseholders' experiences with the process, shows how the enfranchisement and new lease provisions are working in the real world. These are the key findings:

- Only 4 per cent of leaseholders negotiated the entire formal process of enfranchisement as laid out in the 1993 Act. The legal complexities of the process, problems with receiving sound legal advice and the uncertainty of the financial costs involved were all given as obstacles for those interested in purchasing the freehold.
- Another 16 per cent of leaseholders enfranchised informally, that is, reaching agreement outside the statutory framework. Of those who failed, only a small number thought that changes in the law would revitalise their interest to enfranchise.
- Leaseholders were most likely to enfranchise successfully where there was a sense of commitment, thorough professional advice, an approachable freeholder, stability amongst the residents, knowledge and sufficient financial backing to pursue the proceedings and pay for subsequent management arrangements. Those living in blocks with small numbers of flats were more likely to succeed with the enfranchisement process. Disharmony and dissatisfaction between leaseholders

often undermined group-based action and led to delay or withdrawal.

- Enfranchisement was wanted mainly because of problems with the current living conditions. Three major problems were evident: the high level of service and other charges; maintenance and management difficulties; and poor communication with the freeholder or the managing agent.

- Although a less complex procedure is involved, lease renewal was less popular than enfranchisement. Usually it was a second-best position for leaseholders unable to enfranchise. Nevertheless, renewal presented many difficulties similar to those with the enfranchisement process: unawareness of the legislation, poor professional advice, doubts as to costs and disputes with the freeholder. Also, the problems that arise have to be dealt with by a leaseholder alone and not on a collective basis.

- The Leasehold Valuation Tribunal★ was well regarded by leaseholders; however, they felt that their legal advisers lacked knowledge about the LVT's procedures. There was also complaint about the time it took before decisions were announced after the hearing.

- Leaseholders who had successfully enfranchised were very satisfied with their new arrangements, whether they chose to manage themselves or through a managing agent.

Practical difficulties

A number of obstacles may exist on the road to enfranchisement, in addition to unfamiliarity with the new scheme. These could include:

- some leaseholders (e.g. elderly tenants or those who intend to move) being reluctant to become involved in the enfranchisement process or take managerial responsibility for the property

- late changes in occupancy occurring before the initial notice to enfranchise is served, bringing the number of participating tenants below the required threshold. This problem is minimised by the recent reforms

- some leaseholders being unable or unwilling to pay the purchase price required for the freehold

- some leaseholders being deterred by a fear of costs and professional fees
- landlords using delaying tactics and threatening time-consuming and expensive appeals to the Lands Tribunal★
- some leaseholders excluding others unfairly from the enfranchising group. This possibility is reduced by the new reforms
- finding the landlord. If the landlord cannot be tracked down, the Right to Enfranchise (RTE) company or the individual tenant (if it is for a lease renewal) can ask the court to order the purchase. The purchase money will be set by the Leasehold Valuation Tribunal (LVT)★ and the sum paid into court awaiting the landlord's reappearance.

The need for change

In its 1998 consultation paper (*Residential Leasehold Reform in England and Wales*), the government admitted that collective enfranchisement would never be an easy option. It accepted that enfranchisement is worth pursuing only when there is a strong body of motivated tenants with energy, commitment and resources. Nevertheless, the government acknowledged that there were more difficulties than there should be. It suggested that:

- unnecessary obstacles in the current qualifying rules should be removed
- the valuation rules should be altered so as to prevent heavy expenditure on professional fees
- the rights of a landlord to appeal beyond the LVT★ to the Lands Tribunal★ should be further curtailed.

In response to the 1998 consultation paper, there was much support amongst tenants for the simplification and widening of eligibility for collective enfranchisement. Strong support emerged also in favour of simplifying the valuation procedures. In particular, tenants wanted the abolition of marriage value (see page 273) while landlords wanted a fixed 50/50 apportionment. As will be shown, a compromise has now been achieved.

The Commonhold and Leasehold Reform Act 2002 introduces a number of changes affecting enfranchisement and lease renewal, as set out in the table on pages 256–7.

The old law	The new law
Enfranchisement	
At least two-thirds of the flats in the building had to be owned by participating leaseholders.	Only half the flats in the building need to be owned by participating leaseholders.
At least half of the participating group had to satisfy a residence test.	Residence test is abolished.
In a few cases, a low rent test applied.	Low rent test is abolished.
The proportion of the building that could be occupied for non-residential purposes was a maximum 10%.	Non-residential proportion of the building can be up to 25%.
In a converted building, no requirement that the landlord must have been in occupation when the conversion took place.	The present landlord must have been the landlord when the conversion took place.
The freehold had to be purchased by a 'nominee purchaser'.	Nominee purchaser is replaced by a Right to Enfranchise (RTE) company (page 252) of which all participating leaseholders are members.
At least 50% of marriage value had to be paid by tenants and this was regardless of the unexpired term of their leases.	Where marriage value exists (page 273), it is divided equally between the landlord and the leaseholders in all cases. If the unexpired term of all the leases held by qualifying tenants exceeds 80 years, no marriage value is payable.
The freehold was valued on the date when the Leasehold Valuation Tribunal gave its decision.	The freehold is valued on the date on which the notice of claim (pages 266–7) is served.

The old law	The new law
Lease renewal	
A low rent test applied.	Low rent test is abolished.
At least 50% of marriage value had to be paid.	Where marriage value exists, it is divided equally between the landlord and the leaseholders in all cases. Although unlikely, if the existing lease has 80 years to run, no marriage value is payable.
As a residence test, the leaseholder had to have lived in the flat for the previous three years (or periods totalling three years in the last ten years).	The leaseholder must have held the lease for at least two years. Whether he or she has lived there is not relevant.
After the death of a leaseholder, his or her personal representatives could not buy a renewal because they did not satisfy the residence test.	Where deceased leaseholders would have been entitled to buy a new lease immediately before they died, their personal representatives will qualify for a period of one year after obtaining probate of the will, or letters of administration if the leaseholder died intestate.

Attractions of enfranchisement or renewal

There are a variety of reasons why long leaseholders might be tempted either to buy the landlord's freehold collectively or to take a new lease. As regards enfranchisement, the motives of the lease-holders are based largely on negative experiences with landlords. Enfranchisement offers leaseholders the following benefits.

- **Control** On purchasing the freehold they will, to most intents and purposes, own the building in which their flats are situated, albeit normally through a nominee company. This means that through their voting rights within the company they can exert control over repairs and maintenance of the property as well as the cost and quality of services provided to them. There will no longer be a conflict of interest between the landlord and the leaseholders as a body. Of course, disputes could arise between the tenants themselves.

- **Security** On enfranchisement, the tenants' RTE company will control the grant of any new leases in the block and will be able to renew the leases of the existing tenants at a reduced price. Once a renewed lease is next sold on, the individual tenant may make a substantial gain.

As regards the right to renew (which has proved to be the more popular option), the principal benefits for an individual tenant include the following:

- **Independence** Unlike enfranchisement, there is no need to obtain the co-operation of other tenants. If, however, a notice is later served for enfranchisement, the pre-existing lease renewal application is suspended.
- **Security** Taking a new lease avoids the problems associated with the old lease being a wasting asset (i.e. that it runs out). Further renewals can be obtained.
- **Management** The landlord (or where relevant the management company) will still continue to manage the building and there is no need for the tenant's involvement.
- **Cost** The price paid for renewal will tend to be similar to that payable for enfranchisement, but might be lower than the new lease will be worth in the longer term.
- **Procedure** The procedure is easier for renewal than for enfranchisement in that it is an individual making the running rather than a group. Moreover, the landlord is less likely to be opposed to renewal than to enfranchisement.

Conditions for qualification

Do the premises qualify?
Although both rights apply only to domestic residential premises, as regards collective enfranchisement the 1993 Act sets out more elaborate conditions to be satisfied. With renewal, the straightforward

rule is that, if the premises contain a 'flat', the right will apply to that flat. For these purposes, a 'flat' is defined as a separate and horizontally divided part within a building which is constructed or adapted for use as a dwelling (that is, a home); the definition includes a maisonette.

As regards the enfranchisement of blocks of flats, however, there are a number of further conditions to be met:

- the premises must be, in whole or in part, a self-contained building; that is, it must be structurally detached or, if not, be such that it could be redeveloped independently of other buildings
- the building must contain at least two flats
- those applying must represent at least half of the flats in the building.

The scheme applies even if there is a mixture of long and short leases. If the premises do not satisfy these conditions, a tenant may still be able to acquire a lease renewal.

Exceptions
Tenants cannot buy the freehold or renew the lease if, for example, the building is within the precinct boundary of a cathedral or on certain land owned by the National Trust or the Crown.

In addition, tenants cannot buy the freehold (but can renew their leases) if:

- there are no more than four flats in a converted property and the freeholder (or an adult member of his or her family) has lived in one of the flats as his or her only or main home for the last 12 months. This does not apply if the building was originally constructed as a block of flats. Moreover, the resident landlord must have carried out the conversion works
- more than 25 per cent of the internal floor area of the premises, excluding common parts, is used for non-residential purposes. Previously, many tenants who had flats above business premises were outside the enfranchisement scheme. By raising the ceiling to 25 per cent, the government is allowing enfranchisement of most blocks of four storeys or higher which contain shops.

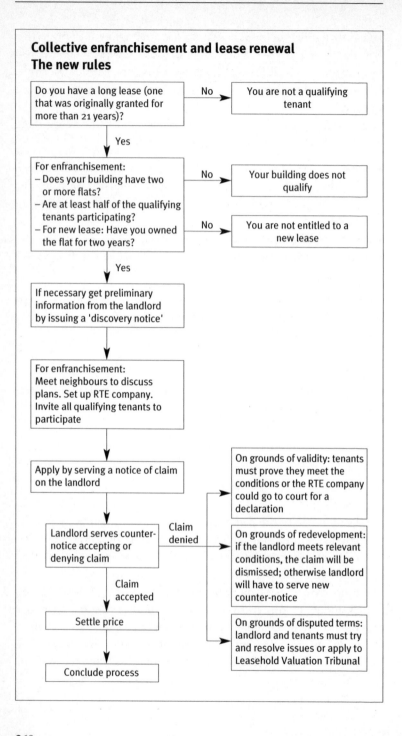

Collective enfranchisement and lease renewal
The new rules

Do you have a long lease (one that was originally granted for more than 21 years)? — **No** → You are not a qualifying tenant

↓ **Yes**

For enfranchisement:
– Does your building have two or more flats?
– Are at least half of the qualifying tenants participating?
– For new lease: Have you owned the flat for two years? — **No** → Your building does not qualify

— **No** → You are not entitled to a new lease

↓ **Yes**

If necessary get preliminary information from the landlord by issuing a 'discovery notice'

↓

For enfranchisement:
Meet neighbours to discuss plans. Set up RTE company. Invite all qualifying tenants to participate

↓

Apply by serving a notice of claim on the landlord

↓

Landlord serves counter-notice accepting or denying claim — **Claim denied** →

On grounds of validity: tenants must prove they meet the conditions or the RTE company could go to court for a declaration

On grounds of redevelopment: if the landlord meets relevant conditions, the claim will be dismissed; otherwise landlord will have to serve new counter-notice

On grounds of disputed terms: landlord and tenants must try and resolve issues or apply to Leasehold Valuation Tribunal

↓ **Claim accepted**

Settle price

↓

Conclude process

Is enfranchisement voluntary?

It is important to realise that no tenant can be forced – by either the landlord or other tenants – to participate in collective enfranchisement.

- A notice to start off the process for enfranchisement must come from the tenants – that is, the landlord cannot force them to buy the freehold.
- If a qualifying tenant decides he or she does not want to be a part of the process to buy the freehold, and the RTE company is successful in buying it, the company will then become his or her new landlord, and he or she will continue to be a tenant.
- A tenant can join in the process later, but if he or she is not an assignee of a participating tenant, the agreement of all the existing participating tenants might be required. If the tenant is the assignee of a participating tenant, he or she has the right to join in the process, but the RTE company must be notified within 28 days of the assignment of the desire to join in.

Do the tenants qualify?

Not all tenants have the right to join in and buy the freehold or to obtain a new lease. The scheme aims to ensure that only long lease-holders and genuine residents (as opposed to property investors) can qualify. Tenants of a charitable housing trust, tenants of business premises, and sub-tenants whose sub-leases were created in breach of a covenant in the head-lease fall outside the 1993 Act. Such tenants are disentitled and can claim neither right. Those who own qualifying leases on more than two flats in the building cannot be qualifying tenants for collective enfranchisement, but may be for lease renewal.

There can be only one qualifying tenant per flat. The 1993 Act states that joint tenants of a flat are to be regarded as one legal unit and that, when a long sub-lease has been granted, it is the sub-tenant who qualifies. In that case, the interest of the person sub-letting (that is, the sub-lessor) will be bought out.

EXAMPLE OF COLLECTIVE ENFRANCHISEMENT

Rivermead Court consists of six flats, all held on long leases for 99 years granted in 1980 at nominal ground rents. Four of the flats are occupied by their owners. The other two flats are sub-let on short-term tenancies.

Of the four owner-occupiers only three are interested in buying the freehold (the fourth is an elderly tenant who has no desire to get involved). In such a case, the qualifying conditions appear to be met:

- the three who wish to buy have long leases
- the block contains more than two flats, and no part of it is non-residential
- the participating tenants own, between them, at least half the flats in the block (that is, the three who want to buy own half of the six flats in the block).

Therefore by setting up an RTE company, the three tenants who want to buy can, if they wish, proceed. If they are successful, the fourth qualifying tenant (who did not participate) will now be the tenant of the RTE company.

Residence conditions

Under the new law, the residence test for collective enfranchisement is abolished. For lease renewals, the test is simplified so that now the tenant must have owned the flat for at least two years, and whether he or she has lived there is no longer of relevance.

Long lease

Generally speaking, a long lease is one which was originally granted for a period exceeding 21 years. It does not matter if the lease has now less than 21 years to run or the tenant claiming the right is not the original tenant.

> ## Collective enfranchisement: qualifying criteria at a glance
>
> Tenants can buy the freehold if the following conditions are satisfied:
>
> - they have long leases (leases originally granted for more than 21 years)
> - there are at least two flats in the building occupied by qualifying tenants
> - no more than 25 per cent of the building is occupied for non-residential purposes (for example, as offices)
> - the participating tenants hold leases of at least half the total number of flats in the block.

The key characters

RTE company

The Right to Enfranchise (RTE) company replaces the 'nominee purchaser' who had to act for the qualifying tenants under the old law. The new arrangements, introduced by the Commonhold and Leasehold Reform Act 2002, permit collective enfranchisement only to occur through the vehicle of a management company (the RTE company), because it proved unsuitable to allow this to happen by way of individuals, or a group of individuals, acting for the tenants. The RTE company is a private company limited by guarantee and its memorandum of association must state that its purpose is to exercise the right to collective enfranchisement. There has emerged a standardised, specifically designed company structure which is adequate to complete the enfranchisement process and subsequently manage the building. Share certificates are not issued and membership will pass automatically to any new purchaser of a flat. There is no exception in relation to small house conversions.

The membership of the RTE company is open to all qualifying tenants of flats contained in the building. To begin enfranchisement proceedings, at least half of the qualifying tenants must become members of the RTE company. Other tenants must be invited to join the company and, at least 14 days in advance, invited to participate in the enfranchisement process. This entitlement to join in ends on the expiry of six months following service of the initial notice (the notice of claim) or the date that contracts are exchanged with the landlord, whichever is the earlier. The formal invitation to participate will provide the details of the proposed enfranchisement, including an estimate of the cost involved. If a member does not participate in buying out the landlord's interest, that tenant's membership of the company will cease on the purchase of the freehold.

On taking the assignment of a lease from a participating member, a new tenant must notify the RTE company of the change within 28 days of the assignment, and can during that period also notify that he or she wishes to participate. If a participating member dies, his or her personal representatives automatically take over the membership but can notify the company that they do not wish to participate, at any time.

Reversioner (in enfranchisement)

The other party to the enfranchisement claim is the 'reversioner', usually the freeholder (landlord) of the premises. When the tenants apply to buy the freehold, it is the reversioner who must respond to the claim. If the freeholder cannot be found, the court can nominate any other intervening landlord (that is, a sub-lessor) to act in that capacity. Special provision now exists for when the freehold is owned by more than one person. This avoids the freeholder side-stepping the act by creating a 'flying freehold' of one flat in the block.

Although the reversioner represents the interests of any sub-lessors involved in the claim, those landlords can ask for a replacement to be appointed if the reversioner is unwilling to act, incapable or absent. They or the RTE company can also seek a replacement when it is believed that there is or is likely to be delay or default by the reversioner. In any event, any landlord may elect to deal directly with the RTE company and to be separately represented in proceedings.

Competent landlord (in lease renewal)

The claim for lease renewal is made against the tenant's immediate landlord provided that, if that landlord is also a tenant, he or she holds a sufficiently long lease from which the proposed new lease can be carved. For example, if a long sub-lease has been granted, the sub-tenant applies to the sub-lessor only if the latter has over 90 years of his or her own lease left to run. If not, the competent landlord will be the next landlord in the chain who does satisfy that condition or, if none, the freeholder. Once more there is a facility which deals with situations when the competent landlord cannot be found. The competent landlord has the ability to bind all other landlords, but they can elect for separate representation in the proceedings.

What is purchased?

Owing to the differences between buying the freehold and obtaining a new lease, the physical extent of the property bought and the nature of the interest acquired will vary.

On enfranchisement the purchase covers not only those flats let to the tenants, but also includes the freehold of the building and any ancillary property which is either 'appurtenant' to the leased areas (for example, garage, outhouse, garden or yard) or which constitutes common parts (for example, lifts, stairways, corridors and shared storage rooms).

Where sub-leases have been created, the interest of any intervening (that is, superior) leaseholder will, at additional cost, also be bought out.

Although the general rule is that the tenants decide what premises they want to buy, they can be required by the freeholder to purchase other parts which otherwise would be either of no practical use or benefit to the freeholder (or intervening landlord) or would be incapable of reasonable management or maintenance by that person.

With lease renewal, the position is more straightforward. The tenant will obtain a new lease of the flat together with, for example, any garage, store room, outbuildings, garden and yard belonging to, or usually enjoyed with, the flat and which are let to the tenant under the terms of the existing lease or by a separate letting. The landlord retains the freehold estate.

The procedure

A major feature of the enfranchisement and renewal processes is the service of written notices and counter-notices. Before proceedings are commenced, it is imperative that the qualifying tenants can identify the freeholder, any intervening landlords and, in the case of enfranchisement, other tenants and licensees of the premises or common parts.

Discovery notice

A tenant can request preliminary information from the landlord even before he or she gets any formal process under way. This is done by means of a discovery notice, which the landlord must reply to within 28 days. Such a notice could help a tenant to find out if his or her building fulfils the criteria for collective enfranchisement; whether there are other parties with an interest in parts of the premises, and if so their names and addresses; and whether there are any ongoing enfranchisement claims. The last of these is important for those who wish to renew their leases too. If the tenant seeks renewal and an enfranchisement claim has been issued, or is subsequently made before the new lease claim is settled, the new lease proceedings will be suspended until the freehold claim has been dealt with.

Dealing with neighbours

For collective enfranchisement, it is necessary that tenants join in the claim to buy the freehold, so there will need to be a meeting between the tenants. This should preferably be before the setting up of any company. The meeting should decide:

- whether the building satisfies the qualifying conditions
- how many tenants will participate in the claim (that is, qualifying tenants representing at least half the flats in the building)
- whom to employ as a surveyor or valuer
- how the finance is to be raised
- who is going to represent the tenants legally.

Notice of claim

The claim for a new lease or enfranchisement must be started by one of the participating tenants or, if it has been formed, the RTE company. This is done by serving on the competent landlord (new lease) or the reversioner (enfranchisement) an additional notice. For enfranchisement, the notice must:

- fully identify the qualifying tenants and their leases
- contain particulars identifying the participating tenants as having long leases
- name the RTE company
- give details of the property to be purchased and include a plan of the premises

- specify any leasehold interest which is to be purchased
- normally after a surveyor's valuation, suggest a purchase price for the entire transaction
- in the case of council tenants, provide particulars of the flats to be the subject of 'leaseback' (see below) to the council.

In the case of a new lease, the notice must:

- identify the tenant making the claim
- identify the flat concerned
- provide details of the tenant's lease
- specify the price to be paid
- suggest the terms of the new lease.

In both cases, the notice of claim must demonstrate also that the premises and the tenant(s) are within the scope of the 1993 Act and state a date, at least two months hence, by which time the recipient of the notice must respond by serving a counter-notice.

Counter-notice

The 1993 Act obliges the reversioner (enfranchisement) or the competent landlord (new lease) to give a counter-notice in response to the notice of claim, which must be served by the date specified in it. This counter-notice must either:

- accept the claim if appropriate, and suggest counter-proposals as to terms. Unless there is misrepresentation or concealment of a material fact, any acceptance of the claim is binding upon the reversioner/competent landlord; or
- state that the tenant(s) is (are) not qualified under the 1993 Act or that the claim will be opposed in court on the basis that the premises are intended for redevelopment (see pages 271–2).

Leaseback

As regards enfranchisement, the reversioner can obtain a 999-year leaseback (at a nominal ground rent) of those flats that are not occupied by the qualifying tenants (for example, unlet flats and business premises). In some circumstances (for example, where the landlord is a local authority or housing corporation) this leaseback is mandatory, while in others it is the reversioner's choice. The reversioner may then make a profit from any rent payable on those premises or any premium if the leases are sold. Nevertheless, taking a leaseback will reduce the price which the reversioner will receive for the freehold. The reversioner should take valuation advice before embarking on this course of action. Details of this must be included in the reversioner's counter-notice.

Non-service of counter-notice

If the counter-notice is not served within the time specified in the notice of claim, the RTE company (enfranchisement) or tenant (new lease) has a further six months to apply to the County Court for the terms of the transaction to be decided. Before this can occur, however, the court must be satisfied that the tenant(s) can make a valid claim under the 1993 Act and that the other party has been served with the appropriate notices. The court can then, after the expiry of a further two months, make an order either vesting the freehold in the purchaser or granting a new lease, as appropriate.

Renewing your lease: the process in outline

Most tenants under a long lease and who satisfy the ownership test can apply to renew their lease at any time while the long lease is still in existence. The process will involve:

- serving a discovery notice asking for information about the free-holder and any intervening landlords
- giving initial notice of your intention (notice of claim) to any intervening landlord whose own lease is longer than yours by 90 years or, if none, to the freeholder. The notice must contain your details, give the price you want to pay, outline any new terms sought and specify a date at least two months after the date of your notice, by which the landlord is to serve a counter-notice
- receiving a counter-notice from the landlord admitting or denying your right to a new lease and accepting or rejecting the terms suggested. If the landlord intends to oppose your right on the basis of redevelopment this must be stated in the counter-notice.

You have at least two months to reach an agreement with your landlord. If you cannot agree, you may apply to the local Leasehold Valuation Tribunal for the dispute to be settled.

Concluding the enfranchisement process

The RTE company and the freeholder are allowed a period of time to agree the terms for buying the freehold. If agreement is not forthcoming, either party is free to refer the matter to the Leasehold Valuation Tribunal*. Applications to the tribunal must be made within six months of the freeholder's counter-notice, otherwise the application for enfranchisement is deemed to be withdrawn. The tenants do not have to pay the landlord's costs incurred on an application to the tribunal (see page 274). If terms are agreed, the parties must enter into a written contract within two months.

Change of tenant

While the claim is ongoing, it is possible that a tenant may sell the lease, become bankrupt or die. The 1993 Act covers such situations in that it permits the new tenant, trustee in bankruptcy or personal representative to stand in the shoes of the previous tenant. Although this occurs automatically when the claim is for a new lease, as regards enfranchisement different rules operate: the new tenant or the trustee must notify the RTE company of the change within 28 days following the assignment of the lease. If the tenant dies during the process, the deceased's personal representative automatically becomes the participating tenant unless he or she chooses otherwise and notifies the RTE company at any time.

When the freehold has been purchased by an RTE company, a share in the company will pass to any new tenant. The company will be set up such that it allows only qualifying tenants to be members.

Change of heart

Once the process for either collective enfranchisement or lease renewal is initiated, the application can be withdrawn and an end put to the proceedings at any time. The means of achieving this, however, varies according to which right was claimed. In the case of a new lease, the tenant can serve a notice of withdrawal on the landlord(s) at any time before a new lease is granted. As regards enfranchisement, the participating tenants may withdraw their claim by serving a withdrawal notice on the reversioner and any other relevant landlord involved in the proceedings. This notice must be served before a binding contract has been entered into (or a vesting order – see page 272 – has been made). In enfranchisement, if one tenant refuses to proceed, with the result that the total number of flats together falls short of the qualifying number required, the whole process will fail. The other tenants may have to content themselves with applying for a renewal of their individual leases.

In both situations (and until withdrawal) the claimant(s) remain jointly and individually liable for the costs incurred by the other side (see page 274). A claim can be deemed withdrawn when the claimant(s) fail to adhere to the time limits and procedures set out in the 1993 Act. If withdrawal occurs, no new claim can be entertained for 12 months.

In relation to enfranchisement, it may be that a qualifying tenant who had chosen originally not to participate has subsequently sought to join in. A tenant has a right to join in within six months of the service of the notice of claim or until exchange of contracts, whichever is earlier. If the tenant does not join in, when the freehold is bought he or she will be in the same position as before, but with a different landlord.

Reasons for refusal of a claim

Although it is not possible to contract out of the 1993 Act, there are several ways in which a reversioner or competent landlord can attempt to prevent the enfranchisement or renewal claim proceeding either at all or, at the least, on the terms proposed.

Questioning status

The reversioner or competent landlord could wish to challenge the status of the tenant(s). In the context of enfranchisement, this is helped by the right of the reversioner, exercisable within 21 days of the tenants' claim, to serve a counter-notice on the RTE company requesting that the leasehold title of certain named tenant(s) be proved. The RTE company has a further 21 days to respond and, on failure to do so, if the named tenant(s) are crucial to the qualifying number count, the notice of claim is deemed to be withdrawn; this right to respond, and potential trap, does not apply to leaseholders claiming a renewal.

If a challenge to status is made, the RTE company (enfranchisement) or the competent landlord (new lease) is entitled to apply to the County Court, within two months of the counter-notice, for a declaration as to the validity or otherwise of the claim. If the court is satisfied as to the qualifying status of the tenants, it must confirm the validity of the notice of claim and will usually require the reversioner or the competent landlord to issue a further counter-notice admitting the right and containing the landlord's proposals. Where the claim is held to be invalid, the claim simply ceases to have effect.

Redevelopment

Another means by which the claim for enfranchisement or renewal can be defeated arises when the landlord shows a definite intention to redevelop the whole or a substantial part of the premises. There are, however, conditions attached to this method of opposition and these make it difficult to establish.

- Where enfranchisement is sought, at least two-thirds of all long leases of flats in the premises must be due to terminate within five years of the notice of claim.
- For lease renewal, it is necessary that the tenant's existing lease will terminate within five years of the notice of claim for a new lease. If this time element is not satisfied, the landlord can make an application to court which, although not preventing renewal, can operate to terminate the new lease after it has been granted. The landlord can make this latter application within 12 months of the time the former lease would have ended or within five years of the end date of the new lease. The tenant will be able to obtain compensation for the loss of the flat.
- The reversioner or competent landlord must intend to demolish, reconstruct or carry out substantial works of construction on the premises which are intended to be bought (enfranchisement) or in which the tenant's flat is contained (new lease).
- The reversioner or competent landlord must demonstrate that the works could not reasonably be carried out without obtaining possession of the flats (enfranchisement) or flat (new lease).

If these conditions are satisfied, the reversioner or competent landlord can apply to the court, within two months of the service of the counter-notice, for the claim of the tenant(s) to be dismissed. Where it is stated in the counter-notice that there was an intention to develop but the intention cannot be proved, the original counter-notice is invalid and a replacement will need to be served by a date specified by the court. Similarly, a new counter-notice is required if the reversioner or competent landlord either fails to make an application to the court or withdraws such an application.

Disputing the terms

The third approach is to allow the claim, but to challenge the terms of the proposed bargain. Within two and six months from the service of an effective counter-notice, and where the terms of the transaction have not been settled, either party may apply to the Leasehold Valuation Tribunal (LVT) for any outstanding matters to be decided. The tribunal has the power to make an order which binds both parties. When the terms are agreed or determined by the tribunal, and either a binding contract is not entered (enfranchisement) or a new lease is not granted, within two months of that agreement or order the tribunal has the power to make a 'vesting order' (equivalent to a binding contract). This order then enables the purchaser to pay the appropriate purchase price to the court in return for the court executing the conveyance of the freehold or a new lease.

Valuation and costs

Following service of the notice of claim, the reversioner, competent landlord and any other affected landlord are given a statutory right of access to the flats in order to obtain an independent valuation. The RTE company is also awarded the right to enter the premises (including appurtenant property, common parts and the flats of non-participating tenants) for valuation purposes provided that it is reasonable and relates to the proceedings. These rights are exercisable at any reasonable time provided at least three days' notice is given to the occupier.

Ascertaining the price

The price will often be the deciding factor as to whether collective enfranchisement (or lease renewal) is sought. It is preferable that the parties involved agree on the price of the freehold or the new lease. However, if agreement is not achieved, the price will be calculated by the LVT according to elaborate formulae prescribed in the 1993 Act. The valuation date for both enfranchisement and lease renewal is as at the time the notice of claim is served.

A notice of claim that specifies a nominal purchase price will be invalid. Enfranchisement, in particular, will not come cheaply. Unlike the Leasehold Reform Act 1967 which governs leases of houses, there is no discount for the purchasing tenants. In essence, the calculated price will represent the market value of the freehold, disregarding the effect that the ongoing enfranchisement proceedings will have on it or the value of the new lease to a willing purchaser. The freeholder is entitled also to 'marriage value' (see below). In some cases, compensation will be payable to the landlord for what is called 'severance' and other losses.

Marriage value

As mentioned, the claimant(s) will have to pay 50 per cent of what is termed 'marriage value' and this can add substantially to the purchase price. The proportional share is fixed at 50 per cent in all cases. If the leases have more than 80 years to run, however, marriage value is disregarded.

Marriage value is a difficult concept which, as regards enfranchisement, reflects the net increase in value to the buying tenants of 'marrying' the leasehold and freehold estates. This necessitates a valuation of the leaseholders' interest (ever-diminishing as time passes) and balancing that against the increased value of the freehold. Clearly, the freehold and leasehold estates will be worth more as one entity than when owned by different persons (because, for example, the flat-owners could now grant themselves new leases on more favourable terms than before without the payment of a capital premium or any restriction on the length of the term). If property values are high and the leases in the block are down to their last 60 years or so, this marriage value may run into thousands of pounds. Conversely, if the leases have longer terms left to run, the marriage value will be depressed.

In the context of a new lease, marriage value is the difference in value between the interests of the parties under the current lease and what they will be when a new lease is granted. If the existing lease has over 80 years to run, however, marriage value becomes irrelevant.

Other sums

In addition, if the value of other property near the premises and belonging to the reversioner/competent landlord is diminished, the tenant(s) will be obliged to pay 'reasonable' compensation to that person. Compensation for any unrealised development value ('severance') is limited to any other property of the landlord, not the premises which are the subject of collective enfranchisement. This is sometimes called 'injurious affection'.

As regards any intermediate leasehold interests (held by sub-lessors) which are acquired, a separate price will be paid for each. Generally, the calculation will be based on the same footing as the freehold. Nevertheless, a complicated mathematical formula is specified as regards 'minor' intermediate leases which have no real market value.

Costs

It is the RTE company (enfranchisement) or the tenant (new lease) who must discharge the reversioner's/landlord's legal and valuation expenses, reasonably incurred in connection with the claim. The costs must be paid even if the claim is abandoned. This does not, however, extend to costs associated with proceedings before the LVT. Until the purchase price is paid and costs discharged, the seller retains a charge over the property for those amounts.

Leasehold Valuation Tribunals

The LVT is an independent local body whose members are drawn from valuers, lawyers and the general public. Their hearings are less formal than court proceedings.

There are two types of LVT – one dealing with service charges, the other with enfranchisement matters. Some disputes occurring during the enfranchisement process are dealt with by the court (for example, those concerning the validity of a notice or the claim). Most disputes, however, are dealt with by the LVT. Either party may then appeal with permission to the Lands Tribunal. The Lands Tribunal and the LVT have the power to award reasonable costs, but only when one party has acted improperly in connection with the appeal.

A major criticism of the current procedure concerns the time it can take (particularly in London) for cases to reach a hearing. There are also claims of inconsistencies between the decisions of different LVTs. The government intends to speed up the process by simplifying the application forms, setting time limits on cases and paving the way for single-member tribunals. Currently, one-member tribunals can only be used when an oral hearing is dispensed with. Better training, more guidance and a system of monitoring performance of individual members of the tribunal are to be introduced.

In addition, tenants often feel disadvantaged because of their landlord's ability to employ specialist and expensive advisers and the confrontational tactics adopted by them. Landlords commonly put pressure on the tenants by threatening to appeal – the fear of the associated increased costs sometimes persuades the tenants to withdraw their claim. In order to minimise this form of pressure, the Commonhold and Leasehold Reform Act 2002 allows appeals to the Lands Tribunal only with the consent of the LVT or Lands Tribunal. Such consent is to be given only where the LVT has clearly erred or where the case invokes important issues of principle.

Applying to an LVT

- You do not have to be represented by a lawyer, but professional assistance is recommended.
- If you represent yourself, you will have to present arguments and evidence in support of your case.
- A pre-trial review of the case may be held where the tribunal gives directions as to filing of evidence, statements and documents, and questions are asked about which (if any) legal authorities the parties are going to rely upon.
- A failure to comply with directions may result in evidence being inadmissible or, in the case of the applicant, the application being dismissed.
- The LVT's decision is, subject to limited rights to appeal to the Lands Tribunal, final and enforceable.
- Each party will normally pay its own costs of appearing before the LVT.

Estate management schemes

Generally, on enfranchisement, the flat-owners will themselves take over responsibility for the management of the block. The building may, however, be within the area of an estate management scheme. Such a scheme allows the landlord to retain management control after selling the freehold to the tenants. A scheme is set up for an area where properties are let by the same landlord, and the basic aim of the scheme is to ensure that the appearance and quality of the area are maintained. Nevertheless, a scheme might provide solely for the upkeep of communal gardens and other common areas. If your building is within an estate management scheme, enfranchisement can still go ahead, but afterwards the building will still be subject to the scheme. The tenants will pay a service charge to the manager much the same as before. Following the Commonhold and Leasehold Reform Act 2002, this can now be challenged on the ground of unreasonableness. If an application for a scheme has been made to the Leasehold Valuation Tribunal the enfranchisement will be stalled until the application has been determined. It does not matter whether the landlord's application is made before or after the service of your notice of claim.

The scheme must, however, be in the 'general interest' and be required in order to maintain standards of appearance and amenity and to regulate development. In deciding whether to approve the scheme, the tribunal must take on board such matters as fairness, reasonableness, architectural and historical values, neighbouring areas and general circumstances. Often it will be in the tenants' interests for the former landlord to continue to apply organisational ability and experience in maintaining the quality of such property. If the tenants object they can make representations to the LVT.

Tactics used by landlords

It has become clear that some landlords are attempting either to prevent or to dissuade their tenants from exercising the right to buy the freehold. Some of the tactics used by them are discussed below.

First, landlords may routinely deny the validity of the claim by, for example, alleging that the premises or the tenants do not qualify. This prolongs the procedure and brings with it added costs.

Second, landlords may decline to negotiate and threaten a drawn-out and expensive hearing before the LVT.

Third, landlords anticipating an imminent claim may engage in major works on the premises which drain any sinking funds and are claimable under the service charges from the tenants. This could ensure that the tenants have depleted funds and reduced incentives to proceed.

Fourth, another tactic used by landlords – selling the freehold to a third-party developer – is leading in many cases to tenants being forced to pay extremely high service charges, thereby again reducing their chances of having enough funds to participate in enfranchisement.

Chapter 19

Private options and the statutory right of first refusal

Options and pre-emptions

A tenant may wish to renew his or her lease or buy the freehold, but not qualify under the 1993 legislation (see Chapter 18). This tenant may have an alternative: the lease to his or her flat may contain a clause which allows an option to renew a long lease at the end of its term or to buy the landlord's freehold. Such options are not subject to the rigorous requirements and restrictions of the 1993 Act. The tenant might be given the right of first refusal (pre-emption) if the freehold is subsequently put on the market. As will be shown, there exists, in some situations, a statutory right of first refusal under the Landlord and Tenant Act 1987.

If not expressly contained in the lease, the option or right may be agreed separately between the parties in a distinct written contract.

Private options

Options to renew a lease

The presence of such an option can offer the tenant a valuable right in circumstances where he or she does not qualify under the 1993 Act. The option, as with all other aspects of the lease, should be drafted carefully; the buyer should check that the following matters are made clear:

- **The time at which it may be exercised** Normally, the option would be made exercisable within a few months before the original lease is to end. It is possible that a specific date might be used as an alternative. Any time limits imposed must be strictly adhered to unless the lease provides otherwise. An option may be lost once the time stipulated for its exercise has passed.

- **The manner of its exercise** The option is usually made exercisable by notice in writing served on the landlord. No set form for this notice will be required.

- **The conditions that the tenant must fulfil** It may be that the option requires that, at the time the notice is served, the tenant has paid all the rent and observed all the covenants. If so, a breach of any covenant (no matter how minor) will prevent the tenant from exercising the option.

- **The terms of the new lease** Normally, the new lease will (except from containing an option to renew) be the same as the old one. The option will usually provide that the tenant will pay the landlord's costs connected with the granting of the new lease.

Once created, the option contractually binds the landlord. However, the problem arises when the landlord sells the freehold to a third party and the buyer refuses to acknowledge the tenant's option. While the tenant can sue the former landlord for breach of contract, this may not be the ideal remedy for a tenant who really wants a new lease of the flat. The tenant should, therefore, protect the option by the entry of a land charge (unregistered land) or a notice (registered land). Consult a solicitor for advice. If this occurs, the tenant will be able to enforce the option against the new freeholder.

Private options to buy the freehold

An option to buy the landlord's freehold is regarded as a separate agreement rather than a term of the lease. The original landlord will remain under the contractual obligation to grant the option and can, if relevant, be sued for damages for breach of contract. This remains so even if the landlord has sold the freehold to a third party. The landlord can avoid this liability by inserting a clause into the lease that the option shall become void unless protected by registration within a specified period. Registration, as demonstrated above, will also ensure that a buyer of the freehold is bound by the tenant's rights.

Two issues are usually of importance in this type of option: who may exercise the option and for how long does it remain open? Much turns on the wording and expression of the clause itself and the option can be exercised only in strict accordance with its terms. Accordingly, the option should state how it is to be exercised, whether written notice has to be given by the tenant, and the time frame within which it is to be exercised. Normally, the option will also state how the purchase price is to be ascertained (for example, a reference to market value). As with the option to renew, the option to purchase can be made conditional upon all the terms of the lease having been performed by the tenant.

Private right of pre-emption

The landlord may not be prepared to grant the tenant the future right to buy the freehold, but may instead offer the tenant first refusal when the freehold is to be next sold. The initiative clearly remains with the landlord. If and when the landlord decides to sell, the tenant will have to be notified and given the opportunity to buy.

The right of pre-emption (first refusal) may provide that the landlord must offer the freehold at a price stated in the lease or at a sum 'to be agreed'. The tenant must then decide whether or not to accept the offer. If the sum is 'to be agreed', the landlord has to accept a *bona fide* bid which reflects current market values. The right may, on the other hand, be drafted in such a way as to make the tenant responsible for offering a price, leaving the landlord to decide whether to accept it. In either case, if a contract is not concluded, the landlord will be able to sell on the freehold to someone else.

Problems that sometimes arise focus upon when the landlord is supposed to notify the tenant, and whether the right exists beyond the first occasion that the freehold is offered to the tenant. These points should be spelled out in the lease contract.

Once the right has been created, the issue arises as to when it will bind third-party buyers. In unregistered land, the buyer will be bound by the tenant's right only if the buyer or agent (for example, solicitor) knew or ought to have known of its existence. In registered land, the right can now be protected by the entry of a notice on the Land Register. In any event, if the tenant is in actual occupation of the flat, the right is protected as an 'overriding interest' and any buyer will then buy the freehold subject to it.

Statutory option

First refusal: the statutory right

The Landlord and Tenant Act 1987 gives to the tenants a right of first refusal when the landlord intends to sell the freehold of a block of flats. Under the Act the landlord has to offer the right of first

---

Statutory right of first refusal: standard procedure

The most common way of selling property is when the conveyance is preceded by a contract. If the landlord intends to sell the freehold in this manner, the procedure is as follows:

- The landlord must serve a notice on at least 90 per cent of the qualifying tenants stating the proposed terms of sale.
- The landlord's notice must give the qualifying tenants an initial period of two months in which more than 50 per cent of them may accept by serving an acceptance notice on the landlord.
- The landlord's notice must give a further extension of at least two months within which the tenants can organise themselves financially and nominate a purchaser.
- The nominated purchaser might be either a company set up by the tenants, a third party or (up to four of) the tenants themselves.
- Once notified of the nominated purchaser, the landlord must send a contract within one month of the notification.
- The nominated purchaser then has two months in which to sign the contract and to pay the deposit (maximum 10 per cent of the agreed price).
- The landlord has seven days from the receipt of the signed contract to exchange contracts or to withdraw; the tenants can also withdraw, until the contract is entered. The withdrawing party will be liable to pay the other party's costs.
- If the tenants withdraw, the landlord has a period of 12 months within which to sell on the open market at the same terms as offered to the tenants.

---

refusal to all the tenants. The tenants can then accept or reject this offer. This does not, however, take precedence over the right of first refusal (pre-emption) given to any one individual tenant by his or her lease. The essential feature of the statutory right is that the landlord cannot dispose of the premises unless a notice has previously been served on the 'qualifying tenants' offering them first refusal. The Act extends only to certain types of property, benefits a limited number of tenants and can be side-stepped easily by landlords. The conditions imposed are less stringent than those under the 1993 Act (as regards collective enfranchisement, see Chapter 18) because under the latter the sale may be against the freeholder's wishes, whereas under the 1987 Act the sale is voluntary.

Although simplified in 1996, the statutory right of first refusal has not proved popular. The Act is still recognised as being poorly drafted, complicated and confusing. Many tenants are unaware of the law and it is not always easy to raise the necessary finance and to act within the time limits. The procedure is also time-consuming and can be stressful. Traditionally, many landlords tend to sell their properties at auction for speed and convenience. Often the tenants are not aware of the auction and lose the chance to buy the freehold. To counter this, it is made a criminal offence (maximum fine £5,000) for the landlord to dispose of the freehold without first giving the tenants the opportunity to buy. The new landlord is, moreover, obliged to notify the tenants of the purchase. A failure to do so is also made a criminal offence (maximum fine £2,500). The tenants then have the right to buy the freehold back from the new landlord on the same terms as he or she acquired it. The time limits for tenants to exercise this right do not start until they have been notified of the sale.

The prospective freehold purchaser
As the 1987 Act ensures that the tenants' right to buy the freehold is potentially binding on any other purchaser and, because there are criminal sanctions if the new purchaser does not inform the tenants of the purchase, the Act affords a prospective purchaser of the freehold some protection. The intended purchaser can serve a notice on at least 80 per cent of tenants of flats (whether held by qualifying tenants or not), informing them of the terms of the proposed sale and asking whether the landlord has offered them

first refusal. If the landlord has not done so, the notice must ask whether the tenants wish to exercise their statutory right. Unless at least 50 per cent of the tenants who have received the purchaser's notice reply within two months (or, if more than 50 per cent reply, and do not wish to exercise the right), the prospective purchaser may treat the premises as being free of the tenants' right to buy.

Qualifying conditions

The following conditions must be satisfied before tenants can claim rights under the 1987 Act:

- the premises in which the flats are situated must fall within the scope of the Act
- the landlord must not be an exempt landlord
- the tenants must be qualifying tenants
- the landlord must be intending to dispose of the freehold.

The premises

The premises must consist of a building which is divided into at least two flats occupied by qualifying tenants. No more than 50 per cent of the floor space (discounting common parts) can be used for non-residential purposes and the number of flats held by qualifying tenants must exceed 50 per cent of the total number of flats.

The landlord

The landlord must not be exempt – for example, he or she must not be a resident or public-sector landlord. For these purposes, a resident landlord is one who lives in another part of the same building as his or her only or main home. The landlord must have lived there for the preceding 12 months and the premises must not be a purpose-built block.

Qualifying tenants

Many tenants of flats have the right collectively to purchase their landlord's interest in the block when the landlord wishes to sell it on the open market. The landlord has to give the tenants the opportunity to buy the freehold (that is, first refusal) before selling it elsewhere. It is a criminal offence for the landlord to fail to do what is required by the 1987 Act.

All residential tenants qualify unless the tenancy falls into one of the following categories:

- a protected shorthold tenancy
- a business tenancy
- a tenancy terminable on the ending of employment
- an assured tenancy.

Relevant disposal

This includes any disposal by the landlord of any interest in the block except the grant of a lease or mortgage, transfer to charity or family, transfer to a trustee in bankruptcy or liquidation, disposal within a group of companies (provided that the companies have been associated for at least two years), and disposal to the Crown or subsequent to a compulsory purchase order. The premises to be disposed of may be all or part of a building. A relevant disposal normally occurs when contracts are exchanged. If a transaction reaches that point without first refusal being offered to the tenants, the landlord will have committed a criminal offence.

If the landlord intends to make a relevant disposal, he or she must first serve a notice on at least 90 per cent of the qualifying tenants. The notice must detail the terms of the proposed transaction and constitute an offer to sell to the tenants on the same terms. More than 50 per cent of the qualifying tenants must accept the offer within the period stated in the notice (not less than two months). Irrespective of what the tenants want, the landlord can then change his or her mind and serve a notice stating that the disposal is no longer to occur. Otherwise, a contract will be sent to the tenants' nominee and the latter has two months within which to exchange contracts.

The nightmare scenario – and solutions

When a landlord sells the freehold to a third party (that is, not to the tenants, and usually by auction), it is often the case that the buyer wants to make as much money as possible from the property. One tactic of abuse is to carry out unnecessary and expensive repairs to the building, charge high management fees and incur legal and surveying expenses or inflated insurance premiums (see Chapter 12), and then bill the tenants for this under the service charge. The tenants may not be able to afford the payments and may be driven to taking out a loan to cover the debt.

Auction sales

Since 1996, a new procedure has allowed landlords to obtain the market price for their property. It operates by enabling landlords to sell their property at auction, and allowing the tenants' nominated purchaser to take the place of the successful bidder at the auction. At the auction, the auctioneer will make it clear that there is a possible risk of first refusal which might be exercised by the tenants. The steps are as follows:

- The landlord must serve a notice on at least 90 per cent of the qualifying tenants between four and six months before the auction.
- The notice must give an initial period of at least two months for more than 50 per cent of the qualifying tenants to accept. This initial period must end at least two months before the auction.
- The notice must give a further period of at least 28 days for the tenants to nominate a purchaser. This further period must end at least 28 days before the auction.
- If the information was not given in the initial notice, the tenants must be notified of the time and the place of the auction at least 28 days before it occurs.
- If the tenants accept the landlord's offer, they have 28 days in which to organise themselves financially and to nominate a person to act as purchaser.
- The nominated person then serves a notice on the landlord at least 28 days before the auction, electing to proceed.
- The successful bidder will enter a conditional contract with the landlord and a copy of this must be sent to the nominated person within seven days of the auction.
- The nominated person then has 28 days to accept the terms of the contract and take the place of the successful bidder.
- Completion cannot be less than 28 days after acceptance and either party has the right to withdraw.
- If the tenants withdraw, the landlord is free, if necessary, to sell at auction for a period of 12 months without consulting the tenants.

The unscrupulous landlord may then continue in the same vein until the tenant can no longer afford to pay or even borrow the necessary sums. The landlord might then try to forfeit the lease (but not if the service charge is disputed) and, if successful, can sell the flat on to a new buyer and keep the proceeds of sale. If the flat-owner had bought with the aid of a mortgage, the lender will normally avoid forfeiture (and thereby save its security for the loan) by paying the landlord what the tenant owes, and adding the sum to the mortgage debt. In such a case the tenant may not be able to pay the increased mortgage repayments and, eventually, it might be the lender who sells the flat in order to recoup its loan (see Chapter 4). The lender will then continue to pursue the borrower for any amounts still outstanding. Meanwhile the landlord has a much-improved building following the expensive repairs carried out and still receives ground rents.

Tenants who find themselves in this situation have some legal rights under the Landlord and Tenant Acts of 1985 and 1987 to challenge the service charge bill before the Leasehold Valuation Tribunal and to apply to the court for the appointment of a manager to run the property (see Chapter 15). These rights have been strengthened by the Housing Act 1996 and are extended further in the Commonhold and Leasehold Reform Act 2002. This route is, however, costly and time-consuming, and will normally require the services of a solicitor. Tenants will still be able, in theory, to buy out the landlord's freehold under the 1993 Act, but in practice are likely to be unable to get together the necessary finance.

It should be pointed out that although such a nightmare scenario could – and does – occur, not all landlords are unscrupulous. Moreover, organisations such as the Leasehold Advisory Service★ and the Coalition for the Abolition of Residential Leasehold (CARL)★ campaign for changes to the law in favour of leaseholders, and offer advice to tenants facing the kind of abuses described above. The government is still considering ways of increasing protection for leaseholders from the more ruthless landlords, but recent reforms have gone some way towards minimising this sort of abuse.

In the long term, however, commonhold – whereby tenants buy the freehold of individual flats, thus doing away with leases and landlords (see Chapter 2) – is the most beneficial measure for flat-owners.

Chapter 20

The right to buy and rent-to-mortgage

The right to buy council houses and flats at a discount is similar to leasehold enfranchisement in the private sector (see Chapter 18), but has proved more popular. Over 1.5 million council tenants have now become owner-occupiers (more than 200,000 of them in flats). The idea is that the right to buy ensures the wider spread of wealth through society, encourages the desire to improve and modernise property, allows an inheritance to be passed to future generations and stimulates independence and self-reliance. Critics of the system might argue that, when assessed against the existing background of an urgent need for inexpensive, good-quality rented accommodation, the depletion of public housing stock is to the disadvantage of the most needy. Moreover, in practice some purchasers have found that because of design defects in their flats, they have become saddled with virtually worthless properties or face huge service charge demands. The government intends to assist these unfortunate buyers (see page 295).

The Leasehold Reform, Housing and Urban Development Act 1993 abolished the council tenant's rights to a mortgage and to postpone completion of the conveyancing process until finance was arranged, and (while preserving existing ones) the concept of a shared-ownership lease. The latter was a scheme whereby the tenant paid a capital sum to buy a portion (at least 50 per cent) of the lease and retained the right to buy successive portions (in blocks of 12½ per cent) until the entire lease was acquired. This 'staircasing' had not proved popular with potential buyers. Instead, there is now a new scheme and with it a new right to acquire on rent-to-mortgage terms. This will be considered later in the chapter. Some changes restricting eligibility under the right-to-buy scheme are to be introduced in the Housing Act 2003. It is unclear, however, when these changes will actually be implemented.

The right to buy

The Housing Act 1985 confers on certain 'secure' tenants the rights to buy the freehold of their houses or to take long leases of their flats at a ground rent not exceeding £10 per year. A secure tenant is generally a council tenant who has the benefit of residential security offered (to renting periodic tenants) by the Act. The right to buy also extends to property let by the Commission for New Towns, housing action trusts and various other registered social landlords.

Normally the duration of any long lease granted will be 125 years, but in two situations the term can be shorter:

- where the landlord does not own the freehold and merely has a leasehold estate for less than 125 years, in which case it can grant to the tenant a lease which is only as long as its own, less five days
- where there is a block of flats and one (or more) of those flats has been sold since 8 August 1980, in which case the landlord can grant a long lease, but only for as long as the period that remains unexpired under the first long lease granted after 8 August. For example, if the first flat in the block was sold in 1981 on a 125-year lease, a flat sold in 1982 would be granted a lease for 124 years. Accordingly, if a long lease was granted in 1995, it would be for a term of 111 years.

Who can buy?

The tenant must have been the secure tenant of a public-sector landlord for at least two years, or for periods amounting to two years, before the right to buy arises. The government is to raise this period to five years. A secure tenant whose property transfers to a non-right-to-buy landlord has a 'preserved right to buy', which is, essentially, the same as the main right to buy. (For the differences see page 295.) This is important where a local authority housing estate is transferred to another social landlord. Tenants of registered social landlords who fall outside the right-to-buy scheme now have a right to acquire their property on rent-to-mortgage terms under the Housing Act 1996.

A wise buy?

Before going ahead and buying your council flat, it is sensible to make a number of enquiries:

- Speak to the landlord authority about service charges and ask whether there are any future repair/maintenance plans.
- Find out whether there is a leaseholders' or residents' association operating in the block or on the estate.
- Ask the landlord whether it would grant you a mortgage.
- Ask a high-street lender whether it would readily give you a mortgage on the flat.
- Talk to current occupiers of flats in the block/estate and see if they have experienced difficulties in selling their flats.
- Speak to local estate agents to find out whether flats in the area sell easily; and how this might be affected by a change in the housing market.

The provisions concerning what constitutes the qualifying period are complex, but it is clear that the tenant need not necessarily have lived in one property or have kept to the same landlord during the qualifying period. The two years' occupation does not have to be

So who does buy?

Recent government research demonstrates that:

- 81 per cent of buyers are in households with four persons or fewer
- 35 per cent of buyers are two-parent families and 10 per cent are one-parent families
- 39 per cent of buyers are aged from 35 to 44 years
- 79 per cent of buyers are white
- 59 per cent of buyers are in households where at least one member is in employment
- 10 per cent of buyers are retired
- 19 per cent of buyers are in households where someone is disabled or suffering from a long-term illness.

continuous and a number of shorter periods of occupation as a secure tenant can be added together. Hence a person who, at some stage in the past, had been a secure tenant for the necessary length of time can exercise the right to buy when next living in public-sector property. Subject to certain conditions, a joint tenant, spouse, parent or child (over 16) of a secure tenant, having lived in the property for the two-year period, will also satisfy the criterion to qualify as a tenant. If the flat is to be purchased jointly, only one of the buyers needs to satisfy the time requirement.

Excluded property

The right to buy extends generally to both houses and flats. Certain types of property are, however, excluded from the Act. Among the categories of excluded property are those where the landlord is a charitable housing trust or co-operative housing association. Temporary housing about to be developed also falls outside the scheme. Also outside the right-to-buy provisions are those prop-erties which have been modified for occupation by physically disabled persons. The right, moreover, does not extend to property which is particularly suitable for occupation by pensioners and which has been let in the past to either a pensioner or physically disabled person. Similarly, the Act prohibits sale to a tenant who is bankrupt or against whom a court order for possession has been granted to the landlord. A tenant who has obtained the house or flat in consequence of employment (for example, a caretaker of a school) also falls outside the right-to-buy scheme.

Special property

On the sale of a flat situated in a designated rural area (at the time of writing this includes the Ribble Valley), the local authority may insert into the lease:

- a covenant requiring its consent to any further sale. This consent cannot be withheld if the purchaser has lived or worked in the designated area for the preceding three years
- a right of first refusal if consent is applied for.

Price and discount

The tenant will pay the market value of the property, less any discount. The property is valued at the time the right is exercised. On the grant of a long lease, the valuation is of a flat with vacant possession (that is, as if it was unoccupied) and with a ground rent of £10 per year. The valuation disregards any improvements made by the tenant and any failure to keep the flat in good internal repair. The landlord carries out the valuation, but the tenant has the right to appeal to the district valuer if there is any disagreement. The district valuer's decision is final.

The secure tenant will buy the property with a discount which is determined by the length of the secure tenancy and whether it is a flat or a house which is being bought. A preferential discount has been introduced in relation to flats in order to encourage more purchasers. The calculation of the discount for a flat is 44 per cent of its market value and, when the purchaser has been a secure tenant for over three years, an additional 2 per cent discount for each year as a secure tenant. There is a maximum ceiling of 70 per cent discount (that is, after 15 years' residence), and the discount can never exceed set sums which change from time to time.

The government has recently reduced the maximum discount cash limit and this will now vary across the nine government office regions. For example, in London and the south east it is £16,000; in the north east it is £22,000. The lower maximum is designed to operate in areas where there is pressure on the housing market. These areas are characterised by high house prices and a high level of homelessness. It is a response to criticism that a shortage of affordable homes has contributed to the explosion of property prices during the last few years. The reduction is also intended to deter profiteering, particularly by right-to-buy companies (see page 296).

A further restriction on the discount applies in situations where the landlord has spent more than £5,500 on acquiring, building or improving the property during the ten years preceding the tenant's application to buy. In these circumstances, the discount cannot push the purchase price below the total of these costs. This is called the 'cost floor' rule.

Note also that if you have previously bought another council property, any discount than obtained will be deducted from the discount that you get on a future purchase.

The clawback
A tenant who has bought a long lease is prevented from profiting from the discount by immediately re-selling the flat for its true

value. If re-sale occurs within a specified period, the tenant will have to repay the discount either in whole or in part; this is known as the clawback. The landlord will have a charge over the flat in order to enforce any repayment.

The clawback occurs when the property is disposed of within three years of the sale to the tenant. In such a case, the whole of the discount is repayable, but is reduced by one-third for each year which has elapsed between the grant of the lease and the disposal. Therefore, if the flat is sold within one year of being bought, the tenant must refund the whole of the discount. If sale occurs between one and two years of the lease being granted, the amount to be repaid is two-thirds of the discount. On a sale arising between two and three years from the initial purchase, the tenant must repay one-third of the discount. No discount is repayable on a sale occurring three years after the lease was granted. The government is to raise this period to five years. For each year which elapses, the maximum amount of the clawback will be reduced by one-fifth. The amount to be repaid is also to be calculated differently; it will be a percentage of the resale value of the property less the value of the tenant's improvements.

The clawback does not operate when the property passes on death of the tenant, is re-allocated on divorce, is compulsorily purchased or is sold to the tenant's spouse (including former spouse) or a member of the tenant's family who has resided with the tenant for the previous 12 months. Landlords also have a discretion not to require repayment of the discount.

Exercising the right

The tenant must serve on the landlord a written notice stating that he or she wishes to exercise the right to buy. The landlord has four weeks in which to reply (eight weeks if you have been a tenant for less than two years). It may either accept the tenant's right or deny that the tenant or the property is eligible. If the right is denied, the landlord must give reasons and the tenant must prove eligibility, if necessary before a court. If the right is accepted, the landlord must serve a notice on the tenant stating the price, the discount, the proposed terms of the lease, the service charges that are payable and the right to appeal to a district valuer. This notice must be served within 12 weeks of the landlord's acceptance notice. The estimate of service charges (including repair costs) will remain binding on the landlord for the first five years of the lease. The landlord also has to give quite onerous repairing covenants and an insurance covenant.

Once the necessary steps have been taken, the landlord is bound to execute the lease. On completion, the secure tenancy comes to an end and the tenant will become the registered proprietor of the flat following registration at the Land Registry.

Service charges and repairs

A purchaser of a flat under the right-to-buy scheme may have the right to a loan in respect of service charges for repairs carried out by the landlord. This gives the tenant the ability to leave the service charge outstanding for a certain period while paying interest on the debt. The main features of this loan scheme are:

- the service charge must accrue within the first ten years of the lease
- the service charges due must exceed £1,500
- the loan must be for a sum over £500 and may be up to a maximum of £20,000
- the principal and interest on the loan must be paid back in equal instalments over three years (for loans under £1,500); five years (for loans between £1,500 and £5,000) or ten years (for loans exceeding £5,000)
- the lender/landlord can charge up to £100 to cover administrative costs.

Rent-to-mortgage

The shared-ownership lease has been replaced by the extremely complex rent-to-mortgage scheme, which caters for those tenants who want to buy, but cannot afford to pay or borrow the entire, although discounted, purchase price in one go. The idea is to extend home ownership to the lower paid. The scheme allows the tenant's current rent payments to be converted to mortgage repayments for a share of the flat, along with the right to purchase the remainder of the lease at a later date. In essence, the rent currently payable on the flat is equated with the portion of a 25-year mortgage that those payments would finance. This is the initial share which the tenant acquires. He or she can subsequently increase the payments and thereby increase the share in the property. If the tenant then sells the flat, the landlord's remaining share is redeemed from the purchase money. Assistance and advice can be obtained from the local authority housing department. It is predicted that this type of buying will remain very unpopular. In 1996–7, for example, only four properties were sold in England and Wales under this scheme. Because of the exclusion of those on housing benefit, it is likely that those who seek to buy will be able to take out a mortgage for the full price and have no need of the scheme.

Who qualifies?

To fall within the rent-to-mortgage scheme, the tenant must satisfy all the requirements that apply to the right-to-buy scheme (see page 288). In addition, the tenant must not have made a claim for housing benefit, or have been entitled to claim housing benefit, within the 12 months preceding the application for rent-to-mortgage. Also excluded is a tenant whose rent is more than 80 per cent of the mortgage payments on a mortgage that would buy the flat outright. Such a tenant is expected to purchase directly rather than use the new scheme. The calculations involved here are horrendously difficult.

Exercising the right

The procedure involves the tenant serving a notice on the landlord stating that he or she wishes to exercise the right and suggesting a purchase price. The landlord must then respond as soon as practicable by a notice either denying or admitting the claim. If admitted, the tenant must then, within 12 weeks, serve a further written notice on the landlord stating the intention to proceed or to withdraw. If the transaction is to go ahead, the landlord will serve another notice which will set out the landlord's share in the flat and the amount of the discount reduced in proportion to the tenant's share. If there is no response from the tenant, the landlord will serve yet another notice and, if there is still no response within 28 days, the claim is then deemed to be withdrawn.

The landlord is, therefore, really granting the tenant a mortgage, and the mortgage repayments take the form of the continued payments of rent. The lease when granted will be essentially on the same terms as under the right to buy, except that the service charges are scaled down to reflect the tenant's share in the flat. The mortgage must be paid off if the tenant sells the flat outside the family or, if the tenant dies during the term of the mortgage, after one year following death.

Preserved right to buy

If you are an *assured* tenant of a housing association, you will not usually have a right to buy your flat. If, however, you were a secure tenant of a local authority prior to the transfer of the freehold to the Housing Association, you can benefit from what is called the preserved right-to-buy. Although the two schemes are similar, some differences exist:

- you must have been living in the flat at the time of the transfer
- the cost floor rule is wider and includes works carried out over the preceding 16 years and can include acquisition and building costs
- the rent-to-mortgage scheme does not apply.

Buying back ex-council flats and houses

At present, local authorities have the power to buy back property, but normally do not have the funds available to do so. The government is planning to give them financial incentives to buy back 'problematic' properties which they had previously sold. This measure is designed to help those former tenants who cannot re-sell their properties or who are unable to pay service charges. It will replace the 'exchange sale scheme' introduced in 1995. If the landlord buys the flat back, you may be offered less than you paid for it. It is the flat's value at the time of sale that is crucial.

The homebuy scheme

Since 1988, local authorities and social landlords have been given powers to operate cash incentive schemes, which are designed to help council tenants and others buy homes in the private sector. If you qualify for the scheme you will need to contribute 75 per cent of the purchase price. The landlord will lend you the outstanding 25 per cent. The loan will be repaid when you sell the flat on at a future time. The amount to be repaid will be 25 per cent of the value of your home when it is sold. These grants, therefore, create vacant properties in the public sector, which can then be used for others in need of housing.

Ask your landlord whether such assistance is available. The grant is at the discretion of the landlord and may be means tested. The landlord will consider the length of the existing lease, the size of the council property the applicant is moving out of, and his or her income and savings. If you are buying a flat, the lease must have at least 55 years left to run.

Right-to-buy companies

In 2003, a substantial government report was published concerning the involvement of (and possible exploitation by) companies in the right-to-buy scheme. There are two types of company in operation: the Right-to-Buy Service Company and the Right-to-Buy Incentive Company. The *service company* helps those who wish to exercise their right to purchase their homes by providing advice, filling out forms, arranging finance and contacting solicitors. The usual cost of the total package provided (including legal fees) is over £2,000. Although this type of assistance is useful, these companies are viewed with suspicion by local authorities. It is claimed that some companies engage in sharp marketing practice targeted at people who cannot afford to buy their homes and that they often provide inaccurate advice and information to the purchaser. These companies usually work on one housing estate at a time and, as a result, the work of the local authority is dramatically increased dealing with the new applications. Much of this work is fruitless, however, as a high proportion of applications are subsequently withdrawn.

The *incentive company* is a very different creature and deals with people who would not otherwise wish to buy their homes or could not raise the necessary finance (e.g. because they have County Court judgments entered against them or their property is not mortgageable on the high street because it is a high-rise flat). These companies provide the tenant with the money to purchase the flat. At the same time, the tenant agrees to sell the lease to the company in three years' time at less than the market value (soon this will be five years). The tenant also grants the company a sub-lease of the property to cover the intervening period. On exercising the right to buy, the tenant immediately moves out of the property in return for a cash payment (usually ranging between £5,000 and £26,000) made by the company. This cash payment is normally less than a quarter of the discount that the tenant would otherwise have been entitled to. This practice is perfectly lawful and has so far affected thousands of properties, primarily in inner London. It offers the company a cheap way of building up a portfolio of properties to rent and the tenant leaves financially enriched by the experience. The potential for exploitation of the right-to-buy scheme by *incentive companies* is one reason why the government has reduced the maximum discount available to tenants.

Watching the relatives?

Local authorities have voiced concern over the exploitation of the elderly by relatives using the right-to-buy scheme in order to acquire a housing asset. Relatives play an important role in the exercise of the right to buy. At least 13 per cent of right-to-buy purchases are funded by non-occupying relatives, particularly children. The government report showed that more than 20 per cent of funding relatives expected a formal financial return, not just to inherit. More than 30 per cent either lived or expected to live with the applicant. The possibility arises, however, that a relative could, possibly following a pre-agreement, claim the property after three years (so as to avoid the clawback provisions) and evict the original applicant. In such transactions, the applicants should take care to ensure that there is, at the least, a right for them to continue to live in the property indefinitely.

Chapter 21

Buying and selling in Scotland

There are major differences between Scottish and English law in relation to the purchase and sale of houses and flats. However, the procedure for buying and selling flats in Scotland is very similar to that for buying and selling houses in Scotland.

One of the most important things to remember when buying a flat is that it is part of a larger building or 'tenement' and you should therefore look at the condition of the whole property, as well as of the flat itself. In particular, you should make sure that the cost of repairing the structure and common parts of the property is shared fairly among the individual flat-owners. These matters are considered in more detail later in this chapter.

Tenure

The English concept of leasehold does not apply to the purchase of flats in Scotland: until 28 November 2004, the traditional system of land tenure continues to operate. Most flats, and indeed most other kinds of land and property, are possessed on **feudal tenure** and property offered for sale is sometimes referred to in Scotland as the **feu**. In principle, feudal tenure means that the owner possesses the property on perpetual tenure from the estate-owner, who is known as the **superior**, who in turn is likely to possess from his/her superior and so on in a chain that ends with the Crown. However, for most practical purposes, the property is owned absolutely and can be disposed of freely rather than being held on long lease as in England or Wales.

The main practical distinguishing feature of feudal tenure is that the original developer of the land or estate-owner (the superior) can impose conditions on its future use – for instance, by prohibiting commercial use, extensions or alterations without his or her consent. It is also usual for the superior to require the future maintenance of the property in good condition and reinstatement following damage or destruction. This is particularly important for flat-owners, who will have a shared interest in the upkeep and maintenance of various common parts of the building. These and other terms are called **feuing conditions** or **real burdens.** They may be found in a legal document called a **deed of conditions** or **feu charter**. These conditions are, in principle, binding on all owners for all time. In addition, **feu duty** (see below), particularly in flats, may be payable annually.

Any buyer will be bound by the feuing conditions, but it may be possible, once he or she has bought the property, to negotiate with the superior for a waiver. Normally, the superior charges a capital payment for agreeing to waive feuing conditions. If he or she refuses to vary unreasonable conditions, or if the existence of a condition impedes some reasonable use of land, such as making external alterations or building a garage, the owner (or **feuar**) can apply to the Lands Tribunal for Scotland★ for an order to vary them. A leaflet on land obligations and how they may be varied or discharged, and the fees payable, is obtainable from the tribunal. If you think that you may be justified in seeking such an order, consult your solicitor in the first instance.

In the past, the feuar nearly always paid a small annual cash sum or **feu duty** (similar to a ground rent in England and Wales) to the superior. (The superior therefore retained a link with a flat built on his or her property or developed by him or her.) Since 1974, the creation of new feu duties has been prohibited and redemption of the feu duty (when the property is sold) has become the norm. Accordingly, it has become much less common since then for feu duties to be payable. As far as flats are concerned, if the overall feu duty for the building has been formally divided (known as 'allocation' of the feu duty) between each flat, the feuar is obliged to redeem the feu duty when he or she sells the property, leaving the flat forever free of any further charge. If the feu duty has not been allocated, there is a procedure for allocating the feu duty between the various flats in the building. Often however, in flatted property, the feu duty has not been allocated, and feu duty continues to be payable annually. The feuing conditions, however, still apply even if the feu duty has been redeemed.

Changes to come

Two major pieces of legislation have been passed by the Scottish Parliament which will have a major effect on the system of landownership in Scotland. The Abolition of Feudal Tenure etc. (Scotland) Act 2000 and the Title Conditions (Scotland) Act 2002 will be fully brought into force as from 28 November 2004. From that date (called 'the appointed date') the system of feudal tenure in Scotland will be abolished and replaced with a system of absolute legal ownership. This will have a profound effect on the system of landownership and conveyancing in Scotland. Some of these changes are as follows:

After the appointed date, all superiors and superiorities will be abolished. With that will go the right of superiors to demand payment for the waiving of feu conditions (for example, for home extensions). However, many feuing conditions will survive after the appointed date. For example, those feuing conditions which are for the benefit of a neighbour may be preserved if the superior seeks to register them. Also, feuing conditions which have been imposed on a group of related properties (such as a block of flats) are automatically converted into **'community burdens'** on the appointed day. In addition, those feuing conditions which relate to things such as maintenance or management of a facility (such as the common parts of a flatted building) will automatically convert into **facility burdens** or **service burdens** on the appointed day. Community burdens and facility burdens can then be enforced by the owners of the flats or houses which are bound by them. In addition, any burdens which are imposed by the seller as a matter of contract will still be binding on the buyer even after the appointed date. However, if the new law does not preserve the feuing condition, it will cease to be enforceable after 28 November 2004. In any event, after that date a superior will no longer be able to charge money in return for permissions.

Finally, the 2000 Act abolishes payment of feu duties. Your solicitor should be able to advise you on the effects of the 2000 and 2002 Acts. One further Bill is proposed: the Tenements (Scotland) Bill. This will amend the law relating to tenemental property, which includes buildings with four or more flats. It is thought that the Bill may be brought before the Scottish Parliament some time in 2004.

Common parts

As explained above, it is normal in Scotland to purchase each of the flats in a block outright, rather than on a long lease as is the case in England and Wales. However, the law recognises that there are various 'common parts' of the whole building in which all the owners in the block have an interest and that they should therefore be jointly responsible for repair and maintenance of those parts. Normally, the **solum** (the ground on which the block of flats is built), the foundations, the roof, attic, close (stairwell or hall) and stairs are owned by the proprietors in the block equally or on some other equitable basis. Similarly, any garden ground and, in more modern blocks, landscaped gardens, car-parking areas and door-entry systems are likely to be deemed common parts. The title deeds (such as the deed of conditions) normally set out the basis on which the costs of repairs and maintenance are shared between the various owners.

It is also possible that there will be a common insurance policy for the block, covering loss by fire, storm damage, and so on. This will result in an additional cost over and above any buildings insurance required under your mortgage, but it may be possible to persuade your mortgage lender to accept the insurance or at least take it into account.

It is customary in many parts of Scotland (particularly in Glasgow and the west coast) for management of common repairs and insurance to be dealt with by a **factor**, who is a professional property manager. The factor will organise common repairs and will arrange for paying the bills. Every owner in the block will receive a half-yearly account from the factor for their share of the common repairs, plus the factor's management charge. Some factors also ask for a float, normally a small deposit of £50–£100, which will be refunded when you sell the flat. The factor is an agent of the owners. While the title deeds may require that a factor be appointed, it will not usually (except in the case of council flat sales) specify the identity of the factor. If, as sometimes happens, the owners are with good reason displeased by the performance of the factor, they can dismiss him or her and appoint a new one.

Finding a solicitor

As there are very few practising licensed conveyancers in Scotland, you will need to consult a solicitor if you want to buy or sell a flat. In theory you could do much of the legal work yourself, but it is not usually practicable to do so, particularly if you need a mortgage. All Scottish cities and many larger towns have solicitors' property centres which are organisations of solicitors who do estate agency work (see below).

English solicitors are not permitted to practise in Scotland, but if you are moving from England or Wales, your own solicitor may know a Scottish solicitor with whom he or she deals regularly. If you do not know a solicitor, the best recommendation may be that of a friend or colleague who has used one for this type of work and who can give you a personal introduction. There is an excellent collection of links to Scottish law firms at www.absolvitor.com/lawfirms/index.html. Details of solicitors can also be obtained from the Law Society of Scotland★ or your local Citizens Advice Bureau. Leaflets explaining the role of solicitors in buying and selling houses or flats can be obtained from any solicitor or the Law Society of Scotland. You will also find a list of solicitors in the *Yellow Pages*.

You should ask your solicitor at the outset to give you an estimate of the fees involved and the outlays (disbursements) he or she will have to make. The outlays are substantial and should be budgeted for. There are no set fees, so you can shop around for competitive estimates. Do remember, however, that the level of fee quoted may be an indication of the standard of service provided.

Pricing of flats

The general practice in Scotland is that flats are usually offered for sale at '**offers over**' a stated figure, occasionally referred to as the **upset price.** The upset price may be the minimum that the seller will consider accepting, but it may have been set artificially low in order to attract buyers and encourage competitive bidding. Buyers will generally have to pay more, sometimes much more, than the upset price, but much depends on the area, the demand, the condition of the property and market conditions.

Sometimes flats are offered for a sale at a fixed price. This may be because either a quick sale is sought or earlier attempts to sell it at an 'offers over' price have been unsuccessful. If you want to buy a flat which is offered for a sale at a fixed price, you should be ready to proceed very quickly, because the first acceptable offer at the stated price will secure the flat. See further below: 'Making an offer'.

Buying a flat

The main steps involved in buying a flat are:

- finding a suitable flat
- arranging a loan and having the flat surveyed
- making an offer
- obtaining legal title to the flat.

It is advisable to see your solicitor as early on in the procedure as possible. Things can move very fast once the process gets under way, and if you have not made contact you may miss your chance to make an offer for the flat you have decided on. The offer is usually prepared by a solicitor, who can also give useful general advice about buying, and assist you in obtaining a loan. At your first meeting with your solicitor, he or she can give you an outline of the whole purchase procedure from start to finish and discuss various essential matters including your price range, your mortgage and likely expenses.

Finding a suitable flat

There are three main sources of information about flats for sale in Scotland: newspapers, solicitors' property centres and offices, and estate agents.

If you are thinking about buying a brand-new flat, you could contact the sales departments of building firms in the area you have chosen or go to see the various developments.

Newspapers

A wide range of properties for sale is advertised in the principal Scottish 'quality' daily newspapers, and each has its main property day – *The Herald* (Glasgow and Strathclyde) on Wednesdays, the *Press and Journal* (Aberdeen and Grampian) on Tuesdays, *The Scotsman* (Edinburgh and the Lothians) on Wednesdays and *Courier and Advertiser* (Dundee, Perth and Tayside) on Thursdays.

A good range of properties for sale is also advertised in smaller local newspapers.

Solicitors' property centres

Solicitors' property centres can be found in the Aberdeen, Dundee, Edinburgh and Glasgow areas and some large towns. These are run by solicitors on a co-operative basis and are situated in shopping areas. Many of them have websites. They provide details of all properties being sold by solicitors in the area. The solicitors' property centre in Berwick-upon-Tweed is unique in that it deals with properties for sale on both sides of the England–Scotland border.

Most solicitors' property centres operate only as information centres and not as selling agents – the solicitors themselves retain the selling role. The staff at a centre are not qualified solicitors, although they are generally conversant with house purchase and sale procedures. A customer who is interested in a property is directed to the solicitor actually selling it. Full estate agency-type particulars are available for each property (most have photographs too). The biggest centres, in Aberdeen, Glasgow and Edinburgh, each have hundreds of properties on display at any one time. The service is free to people looking for property to buy.

Some solicitors' property centres publish regular property lists, most of them weekly, with full listings of all properties registered at the centre in question. Copies can be mailed to prospective buyers if requested and are available from the particular centre and from all the solicitors practising in the area. A list of solicitors' property centres with addresses and telephone numbers and website addresses is available from the Law Society of Scotland* or the website of the Scottish Solicitors' Property Centres (*www.sspc.co.uk*).

Solicitors are allowed to call themselves 'solicitors and estate agents' and often do so. Some firms of solicitors have their own property department where details of available properties are displayed. Many firms of solicitors employ specialist sales staff who deal with the non-legal aspects of buying and selling property.

Estate agents

There are many estate agents in Scotland, some of which are part of chains owned by UK insurance companies or building societies, while others are local firms. Generally, estate agents in Scotland operate in a similar way to those in England and Wales. However, the conveyancing is done by solicitors.

The larger estate agencies issue regular property lists and most of them maintain mailing lists and have properties on their websites.

When you have found a flat

When you have found a flat that you would like to buy, tell your solicitor immediately. You can discuss with the seller the date of entry (see page 308) and what contents, such as carpets, curtains, light fittings and so on ('extras') are included. Although these may be in the particulars of sale or schedule, it is still important to ensure that they are specifically covered in the offer. You can try to negotiate a price direct with the seller, but most sellers will simply ask you to put in a formal offer via your solicitor. The details of the offer are handled by solicitors rather than by estate agents. An oral agreement for the sale of a flat cannot create a binding contract, and can be repudiated by either party without any consequences. You should never write letters or sign any documents relating to a sale or purchase without consulting your solicitor. Developers of new flats usually have their own legal documents for intending buyers to sign, and it is very difficult to negotiate different terms. Even so, you should get your solicitor to act for you in the sale so that he or she can give you proper advice about the sale before you enter into it, and protect your position.

When you tell your solicitor that you are interested in buying a particular property, the first thing he or she will do is to telephone the seller's solicitor or estate agent to notify him or her of your interest. This is called **noting interest.** The convention is that once a closing date has been set, all those who have noted interest will be told so that they have the opportunity to make an offer before the closing date.

Arranging a mortgage

If you have not already made your loan arrangements, you will need to ensure that you have an agreement with a building society, bank or other source of finance to borrow the money you need (see Chapter 4). If you have any difficulty in finding the loan, your solicitor will probably be able to help you.

All Scottish banks and building societies will lend on the security of Scottish properties, subject to status and the condition of the flat. Preferably, even before you have a specific flat in mind, you should establish that the amount you require will be available on the type of property that you will be seeking and that it will be available when you want it – subject always to a satisfactory survey report on the chosen flat.

Survey

Building societies and banks require the property to be surveyed before committing themselves to a loan. Even if you are paying for the flat without a loan, you are strongly advised to have it surveyed before making an offer. It is customary to have a survey carried out before you make an offer for a flat. An offer made 'subject to survey' is likely to be rejected by the seller unless the flat requires expensive specialist surveys or if market conditions are unusual.

The survey is usually instructed by your solicitor once he or she is informed that you are interested and wish to go ahead. If you prefer, you can instruct the survey yourself. If your offer is unsuccessful you will have wasted the survey fee and your solicitor may expect you to pay for it there and then.

The range of types of survey is similar to that in England and Wales (see pages 80–2). The cheapest type of survey, but the one with the least detail about the property, is the **lender's survey**, which is little more than a mortgage valuation; the **home-buyer's report** gives a wider range of information; a full **structural survey** normally costs much more but gives very detailed information about the condition of the property.

Lenders will always require that at least a lender's survey is done so that they can be satisfied that the flat will provide suitable security for their loan to you. However, it is you who pays the surveyor's fee and you who will be buying the flat so you may choose to have a more detailed survey carried out. A lender's survey report will say whether the property in question is suitable for the loan that you require and its valuation. It will usually also give an overview of the state of the property indicating any major problems observed. The usual practice is that you will be given a copy of the report even if it is only the lender's report.

Making an offer

If the survey report is favourable, the next thing is to make an offer to buy the flat. An offer is a formal document, usually a letter running to several pages, or a shorter letter with a schedule of conditions attached. It specifies all the conditions on which you are willing to buy the flat. You are strongly advised not to make an offer yourself. Your solicitor will prepare it and send it to the seller's solicitor or estate agent.

In making the offer, you will have to decide, with guidance from your solicitor, how much to pay. You should also be clear when you want to move in and what extras you want to buy. If you are the only person interested in the flat, your solicitor may be able to find this out from the seller's solicitor or estate agent and may be able to negotiate an acceptable price. If more than one person is interested in buying the same flat, the seller's solicitor or estate agent will normally fix a closing date and time. He or she will intimate to those who have noted interest that offers must be submitted by a stated time on a particular date. You will have to offer 'blind', without knowing how much other people will have offered. There may be quite a large gap between the highest and the next highest offers but it is not possible to get round this by making a bid of, say, '£100 more than the highest offer you receive'.

Your solicitor will normally help you decide how much over the asking price you should offer – he or she probably has access to information about prices achieved for similar flats to guide you in making your decision. The solicitor's knowledge of the local market is important and usually helpful. However, the final decision will be yours.

The seller is not bound to accept the higher price, or indeed any offer. If an offer is accepted, the convention is that the seller's solicitor telephones the successful bidder's solicitor to advise that the seller intends to formally accept the offer. The unsuccessful bidders are also advised. By convention, none of the bidders is told what the others offered, nor are the unsuccessful bidders told what the successful bid was, although your solicitor may be able to get a rough indication of the position. The way in which the contract is concluded is dealt with below.

Date of entry

Stating the date of entry, the date on which you want to take physical possession of the property is part of your formal offer. Whether this is acceptable is largely governed by when the seller wants to move out. The date of entry is often negotiated after the offer has been accepted. As there are no 'chains' in Scottish practice, the date of entry can be fairly short. If there are no compelling reasons on either side for a very early or very distant date of entry, the period between making the offer and moving in is generally anything between four weeks and three months. However, it is important to ensure that you have sufficient time to sell your own house or flat, if necessary, and to have all the legal work for that sale completed before you take possession of the new flat.

Miscellaneous conditions

You may be interested in buying extras, such as carpets, curtains, kitchen equipment, and so on. Sale particulars normally specify what is, and what is not, included in the price and your offer will normally be drawn up accordingly.

If the extra items included in the price are valuable, you may want to allocate part of the price to them – for example, if the flat with the extras costs £63,000, you could say that the flat costs £60,000 and the moveable property £3,000 – as this will give you a small saving in stamp duty land tax (see pages 96–8). The items must be moveable for the tax to be saved. Ownership of more permanent fittings and fixtures (such as fitted kitchens, built-in bedroom furniture) is transferred together with the flat, under the **disposition** (the legal document transferring the flat) granted to you by the seller.

The remaining conditions in the offer are taken up with technical legal matters such as ensuring that you will receive a good marketable title, that the property is not adversely affected by planning proposals, that structural alterations or extensions have received local authority approval, and that you can withdraw from the contract if there are certain material changes in circumstances before the date of entry.

If there is some special use to which you want to put the flat, such as using a part of it as an office or for a business, or if you plan to make major alterations, you must tell your solicitor so that he or she can include conditions in the offer to make sure that there are no relevant prohibitions in the title deeds. If you are planning alterations or a change of use, you may have to make the offer conditional upon obtaining planning and/or building control permission. Sellers are usually not very keen on such offers but sometimes find that they are unavoidable.

Your offer will stipulate that the flat is not subject to any local authority proposals, notices or orders which might adversely affect it, and will oblige the seller to obtain and exhibit local authority certificates (for which the seller must pay) to this effect. Should the certificates disclose anything adverse, you are permitted to withdraw from the purchase, or you could renegotiate the price. You should ask your solicitor to explain the legal and practical effects of any matters disclosed, such as the building being listed as having architectural or historic interest.

Concluding the contract

An oral acceptance of the offer to buy is not legally binding. The seller's solicitor will deliver a written acceptance by letter. Usually this letter will accept the terms of the offer but subject to qualifications, modifying or adjusting some of the terms such as the date of entry. These terms may include to what extent and for how long any conditions of the contract may remain enforceable after you take possession: for instance, if you find out soon after taking possession that the central heating is not working, you may be able to go back to the seller and ask him or her to pay for repairs. This is called a qualified acceptance which is usually delivered soon after receipt of the letter of offer.

If the qualifications are entirely acceptable to you (your solicitor will advise you on this), your solicitor will send a letter to the seller's solicitor confirming that a binding contract is concluded. This is usually done within a day or so of receipt of the qualified acceptance, so the contract can be concluded within a few days of the offer being made. More usually, however, the buyer's acceptance of the qualifications will itself be subject to further qualifications. This process continues until one or other side accepts the other's counter-offer without qualifications and 'holds the bargain as concluded'.

The written offer and subsequent letters between the buyer's and seller's solicitors relating to it and containing qualifications are known as the **missives**. Once the bargain is concluded, a binding legal contract is created and neither the buyer nor the seller can withdraw without liability to pay damages. However, the conclusion of the missives does not transfer ownership of the flat to the seller. All they do is create a legal obligation on the parties to complete the transaction by payment of the price in exchange for a legal document (the disposition) which transfers title to the flat. Missives are concluded by the solicitors on behalf of the buyer and seller; there is nothing for the buyer or seller to sign at this stage.

Accordingly, it is possible to withdraw from the sale/purchase before the missives are concluded. However, this is rare in practice unless there is a good reason for doing so (such as a problem with the property searches or title). Most solicitors will refuse to continue to act for a person who tries to withdraw from the bargain before missives are concluded, without there being a good reason for doing so relating to the property. Gazumping is therefore rare in Scotland.

Insurance

At common law in Scotland the buyer becomes responsible for insurance of the property from the date when the missives are concluded. However, it is now usual for the missives to provide that the seller will remain liable for any damage to the property and for it to be insured until the date of entry, and that the buyer can withdraw from the purchase without penalty if the flat and any extras included in the sale are seriously damaged or destroyed before the date of entry.

Completing the purchase

Once missives have been concluded, or possibly while they are in the process of being concluded, your solicitor will set in train examination of the title and the conveyancing procedures to ensure that the formal legal documents, which transfer title to the property in your favour, are ready for delivery by the date of entry, in exchange for payment of the price.

If you are buying the flat together with your husband or wife, or some other person, you will need to think about how the title is to be taken. The terms of the title will regulate the ownership, the respective shares of the co-owners and what happens to their shares on their death. You should discuss these matters with your co-owners and your solicitor before the disposition is prepared.

A title simply in the names of two people gives each of them an equal share in the property. If you and your co-owner are to have unequal shares (say, one-third to you and two-thirds to your brother) the title must state this. During their lives each co-owner can dispose of his or her share (by sale or gift) or can demand that the whole property be sold and his or her share of the proceeds be paid over (a **division and sale**). It is possible for co-owners to agree not to demand a sale.

Two co-owners, particularly spouses, often take the title in each of their names and those of their survivor. If this is done, when either of the co-owners dies, the survivor automatically becomes entitled to the whole property. Such a survivorship title cannot usually be altered without the agreement of both co-owners and it will generally prevail over any will made by either of the co-owners.

The mortgage

As soon as the missives have been concluded, you should complete your loan application if you have not already done so.

If you are borrowing from a building society, bank or other lender, your solicitor normally acts for the lender as well as for you. There are various types of mortgage available including repayment mortgages and endowment mortgages (see Chapter 4 for more information). Your solicitor or an independent financial adviser can advise on which type of mortgage suits you best. He or she will report to the lender on the title and prepare the necessary mortgage document, called a '**standard security**'. Your solicitor will arrange for the mortgage funds to be available in time for the date of entry and will ask you to sign the standard security and other documents by the date of entry.

If you are in any doubt about the terms of the mortgage documents, ask your solicitor to explain them to you before you sign them. Almost all such documents prohibit the letting of the property without the lender's consent. They also set out detailed conditions about maintenance, insurance, and so on, and give the lender a wide range of remedies, including ultimately the right to sell the flat if you fail to maintain your payments or otherwise fail to observe the loan conditions.

The funds from the lender will be sent to your solicitor before the date of entry and he or she will ask you to pay the difference between your mortgage loan and the full price. If you are selling another house or flat, whether in Scotland or England, and you are relying on money from the sale which will not be available by the date of entry, you will need to make bridging loan arrangements at an early stage and you should discuss this with your solicitor.

Documents

On the date of entry, a procedure known as 'settlement' takes place, when a cheque for the full price is exchanged for the title deeds, including the disposition in your favour. The keys are usually handed over at settlement unless other arrangements have been agreed.

Your solicitor will then register the disposition and the standard security. Normally the documents will be returned to your solicitor after some time, which may be over a year. If you have a mortgage, the solicitor will send the documents to the lender. If you do not, your solicitor will hand the title deeds over to you once the registration process has been completed. He or she may offer to hold them in safe custody for you, usually free of charge.

Solicitors' charges

After completing the purchase (or sometimes before doing so) your solicitor will send you the account for his or her fees and outlays (disbursements). Solicitors in Scotland do not charge according to fixed scales set by the Law Society of Scotland.

In addition to the solicitors' fees for the preliminary work leading up to and including missives, the conveyancing and the mortgage (on all of which you will have to pay VAT), there will be stamp duty of 1 per cent of the price of the flat if it is over £60,000 (unless the property is in an area designated by the Inland Revenue in which case the limit is £150,000) and registration dues for recording the documents in the Land Register.

Outlays must be paid on the date of entry; the solicitor may agree to accept payments of fees later or payment by instalments.

Succession

If you buy a flat in Scotland and use it as your residence or principal residence, you may acquire Scottish domicile. This may affect, among other things, the way your property is inherited on your death.

If you die without a will, Scottish law will regulate the distribution of your heritable property (that is, land and buildings) in Scotland, and moveable property (all property other than heritable) in Scotland and elsewhere.

If you die leaving a will, it regulates the distribution of your estate, but the provisions of your will are subject to Scottish rules of succession which differ in a number of important respects from English law. The most important difference is that a spouse and children cannot be cut out of the succession to moveable estate, no matter what the will may say. They are always entitled to their 'legal rights' which, depending on the circumstances, may be either one-third or one-half of the net moveable estate. In addition, the spouse is entitled to 'prior rights' to parts of the estate if there is no will.

With heritable property, regardless of the domicile of the owner, succession is governed by the law of the country in which the property is situated. Therefore, even if only a holiday home is bought in Scotland, so that there is no question of the buyer thereby acquiring Scottish domicile, the succession to that flat is governed by Scottish law.

A will made under Scottish law is not automatically revoked if the person making it subsequently marries, nor are provisions in favour of a spouse automatically revoked on divorce.

Selling a flat

If you are selling in Scotland, you are likely to have been a buyer already and thus familiar with the Scottish system. Many matters dealt with in the section on buying will be of interest to you as a seller.

The main steps involved in selling a flat in Scotland are:

- advertising and showing your flat
- dealing with offers
- transferring title to the buyer and repaying any loan.

Before you put your flat on the market you should alert your solicitor to the fact that you are about to sell it. This is to give your solicitor sufficient time to do the preparatory work that has to be done before the flat can be sold. The solicitor will probably have to:

- look over your title deeds to ensure they are in order and that you have good title to the property. He or she will borrow them from your building society or other lender if you have an outstanding loan over the property
- check the amount of any outstanding loan
- order local authority searches to make sure that the property is not affected by any outstanding local authority notices, orders or proposals.

Someone who has been used to the English method of sale, where the solicitor becomes involved at only a relatively late stage, should be aware of the need to bring a solicitor into the picture early in Scotland.

Consent to sale

Where a flat is owned by two or more people, all of them must consent to its sale, although a sale can be forced by the court. Try to get agreement because legal proceedings are expensive.

The Matrimonial Homes (Family Protection) (Scotland) Act 1981 makes it imperative for a married seller whose spouse is not a co-owner to obtain the spouse's consent to a sale at the earliest opportunity and certainly before missives are concluded. Failure to do so may mean that the seller finds he or she cannot give the buyer possession of the property as provided for in the missives. This is especially important where the couple are separated or estranged.

Advertising and showing your flat

The three most common ways of marketing your flat are to:

- employ a solicitor
- employ an estate agent
- do it yourself.

Even if you employ a solicitor or estate agent you will probably be showing prospective buyers around the flat yourself. As the owner, you will show the property to its best advantage and know the answers to all the questions people are likely to ask. Moreover, solicitors and estate agents will generally charge extra for showing prospective buyers around property.

Selling through a solicitor

If you ask your solicitor to sell your flat, you should expect him or her to provide a full estate-agency service. He or she will normally also register your flat in the local solicitors' property centre, for which a charge is made. This covers display of the flat in the solicitors' property centre until it is sold, and insertion in the property centre's regular property listing or mailing where there is one.

A solicitor who acts for you in selling your flat will charge a selling commission over and above the conveyancing fees. The commission will usually be about 1 per cent of the selling price of the flat although some solicitors may seek more or less than this. Specialised properties or very expensive ones may attract a different rate of commission. Ask your solicitor for an estimate of charges before instructing him or her to act for you and, if you are not satisfied with the estimate, discuss it with him or her, or seek an alternative estimate from another solicitor.

Selling through an estate agent

Generally speaking, estate agents' terms of business are similar in Scotland to those in England and Wales. Commissions are generally around 1 per cent or so of the achieved selling price, although lower charges may be negotiated, and higher charges normally apply in the case of large or specialised properties. Ask the estate agent for an estimate and make sure you understand whether items like VAT are included in the charge and whether advertising costs are extra. You may be charged for the insertion of the property in the estate agent's house magazine.

Even if you instruct an estate agent to sell your flat for you, he or she will normally pass to your solicitor any formal offers that are made. It is important to realise that as well as the estate agent's commission, you will have to pay the solicitor's fee for concluding missives and the conveyancing fees.

Many estate agents will agree a 'no sale, no fee' arrangement whereby if the flat is not sold, no fee is charged; although outlays, such as for advertising, will be payable.

Selling it yourself

This entails arranging to advertise the property, showing people around it, letting surveyors inspect it, and answering questions about room sizes, the price and what items are and are not included in the sale. You should prepare written particulars similar to those issued by solicitors and estate agents, but stress to people viewing the flat that these are provided only as a guide and are not to form part of any contract.

If you decide to sell your flat yourself, the only costs which you need incur are those for advertising. Although it is probably not sensible to 'go it alone' the first time you sell, if you have been through the process of buying and selling before, and if you have a readily saleable flat in which a large number of people are likely to be interested, you may feel that the saving in sales commission is justified. However, you will not have the advantage of the large scale of advertising that is practised by solicitors' property centres, other similar groups and estate agents. Nor will you be able to get the same discounts for property advertising that they enjoy.

You will still need a solicitor to do the conveyancing and should tell him or her in advance, and tell prospective buyers that formal written offers are to be submitted to him or her.

The advertisement

If you are selling through a solicitor or an estate agent, he or she will prepare the advertisement for you and agree its terms with you, and will also advise you on the upset price and the price you should expect to achieve.

Arrangements for viewing are normally made with prospective buyers, who should be asked for their names and addresses. There may be fixed viewing times or viewing by appointment, or a mixture of both. Remember that the easier you make it for people to view a flat, the more people are likely to do so and the quicker you may find a buyer. Evenings and weekend afternoons are popular viewing times. Some places have traditional viewing times. For example, in Edinburgh, viewing is usually on Thursday evenings and Sunday afternoons.

The advertisement also sometimes states the 'offers over' (or upset price) and invites offers over that price. The upset price is generally fixed below the actual price that a seller hopes to obtain in order to attract buyers and encourage competition. You should be able to judge what upset price to put on your flat by looking at advertisements for comparable flats in the neighbourhood. A surveyor will carry out a quick pre-sale valuation which will help you to fix a price. Ring around reputable surveyors' firms for a quotation.

After the advertisement

You may gain an impression of whether people are seriously interested or not in buying the flat when they come to view, particularly if they return a second time. However, this is not always the case. The first sign that you may receive an offer is usually when a solicitor telephones your solicitor or estate agent to say that he or she has a client interested in your property. This is called 'noting interest'.

An indication of interest is usually followed by a visit from a surveyor. If the survey is favourable, it is likely to be followed by an offer. If you are doing the selling of your flat yourself, ask buyers to lodge formal offers with your solicitor. Never sign a written acceptance of an offer or exchange letters with a prospective buyer without consulting your solicitor.

Receiving offers

If several people have noted interest in your flat, it is usual to fix a closing date for offers – that is, a date and time at which you will consider all offers which have been lodged. All those people whose interest has been noted will be given the chance to submit formal written offers through their solicitor. Your solicitor or estate agent will advise you whether to fix a closing date or not, and will suggest when it should be. Where there is competition, a higher price may be achieved if you do not rush the sale, but this may be nerve-racking for you.

On the closing date, you will have to decide which offer to accept. You are not under an obligation to accept the highest offer or even any offer at all. If offers are close, you may take into account other factors such as the proposed date of entry, what extras are included in the price, or even whether or not you liked the person making the highest offer. If the price is acceptable but other conditions of the offer are not, your solicitor or estate agent can negotiate them with the person making the offer or his or her solicitor. If the top offer is too low, you may have to re-advertise. It is considered by some unethical, and may be unwise anyway, to try to get the person making the highest offer to pay more without giving the others making offers a chance to re-offer.

Concluding the missives

If you are selling through an estate agent, he or she will normally pass the offers, or at least the offer which is to be accepted, to your solicitor. Once you have received an offer which you want to accept, or identified which of any competing offers is to be accepted, your solicitor will adjust points of detail with the solicitor acting for the person who made the successful offer, through the exchange of letters called **missives**. This process normally takes between two and four weeks. The conclusion of missives constitutes a binding contract from which neither party can withdraw. Your solicitor will accept the offer and conduct the bargain on your behalf. Make sure therefore that you understand exactly what you are agreeing to.

In theory, it would be possible for gazumping to take place between the date when an acceptable offer is received and the date when the missives are concluded, but it would be considered unethical for a solicitor acting for a seller to negotiate with an alternative purchaser during this period. If in such circumstances you decide to withdraw from negotiations with the person who made the successful offer and to negotiate with someone else, your solicitor would probably stop acting for you and you would have to appoint another solicitor. The absence of gazumping, the short time between offers being made and becoming binding, and the absence of 'chains' are advantages of the Scottish system.

Completing the sale

Once the missives have been concluded, or possibly during that process, your solicitor will send the title deeds of the flat to the buyer's solicitor so that he or she can examine them and prepare the legal documents of transfer in favour of the buyer. Your solicitor will also inform your building society, bank or other mortgage lender that the missives have been concluded and obtain a redemption statement to show the amount of the loan to be repaid on completion of the sale. He or she will prepare the discharge document and have it signed by the lender before the date of entry.

Your solicitor will have instructed searches in the registers to demonstrate to the buyer that there are no adverse entries, such as court decrees, in respect of the property or against you as a seller. He or she will answer any questions raised by the buyer's solicitor, and adjust the terms of the disposition with him or her. You have to sign the disposition before the date of entry.

Immediately prior to the date of entry, your solicitor will agree with you what arrangements are to be made about handing over the keys (often it is best to deliver these to your solicitor on or before the date of entry).

On the date of entry, the disposition in favour of the buyer is handed over in return for the buyer's solicitor's cheque or other payment for the full purchase price. Out of that amount, your solicitor repays your outstanding mortgage loan, and any bridging loan, in accordance with instructions received from you or your bank. He or she will then let you have a cheque for the balance of the price payable to you, after deducting fees and outlays. He or she should provide you with a detailed statement (sometimes called a State for Settlement) showing all the financial details; if not, make sure you ask for one. Your solicitor will normally send you the balance of the price and his or her statement on the day on which the sale is completed, or soon thereafter.

Chapter 22

Buying and selling in Northern Ireland

While Northern Ireland has its own distinct form of land law and landlord and tenant law, the procedure for buying and selling property is similar to that in England and Wales. The Landlord and Tenant legislation referred to in earlier chapters is not applicable in Northern Ireland but details of rights, wrongs and remedies are similar.

As in England and Wales the conveyancing process varies depending on the registration status of the property in sale. In Northern Ireland most urban land and property was unregistered while nearly all agricultural land and rural property was held under registered title. The distinction is blurred somewhat by the encroachment of development on to what was originally agricultural land, resulting in an increasing number of residential and commercial properties having registered title. Unregistered land and property is registered in the Registry of Deeds. Such registration does not in any way underwrite the validity of the title, but records the existence and contents of the deed presented for registration without confirming that such contents are correct. Registered land and property is registered at the Land Registry with the title being contained in a folio or folios containing details of ownership, charges etc. The Land Registry has embarked upon compulsory first registration throughout Northern Ireland with all unregistered land transactions being subject to first registration.

A central distinguishing feature of the law relating to conveyancing in Northern Ireland is the absence of exchange of contracts. Under the Northern Ireland conveyancing procedure, a single contract is signed first by the buyer by way of 'offer' and returned to the seller to be signed by way of 'acceptance'. The binding contract is formed upon receipt by the buyer of a copy of the contract accepted by the seller.

There are no licensed conveyancers in Northern Ireland. All conveyancing transactions are carried out by qualified solicitors.

The Law Society of Northern Ireland⋆ operates the Home Charter Scheme which, as with the Law Society Protocol in England and Wales, offers a standardised procedure for conveyancing in Northern Ireland. All residential conveyancing transactions must now be completed in accordance with the Home Charter Scheme.

The right-to-buy scheme in England and Wales is not applicable in Northern Ireland although the Northern Ireland Housing Executive House Sales Scheme is similar in scope. With respect to buying the freehold, different legislation and procedures apply under the Leasehold (Enlargement and Extension) Act (NI) 1971 and the Ground Rents Act (Northern Ireland) 2001.

The Property (Northern Ireland) Order 1997 has introduced considerable change to the conveyancing process in Northern Ireland but the Order's prohibition of the creation of long leases is not applicable to flats. The Ground Rents Act (Northern Ireland) 2001 provides for compulsory redemption of ground rents in due course, in tandem with compulsory first registration, but again the legislation does not apply to provisions in respect of rent and service charge for flats. The Commonhold and Leasehold Reform legislation for England and Wales does not apply in Northern Ireland.

A summary of the buying and selling process

Pre-contract stage

The seller's solicitor is notified by the estate agent that the property is on the market for sale. The solicitor obtains the documents of title relating to the property from the seller or the seller's lender. Unless there are special circumstances which would lead to a seller asking the solicitor to delay, the solicitor applies for property certificates and searches (see page 324) in accordance with the Home Charter Scheme. The expense of providing these certificates and searches is borne by the seller. The solicitor will usually at this stage also obtain replies to standard pre-contract enquiries and, if appropriate, details of management accounts, service charge and insurance cover in respect of the flat development.

Upon an acceptable verbal offer being obtained for the property the estate agent issues a memorandum of sale containing details of the respective parties, the solicitors, the agreed price for the property and any items on the property, a proposed completion date and any other special conditions or matters deemed relevant to the proposed transaction.

The seller's solicitor drafts a contract. In the vast majority of cases the Law Society of Northern Ireland's* General Conditions of Sale are used. The solicitor takes further instructions from the seller. The draft contract, documents of title, property certificates and searches and replies to pre-contract enquiries are forwarded to the buyer's solicitor.

The buyer's solicitor checks the documents of title, property certificates and searches and considers the replies to pre-contract enquiries. If additional matters arise, further pre-contract enquiries are made of the seller's solicitor.

The buyer's solicitor conducts an interview with the buyer at which title to the property is discussed, terms of covenants of the lease explained and the details of the contract considered. The buyer completes the additional terms of the draft contract (that is, details of purchase price, deposit and any sum agreed for fittings or contents). The buyer's solicitor may add further special conditions with respect to the survey or mortgage finance. The contract is then forwarded to the seller's solicitor.

The seller's solicitor receives the signed contract which amounts to an 'offer' to purchase. He or she conducts an interview with his or her client and explains the contract, together with any special conditions added by the buyer. Any amendments to the contract are discussed and agreed with the buyer's solicitor. The seller then signs the contract by way of 'acceptance' and a copy of the accepted contract is forwarded to the buyer's solicitor. The contract is formed upon receipt of a copy of the accepted contract by the buyer's solicitor. The agreed deposit is payable to the seller's solicitor within five days of the contract being formed.

Contractual stage

The buyer's solicitor prepares the draft deed/transfer form and forwards it for approval and signing by the seller. Requisitions on title are made to confirm that no additional matters have arisen since completion of the replies to standard pre-contract enquiries. The buyer's solicitor prepares and forwards a report on title, if appropriate, to the buyer's lender, specifying the completion date and requesting funds in time for completion.

The seller's solicitor writes to the lender with an existing mortgage on the property to establish a redemption figure for payment from the sale proceeds. The seller goes to the solicitor's office to execute the deed/transfer form and confirm replies to requisitions on title. The executed deed/transfer form is held on file pending completion.

Solicitors acting on behalf of both buyer and seller make arrangements for the practicalities of completion – signing over of services, availability of keys, apportionment of service charge, etc.

Completion

The day before completion the buyer's solicitor will usually send by post, or deliver on the day of completion, a completion letter containing a cheque or bank draft for the balance purchase money to the seller's solicitors. Sometimes completion is effected by a telegraphic transfer of funds from the buyer's solicitor's client account to the seller's solicitor's client account.

Upon receipt of the completion money, the seller's solicitor contacts the estate agent or the seller and confirms that keys may be released to the buyer.

A redemption cheque is sent to the seller's bank/building society to redeem the existing mortgage in respect of the property. The seller's solicitor then forwards the executed deed/transfer form to the buyer's solicitor, together with any outstanding original documents of title retained pending completion.

Post-completion

The buyer's solicitor, if appropriate, attends to payment of stamp duty land tax within the specified time scale (otherwise a penalty is payable). Stamp duty land tax rates in Northern Ireland are as in England and Wales (see page 97).

The seller's solicitor writes to the landlord or his or her agent to confirm the change of lessee and the date of completion. When the vacated mortgage deed is returned by the lender it is either registered by the seller's solicitor or the appropriate fee furnished and forwarded to the buyer's solicitor for registration.

If appropriate, the buyer's solicitor attends to the registration of the seller's vacated mortgage, together with the deed/transfer form and the buyer's mortgage. Documents of title are forwarded to be held by the buyer's lender.

Searches and property certificates

Searches

- **Statutory Charges Register** The search is against the property in sale and lists government charges affecting the land, for example, private street agreements, public health charges, tree preservation orders, listed buildings, etc.
- **Bankruptcy Office Register** The search is carried out against the seller. If the seller is bankrupt he or she may not be in a position to give good title. Under some leases if the tenant is bankrupt the landlord has the right to forfeit the lease.
- **Enforcement of Judgments Office** Again, this is a search against the seller. Strictly speaking the only type of enforcement which affects a potential buyer is an Order Charging Land. Such orders are registered at the Registry of Deeds or Land Registry as appropriate but this search highlights Orders Charging Land which have been made but not yet registered.
- **Registry of Deeds** This is a search in respect of unregistered property. While a deed is perfectly valid even if not registered in the Registry of Deeds, it is the date of registration rather than the date of execution that is significant and confers priority.
- **Land Registry** Searches in respect of registered property. Folio Searches and Map Searches confirm details of registered ownership, charges, boundaries, etc., and Priority Searches ensure priority of registration of dealings.

Property certificates

Property certificates are requisitioned by standard application forms and are supplied by the Department of the Environment, the local Council of the area in which the property is situated and in some cases the Northern Ireland Housing Executive. They cover matters such as road schemes, water and sewage systems, planning and building regulation matters, public health notices, compulsory purchase orders, etc.

Glossary

Abstract of title A summary provided by the seller of the history and validity of the legal title to unregistered land; also known as an epitome of title

Action Civil proceedings before the courts

Actual notice Actually knowing of someone's rights over a flat

Advance The mortgage loan

Advancement A presumption that when a husband/father transfers property (for example, land or money) to a wife/child it is a gift

Assignment The sale of a tenant's entire lease to another person; also used for the sale of the freehold

Assured tenancy A tenancy of rented property falling within the Housing Act 1988

Beneficial ownership Having the real ownership of a property without owning its legal title

Beneficiary The person who is entitled to property under a trust

By-law Local legislation created by the local authority for its area

Caution A means of protecting an interest on the Land Register

Caveat emptor 'Let the buyer beware'

Charge Any right or interest over the land securing the repayment of money, especially a mortgage; also used to denote a debt, or a claim for payment

Charge certificate When there is a mortgage, the certificate issued by the Land Registry or Registers of Scotland for areas where land registration has been implemented to the lender on a property which has a registered title

Charges register One of the three parts which make up the register at the Land Registry or Registers of Scotland of a property with a registered title; contains details of restrictive covenants, mortgages and other interests, subject to which the registered proprietor owns the property

Chattel Any moveable possession

Civil law That part of the law (for example, contract and negligence) which confers rights and imposes duties on individuals and deals with resolving disputes between them. Most of the actions between landlord and tenants are matters of civil law

Commonhold A scheme whereby tenants can own the freehold title of their flats, with the major title being owned (and regulations laid down) by the commonhold association for that block

Commonhold assessment Under the commonhold system, the payments made by the occupiers towards the running costs of the block (previously known as service charges)

Commonhold association Under the commonhold system, the body that owns and manages the common parts of a block

Commonhold community statement Under the commonhold system, the formal document governing the rights and obligations of the owners and the commonhold association

Common law That part of the law which is derived not from statutes but from the principles and the precedents set by earlier decisions of the court

Completion The final stage of the legal transaction when buying or selling the long lease of a flat

Constructive notice Knowledge which the buyer should have had about the flat if he or she had made reasonable enquiries

Contract Any legally binding agreement; on the sale of a property it is the document, in two identical parts, one signed by the buyer and the other by the seller, which, when the parts are exchanged, commits both the buyer and the seller to complete the transaction by transferring ownership in exchange for paying the purchase money

Conveyancing The legal and administrative process of transferring the ownership of land or any buildings on it, or a part of a building (such as a flat), from one owner to another

Co-ownership Where two or more people own the flat

County Court Court which deals with small civil cases, including landlord and tenant matters

Covenant An undertaking between landlord and tenant whereby each is bound to do (such as pay the rent or to repair), or refrain from doing (such as misusing property), certain things; may be expressed (that is, set out in the lease), or implied

Criminal law That part of the law which punishes behaviour harmful to the community as a whole, as against the civil law which confers rights and duties on individual people

Date of entry In Scotland, the date a buyer takes physical possession of a property

Dealings Any transaction involving property

Deed A formal legal document which is 'signed and delivered'; the transfer of the legal title to leasehold property has to be by deed

Demised premises Property which is the subject matter of a lease with certain implied covenants

Deposit Part of the purchase price, usually 5 or 10 per cent, which the buyer has to pay at the time of exchange of contracts. The seller's conveyancer will hold the deposit either as stakeholder (in which case it cannot be given to the seller until completion) or agent (in which case it can be passed to the seller at any time)

Disclaimer The right of a tenant's trustee in bankruptcy to get rid of the lease

Disposition In Scotland, the legal document transferring the property to the buyer

Distress An ancient remedy whereby the landlord can seize and sell goods of the tenant to recover rent arrears

Easements The legal rights of a property owner to use the facilities of another's land (for example, a right of way)

Encumbrances Rights held by third parties which adversely affect the use of the flat to be bought (for example, easements and restrictive covenants)

Endowment mortgage A loan on which only the interest is paid throughout the term; the capital is paid off at the end with the proceeds of an endowment insurance policy which is assigned to or deposited with the lender as additional security for the loan

Enfranchisement Tenant with long lease buying the freehold of a house under the Leasehold Reform Act 1967; or tenants collectively buying the freehold of the building in which the flats are situated under the Leasehold Reform, Housing and Urban Development Act 1993

Engross To put into final form (for example, to type a document in deed form)

Enquiries before contract A set of detailed questions about many aspects of a property which the seller, or his or her legal adviser, is generally asked to answer before the buyer is prepared to sign a contract; also called preliminary enquiries

Enquiries of local authority A number of questions asked of a local authority on a printed form about a particular property; the form is usually sent with, and loosely speaking forms part of, the buyer's local search which is made before contracts are exchanged

Equitable interest Rights in a property which fall short of legal title, for example where a lease is not properly created by deed it may be an equitable lease; also used to describe the interest of beneficial ownership (arising under a contract or by co-ownership) when this is not the same as the legal title

Equity Body of law which runs alongside the common law and is designed to ensure that justice and fairness is dispensed by the courts. Equity has its own rules (to do with co-ownership and mortgages, for example) and its own remedies (for example, specific performance, injunctions and rectification)

Equity of redemption The right of the borrower under a mortgage to redeem (that is, pay off) the mortgage at any time

Estate Person's ownership of land (may be freehold or leasehold)

Exchange of contracts The stage at which the buyer has signed one copy of the contract and sent it to the seller, and the seller has done the same in return, so that both become legally bound to go through with the transaction

Exclusive possession The right of a tenant to exclude all others (including the landlord) from the flat

Factor A professional property manager (Scotland)

Feu Property offered for sale (Scotland)

Feuar The owner of a property (Scotland)

Feuing conditions Conditions imposed on a flat- or house-owner by the land-owner (Scotland, similar to covenants in England and Wales)

Feu duty Sum paid annually by flat- or house-owner to the land-owner (Scotland, similar to ground rent in England and Wales)

Fixed-term lease A lease which is granted for a fixed duration (for example, 99 years)

Fixtures Articles which, being attached (by screws, concrete or pipes, for instance) to the property itself, are presumed to have become legally part of the property so that they are included in a sale, unless specifically excluded by the contract

Foreclosure A mortgage lender's remedy whereby it obtains the property rather than repayment of the loan and keeps the money already repaid; needs a court order

Forfeiture The means by which a landlord can bring a lease to an early end following a breach of covenant by the tenant; needs a court order

Freehold The absolute ownership of property until the end of time. In the case of a flat, the freehold will usually be the title owned by the landlord and will relate to the whole building and the land on which the building stands

Freeholder The person who owns the freehold. When this person creates or grants a lease (that is, sells a flat) he or she is known as the lessor, landlord or reversioner

Gazumping When a potential flat-buyer is out-bid by a rival buyer. As well as losing the desired flat, the unlucky victim of gazumping will lose the money already spent on the conveyancing process

Gazundering When a buyer refuses at the last minute to go ahead with the purchase unless the price is reduced, or because he or she has found a more suitable property or had a change of heart

Grant The formal giving or transferring of, for example, a lease or covenant. The person who transfers is called the grantor; the person to whom the lease is transferred is called the grantee

Ground rent Small sum payable periodically to the landlord by a tenant who holds leasehold property on a long lease

Habendum The part of the lease which states how long the tenancy is to run for

Head-lease A lease from which another, shorter, lease is carved out

Injunction A court order requiring a person to do something or to stop doing something

Interest in land A right to, stake in, or any form of ownership of, property such as a flat

Joint tenants Two (or more) people who hold property as co-owners; when one dies, the whole property automatically passes to the survivor(s)

Land Includes the plot of ground and all buildings on it

Land certificate The certificate issued to the registered proprietor of a property which has a registered title, showing what is entered on the register of that property at the Land Registry or

Registers of Scotland. When the property is mortgaged, no land certificate is issued; instead a charge certificate is issued to the lender

Land Charges Registry A government department in Plymouth where rights over, and interests in, unregistered property are recorded; charges are registered against the name of the owner, not the property concerned

Landlord The owner of a property who grants a lease or sub-lease of the property; also known as lessor or reversioner

Land Registry A government department (head office in London and district registries in various other places in England and Wales) where details of properties with a registered title are recorded

Lease The charter setting out the terms and conditions of the leasehold

Leasehold Ownership of property for a fixed number of years granted by a lease

Leaseholder The person to whom a lease is granted (that is, the person who buys a flat); also known as a lessee or tenant

Lessee *see Leaseholder*

Lessor *see Landlord*

Local Land Charges Register A register kept by the local authority, containing charges of a public nature affecting the property, which is consulted when a local search is made

Local search An application made on a duplicate form, to the local authority, for a certificate providing certain information about a property in the area. Also denotes the search certificate itself. Loosely speaking, a local search also includes the answers given by the local authority to a number of standard enquiries, made on another special form

Long lease A lease originally granted for over 21 years; it may have been assigned (sold on) to other leaseholder(s) since the original granting of the lease

Management company A company set up by the landlord or the tenants to manage the services provided and attend to repairs in a block of flats

Marriage value The notion that when the tenants buy the freehold they are obtaining a benefit of the increased value of the freehold and the leaseholds being together

Merger The purchase of the landlord's freehold by a tenant

Missives The written offer and subsequent letters between the solicitors of the buyer and the seller (Scotland)

Mortgage Loan for which a property is the security. It gives to the lender (mortgagee) certain rights in the property, including the power to sell if the mortgage payments are not made

Mortgage deed The document setting out the mortgage conditions

Mortgagee One who lends money on mortgage, such as a building society, bank, local authority, insurance company or private lender

Mortgagor The borrower (whose property is security for the loan)

NHBC scheme This is a form of insurance cover/building guarantee available on most newly constructed houses and flats

Negative covenants Covenants restricting one party from doing something; for example, using the premises for certain purposes

Negative equity Where the sale of the property will not generate sufficient funds to discharge the mortgage debt

Negligence Breach of a legal rule which imposes a duty of care on any person who ought to foresee that his or her act or omission could cause loss or injury to another

Notice to complete A notice served by either the buyer or the seller if completion does not go ahead on the agreed date because of delays by the other. It then becomes a term of the contract that completion will occur within a reasonable period of the notice and that time will be of the essence for both parties

Nuisance The legal duty not to unlawfully interfere with someone's use or enjoyment of land

Official search An application to an official authority (such as a local authority, the Land Registry or the Land Charges Registry), to find out some relevant facts about a particular property

Option A contractual right to buy something (for example, a new lease or the freehold)

Overreaching The ability, by paying the purchase money collectively to two trustees (legal owners), to get free of a co-owner's interest in the flat

Overriding interests Rights which are enforceable against a property, even though they are not referred to on the register of the property at the Land Registry

Parcels The part of the lease which describes the property which is being leased

Periodic tenancy A lease which is not fixed term (that is, a tenancy from week to week or month to month)

Positive covenants Covenants which compel one party to do something (for example, to pay rent or to insure)

Possession Procedure whereby a landlord goes to the court to evict a tenant or other lawful residential occupier

Pre-emption The contractual right to have first refusal (for example, when the freeholder decides to sell the freehold)

Premium Capital sum (the purchase price) paid for a long lease; also the payments to insurers for insurance cover

Privity of contract The contractual relationship between the original landlord and the original tenant

Privity of estate The relationship between the current landlord and the current tenant

Protocol A standardised procedure (and preferred practice) for conveyancing introduced by the Law Society; intended to simplify and quicken the (pre-contract) process

Purchaser The buyer

Quiet enjoyment An implied covenant that the landlord shall not unlawfully interfere with the tenant's enjoyment of the flat

Reddendum The part of the lease which states the ground rent payable and when it is to be paid

Re-entry Landlord lawfully retaking possession of a property with a court order on forfeiture

Register In the case of a property with a registered title, the record for that property kept at the Land Registry, divided into the property, the proprietorship and the charges registers

Registered title Title or ownership of freehold or leasehold property which has been registered at the Land Registry, with the result that ownership is guaranteed by the state

Registers of Scotland Where records of titles under Sasines or land registration schemes are kept

Relief Redress or remedial action sanctioned by law; for example, where the tenant's lease is allowed by the court to continue despite the fact that the landlord has obtained a judgment for forfeiture

Remedy The means of legal redress

Rent-to-mortgage Scheme allowing council tenants to count their rental payments as contributing to the purchase of the flat

Repair Renewal or replacement of part of a building

Repayment mortgage Loan on which part of the capital and interest are paid back by regular instalments throughout the term of the loan

Reservations Rights set out in a lease as being kept by the landlord over the property he or she has let; the converse of easements and usually of similar nature

Reserved property Parts of the building or garden which the landlord keeps under his or her control

Restrictive covenant A covenant which restricts the use of the premises

Reversion An interest in a property which will eventually return to the original owner (or successors) after the period in which another person holds the property comes to an end; loosely used to denote the freehold

Reversioner *see* **Landlord**

Right to buy Right of public-sector tenants to buy the rented flat in which they live

Right to Enfranchise (RTE) company Specific type of company to be used by tenants exercising the statutory right to collective enfranchisement

Right to Manage (RTM) company Specific type of company to be used by tenants exercising the statutory right to manage

Sasines Register System of title registration prior to introduction of land registration

Search An enquiry for, or an inspection of, information recorded by some official body, such as a local authority, the Land Registry or the Land Charges Department

Secure tenant An individual who occupies as his or her only or principal home a property of which the landlord is a local authority, a county council, a housing association or one of a few other public-sector landlords

Security of tenure The right to remain in possession after the original contract has expired

Service charges The cost paid periodically to the landlord or the management company for the services provided to the tenants

Severance The conversion of a joint tenancy into a tenancy in common

Solicitors' property centres Organisations run by solicitors on a co-operative basis providing details of all properties being sold by solicitors in the area (Scotland)

Specific performance Equitable remedy amounting to an order that a reluctant party complete the contract (that is, performs what has been agreed), similar to specific implement in Scotland

Stamp duty land tax A tax payable to the government on land transactions at a price above (at present) £60,000; deeds and documents cannot be used as evidence or registered at the Land Registry unless certified

Standard security A mortgage document (Scotland)

Statute An Act of Parliament

Statutory A right or obligation arising from a statute or subordinate legislation made under it

Subject to contract Provisionally agreed, but not so as to constitute a binding legal contract; either the buyer or the seller may still back out with no legal consequences, without giving any reason

Sub-lease A lease carved out of another lease, necessarily for a shorter period, created by a person who has only a leasehold interest in the property

Sub-tenant Tenant who leases property from a landlord who owns a leasehold, not a freehold, interest in that property. It is possible for a chain of tenancies to be built up running from the freeholder (the head landlord) to his or her tenant and down to a sub-tenant, then to a sub-sub-tenant, and so on. Each tenant becomes the landlord of his or her own sub-tenant down to the last link in the chain – the tenant in actual occupation

Superior Original developer of the land or estate-owner; person to whom a flat- or house-owner pays feu duty (Scotland)

Superior landlord Someone with a higher interest than the tenant's immediate landlord; if A, a freeholder, grants a 99-year lease to B, and B then grants a 21-year lease to C, the superior landlord is A

Surrender The selling or giving up of the lease to the landlord

Survivorship (right of) The right of a surviving joint tenant to acquire automatically on death the interest of a deceased joint tenant

Tenant The person to whom a lease is granted (word is interchangeable with lessee or leaseholder)

Tenants' association A body which is representative of the tenants and recognised as such by the landlord; the importance of such associations lies in the collective bargaining power the members have in relation to the landlord

Tenants' management company A company formed by tenants to manage the block or estate; such a company usually acquires the freehold to the property

Tenants in common Two (or more) people who together hold property in such a way that, when one dies, his or her share does not pass automatically to the survivor but forms part of his or her own property and passes under his or her will or intestacy (this is in contrast with what happens in the case of joint tenants)

'Time is of the essence' A term in the contract indicating that stated time limits must be observed; if a party is late in performing a contractual obligation where time is of the essence, the other party is released from his or her corresponding contractual obligation. Completion time can be made 'of the essence' in a contract for the sale of land by either party serving a 'notice to complete'

Title Ownership of a property

Title deeds Documents going back over 15 years or longer which prove the ownership of unregistered property

Transfer A deed which transfers the ownership of a property, the title to which is registered at the Land Registry (as opposed to the deed used where the title is unregistered)

Trust An arrangement whereby the legal ownership of property is vested in trustees on behalf of the real owners, the beneficiaries

Trustee A person in whom the legal ownership of property is vested, but who holds it for the benefit of someone else (called a beneficiary)

Trustees for sale People who hold property as trustees on condition that they should sell the property, but usually with a power to postpone doing so indefinitely if they want to

Trust for sale Where there is co-ownership the co-owners hold under a trust to sell the property (which can be postponed indefinitely) and account to the beneficiaries for the proceeds of sale

Underlease *see Sub-lease*

Unit Under the commonhold system, the term for each flat within a commonhold development

Unit-holder Under the commonhold system, the term for a flat-owner

Unities (the four) Possession, time, title and interest: the necessary ingredients of a joint tenancy

Unregistered land Property, the title or ownership of which has not been registered at the Land Registry

Upset price The price set for a flat above which offers are invited (the 'offers over' price) (Scotland)

Vendor The seller

Waste An act by the tenant damaging the interest of the landlord in the property

Addresses

Association of British Insurers
51 Gresham Street
London EC2V 7HQ
Tel: 020–7600 3333
Fax: 020–7696 8999
Email: info@abi.org.uk
Website: www.abi.org.uk

Association of Residential Managing Agents
178 Battersea Park Road
London SW11 4ND
Tel: 020–7978 2607
Website: www.arma.org.uk

Chartered Institute of Arbitrators (CIArb)
International Arbitration Centre
12 Bloomsbury Square
London WC1A 2LP
Tel: 020–7421 7444
Fax: 020–7404 4023
Email: info@arbitrators.org
Website: www.arbitrators.org

Coalition for the Abolition of Residential Leasehold (CARL)
PO Box 26369
London N8 7ZL
Email: charlotte@carl.org.uk
Website: www.carl.org.uk

Community Legal Service Fund
See Legal Services Commission

Council for Licensed Conveyancers
16 Glebe Road
Chelmsford
Essex CM1 1QG
Tel: (01245) 349599
Fax: (01245) 341300
Email: clc@theclc.gov.uk
Website: www.theclc.gov.uk

Council of Mortgage Lenders
3 Savile Row
London W1S 3PB
Tel: 020–7437 0075
Fax: 020–7434 3791
Email: info@cml.org.uk
Website: www.cml.org.uk

Federation of Private Residents' Associations
113–115 George Lane
South Woodford
London E18 1AB
Tel: 020–8530 8464
Fax: 020–8989 3153
Email: info@fpra.org.uk
Website: www.fpra.org.uk

Financial Ombudsman Service
South Quay Plaza
183 Marsh Wall
London E14 9SR
Tel: (08450) 801800
Fax: 020–7964 1001
Email: enquiries@
financial-ombudsman.org.uk
Website:
www.financial-ombudsman.org.uk

Financial Services Authority (FSA)
25 The North Colonnade
Canary Wharf
London E14 5HS
Tel: 020–7066 1000
Fax: 020–7676 1099
Website: www.fsa.gov.uk

Lands Tribunal for England and Wales
48/49 Chancery Lane
London WC2A 1JR
Tel: 020–7947 7200
Fax: 020–7947 7215
Website: www.courtservice.gov.uk/
tribunals/lands/frm.htm

Lands Tribunal for Northern Ireland
Royal Courts of Justice
Chichester Street
Belfast BT1 3JJ
Tel: 028–9032 7703
Fax: 028–9054 6187
Email: lands.tribunal@dfpni.gov.uk

Lands Tribunal for Scotland
1 Grosvenor Crescent
Edinburgh EH12 5ER
Tel: 0131–225 7996
Fax: 0131–226 4812

Law Society of England and Wales
113 Chancery Lane
London WC2A 1PL
Tel: 020–7242 1222
Fax: 020–7831 0344
Email:
info.services@lawsociety.org.uk
Website: www.lawsociety.org.uk

Law Society of Northern Ireland
Law Society House
98 Victoria Street
Belfast BT1 3JZ
Tel: 028–9023 1614
Fax: 028–9023 2606
Email: info@lawsoc-ni.org
Website: www.lawsoc-ni.org

Law Society of Scotland
26 Drumsheugh Gardens
Edinburgh EH3 7YR
Tel: 0131–226 7411
Fax: 0131–225 2934
Email: lawscot@lawscot.org.uk
Website: www.lawscot.org.uk

Leasehold Advisory Service
70–74 City Road
London EC1Y 2BJ
Tel: 020–7490 9580
Fax: 020–7253 2043
Email: info@lease-advice.org
Website: www.lease-advice.org

Leasehold Valuation Tribunal
Contact the Office of the Deputy Prime Minister for your nearest tribunal

Legal Services Commission
85 Grays Inn Road
London WC1X 8TX
Tel: 020–7759 0000
Website: www.legalservices.gov.uk

Mortgage Code Compliance Board
University Court
Stafford
Staffordshire ST18 0GM
Tel: (01785) 218200
Fax: (01785) 218249
Email:
enquiries@mortgagecode.org.uk
Website: www.mortgagecode.org.uk

**National Association of Estate Agents
(NAEA)**
Arbon House
21 Jury Street
Warwick
Warwickshire CV34 4EH
Tel: (01926) 496800
Fax: (01926) 400953
Email: info@naea.co.uk
Website: www.naea.co.uk

**National House Building Council
(NHBC)**
Buildmark House
Chiltern Avenue
Amersham
Buckinghamshire HP6 5AP
Tel: (01494) 735363/9
Fax: (01494) 723530
Website: www.nhbc.co.uk

Office for the Supervision of Solicitors
Victoria Court
8 Dormer Place
Leamington Spa
Warwickshire CV32 5AE
Tel: (01926) 822007/8/9
Fax: (01926) 431435
Email:
info.services@lawsociety.org.uk
Website: www.lawsociety.org.uk

Ombudsman for Estate Agents
Beckett House
4 Bridge Street
Salisbury
Wiltshire SP1 2LX
Tel: (01722) 333306
Fax: (01722) 332296
Email: admin@oea.co.uk
Website: www.oea.co.uk

Rent Assessment Committee
*Look in the phone book for your nearest
committee*

**Royal Institution of Chartered
Surveyors**
12 Great George Street
London SW1P 3AD
Tel: 020–7222 7000
Fax: 020–7222 9430
Email: info@rics.org
Website: www.rics.org

**Royal Institution of Chartered
Surveyors in Scotland**
9 Manor Place
Edinburgh EH3 7DN
Tel: 0131–225 7078
Fax: 0131–240 0830
Email: scotland@rics.org
Website: www.rics-scotland.org.uk

Index

Numbers in **bold** refer to the page number in the Glossary where the subject is defined.